# THE
# PREHISTORIC
# WORLD

# THE
# PREHISTORIC
## WORLD

## Giorgio P. Panini

GALLERY BOOKS
An Imprint of W. H. Smith Publishers Inc.
112 Madison Avenue
New York City 10016

First published in Great Britain in 1987 by
Treasure Press

This edition published in 1987 by Gallery Books
An imprint of W.H. Smith Publishers, Inc.
112 Madison Avenue, New York, New York 10016

© 1982 Arnoldo Mondadori Editore S.p.A., Milano
English translation © Octopus Books Ltd, 1987

ISBN 0-8317-7113-5

Printed in Czechoslovakia

# CONTENTS

# Understanding evolution

When you look at your face in the mirror, you recognize it at once. But if you look at a picture of yourself in an old photograph album, you notice obvious differences. For example, your face then was more childish, smaller and rounder. If the photograph includes other parts of the body, you may be struck by the fact that a child's head is bigger, in proportion to the body, than a grown-up's. The photograph and the mirror tell you that you gradually change. Yet you do not alter so much that you cannot recognize yourself. If you were to show a group photograph to a friend, he may pause for a moment but will still pick you out. So although your body and outward appearance may have changed, you have still remained fully recognizable.

As you look through those old photographs you may come across one of your grandfather or grandmother. Your friend may identify one or both as a grandparent, pointing out that there is a 'family likeness'.

We all change in many different ways. For example, you are different today from when you first went to school. You changed when you learned about the history of your town; and tomorrow you will be slightly different again because you will have read this book about animals of the past and your own history. You become different simply by learning new facts.

So although we change, we are still recognizable to ourselves, our

*If you look at a camel or a dromedary (above) and a llama or a vicuña (right), you can see a certain similarity between the two types of animal. The study of the bones of animals that lived long ago shows us that other animals were similar to camels and llamas. By using information gained from observing present-day animals and from studying those of the past, we can deduce the history of many groups of animals and can reconstruct their family trees (drawing on opposite page).*

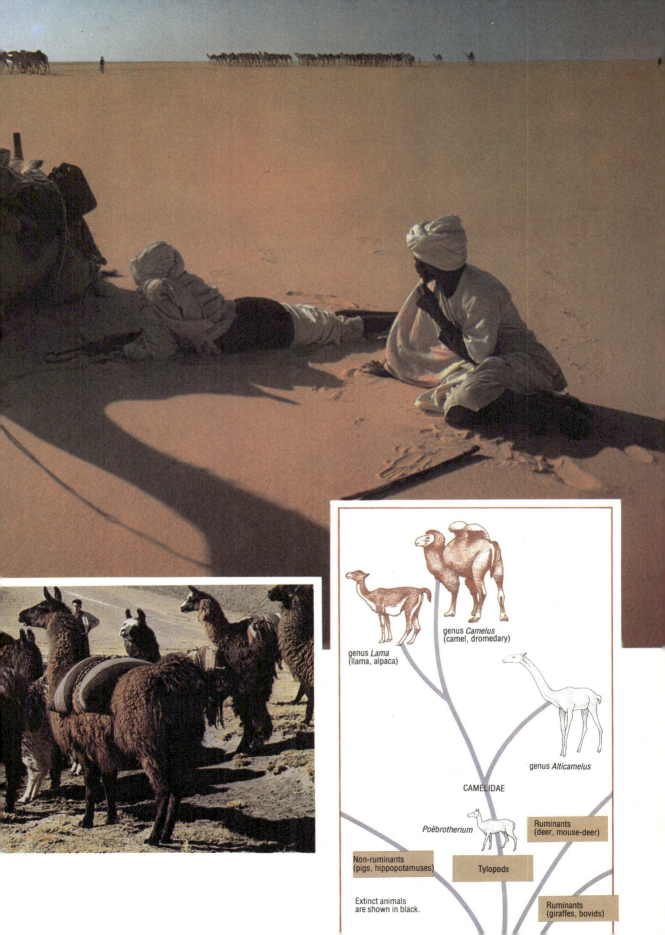

genus *Lama*
(llama, alpaca)

genus *Camelus*
(camel, dromedary)

genus *Alticamelus*

CAMELIDAE

*Poëbrotherium*

Ruminants
(deer, mouse-deer)

Non-ruminants
(pigs, hippopotamuses)

Tylopods

Ruminants
(giraffes, bovids)

Extinct animals
are shown in black.

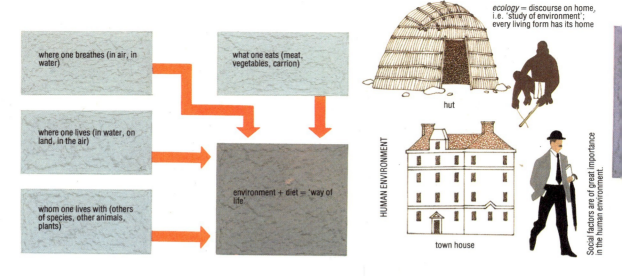

where one breathes (in air, in water)

what one eats (meat, vegetables, carrion)

where one lives (in water, on land, in the air)

whom one lives with (others of species, other animals, plants)

environment + diet = 'way of life'

*ecology* = discourse on home, i.e. 'study of environment'; every living form has its home

hut

HUMAN ENVIRONMENT

town house

Social factors are of great importance in the human environment.

parents, our grandparents and our close friends.

This happens to all livings things. The differences between animals are clear, but we can also see the similarities, which may mean that two different creatures are related. Two similar animals, despite their slight differences, may perhaps have the same mother. Two similar yet slightly different kinds of animal may have a common ancestor.

made yourself (even though only with clothes) slightly different.

This is exactly what has happened to all living things gradually, over millions of years. The environment has changed and living things have adapted to it. Of course, a very considerable time must pass for such adaptations to show.

## Adapting to change

How can a common ancestor have different types of descendant? This is the vital question we have to ask in order to understand the story of living things. The very fact that we talk about the 'story' of living things forces us to admit that many things have happened and that many have changed. A sequence of events in which all the characters stayed the same would not be a real story.

Let us think of a very simple kind of change. It is snowing outdoors and in order to go out in the cold you put on an overcoat and a pair of boots. In this way you have adapted to the different situation outside the house and have

about 200 million years ago

arrangement of the continents about
600 million years ago

today

The Earth is the home of all living things; it has changed
with the passage of time.

Living things have changed so as to make ever better use
of their changing home.

*Tyrannosaurus rex*
A typical carnosaur

Crocodiles (photograph below) are related to the
huge carnivorous dinosaurs which lived 150
million years ago (drawing below); both are
vertebrates of the class Reptilia and share a
number of other characteristics. Yet there are some
obvious differences. The crocodile lives in watery
surroundings, swims and moves around on four
legs; whereas many dinosaurs like the allosaur ran
on dry land, with the large feet of a two-legged
animal. Every living organism is adapted to its
particular environment. The diagram (above left)
shows what is meant by environment and
describes how it is linked to our lives.

9

# Different ways of moving

Any living thing, in order to survive, must be able to find food and shelter. It must therefore be able to move around in its particular environment. Animal that live in water, swim. In the air, animals fly. Different ways of

moving use different parts of the body. Snails crawl with their feet; but a caterpillar moves by leaning on its legs and arching its body. Insects use their four wings. In birds, bats and the prehistoric flying reptiles what in humans are the arms have been adapted for flight.

The human arm may be compared to the wing of a bird or a bat. It develops in a similar manner, and at a certain stage in their development humans, birds and bats have 'hands' which are similar. The human arm also resembles the foreleg of a quadruped or four-legged animal.

4

5

# A question of time

How is it that so many different forms of limb have developed and why are they used in such different ways? For example, even though the human arm bears some resemblance to a bird's wing, and the human hand resembles the support of a bat's wing, they are clearly different. The answer is quite simple. It is a question of time. Creatures have been living on the planet Earth for a very long time indeed. During that time living organisms have gradually adapted to many different types of environment, and this has given rise to a diverse number of animal and plant forms.

The story of living things on Earth has been going on for some 3500 million years. This story is written on Earth itself. The ground we stand on is formed of many strata or layers. It

*There are many ways in which animals adapt to different environments. Movement is a vital activity. It is made according to whether an animal lives in water, on dry land or in the air. The fish swims mainly by moving its tail to and fro (1). Snails crawl by special movements of their foot muscles with help from a sticky substance secreted from their bodies (2). The caterpillar, larva of the butterfly, climbs a twig by using various parts of its body (3). The seed of the parrot plant relies on the wind for movement (4). Dragon-flies (insects) and the pterosaur (a flying reptile of the upper Jurassic) move by flying but their means of flight are quite different (5,6).*

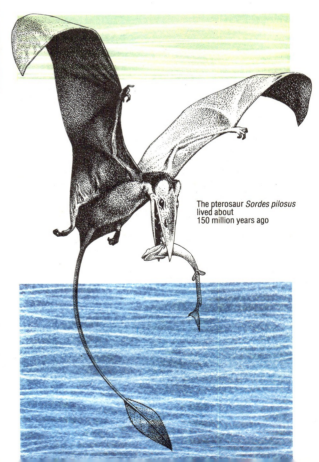

The pterosaur *Sordes pilosus* lived about 150 million years ago

might be compared to a flaky cream pastry. Just as in the preparation of this pastry one layer is added on top of another, so in the Earth, the oldest layers are the deepest. To study the history of life on Earth, we use the traces left by living things, traces preserved in the ground's strata. The deepest of these strata will preserve the traces of the oldest forms of life.

# How did life begin?

The story of living things on Earth began approximately 3500 million years ago. The Earth itself has been in existence for something like 4500 million years; and the Solar System (our Sun, its planets and the Moon) is about the same age. We know that on the other planets and moons of our solar system, there is no life. What, therefore, happened on Earth between about 4500 and 3500 million years ago, that enabled life to begin?

A favourable environment evidently made it possible for certain molecules to develop the ability to reproduce themselves. These molecules changed from non-living things to become living things.

The transition from non-living to living organisms appears so extraordinary that in order to explain it, many learned people have conjured up an 'explanation' outside the material world, a miracle or an inexplicable event. But this form of explanation is not scientific.

By using scientific methods of enquiry (observing, verifying and reconstructing what has been observed in the laboratory), we have managed to learn much about the fundamental mechanisms of living things, about their chemistry and about their composition which enables the phenomenon of life to exist. We also know how energy in organisms is stored and how it is made available.

Laboratory scientists have tried to reconstruct what may have happened in the past; and they have been successful. By giving energy to various substances which they believe existed on Earth during that vital 1000 million years, they have obtained substances just like those found in living things.

Interesting information has come, too, from the study of astrophysics (the physics of heavenly bodies and

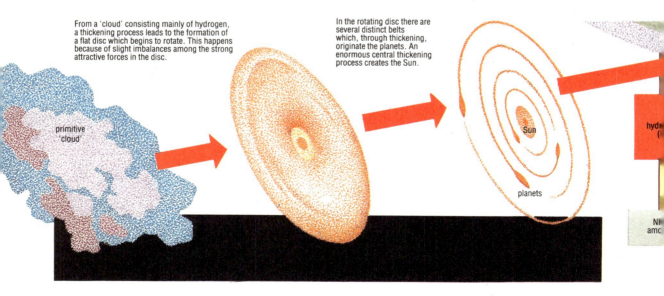

From a 'cloud' consisting mainly of hydrogen, a thickening process leads to the formation of a flat disc which begins to rotate. This happens because of slight imbalances among the strong attractive forces in the disc.

In the rotating disc there are several distinct belts which, through thickening, originate the planets. An enormous central thickening process creates the Sun.

primitive 'cloud'

Sun

planets

of the substances of the universe). Accurate observations, made with radiotelescopes, have revealed, in some zones of space outside the Solar System, the presence of substances peculiar to living things (water, ammonia, ethyl alcohol, methane and others). It is possible that some of the processes involved in creating living substances from non-living material may have occurred in Space.

It is possible, too, that these processes were in some way speeded up during the formation of a star similar to the Sun and its associated planetary system. However, a powerful supply of energy (heat, collisions or pressure) would have been needed while the planets were formed.

Finally, it is possible that on a planet such as Earth, with a plentiful supply of liquid water (not frozen and not in the form of steam), the substances present in the primitive atmosphere, together with energy from lightning, solar rays, volcanic eruptions and radioactivity, may have resulted in the formation of complex atomic substances which gradually became capable of reproduction, and hence life.

# Fossils: evidence of prehistoric life

Living organisms leave traces of their existence in the environment: such traces are called fossils. This word is derived from the Latin and means 'what can be dug up'. A fossil may be a genuine trace, such as the mark left in the sand by a worm or a series of prints left in the mud by a dinosaur. In time, the sand and the mud have been changed into rock.

A fossil may be made up of one part

*From a primitive cloud (containing hydrogen and a few other chemical elements) a disc was formed which, because of internal imbalances or the provision of energy from outside, began to revolve. At its centre, by accumulation, the star known as the Sun was formed; around it, from various bands, the planets were formed (at the left of the drawing). Some, like Jupiter (shown below in a photograph taken during the Voyager missions), have retained many of the gases formed during the initial phases. In other planets there was a slow evolution. This happened with the Earth (at the right of the drawing) which has a solid core, with a large amount of surface liquid (the oceans) and an atmosphere. The atmosphere gradually changed, and with the energy from lightning, volcanic eruptions and reactions in radioactive substances came to have the combinations of substances which resulted in the first living organisms.*

The primitive atmosphere of all the planets was probably similar; that of the Earth contained various elements in several principal combinations, but there was no free oxygen.

nitrogen (N)

oxygen (O)

carbon (C)

sulphur (S)

$H_2O$ water

$CH_4$ methane

$H_2S_1$ hydrogen sulphide

$CO_2$ carbon dioxide

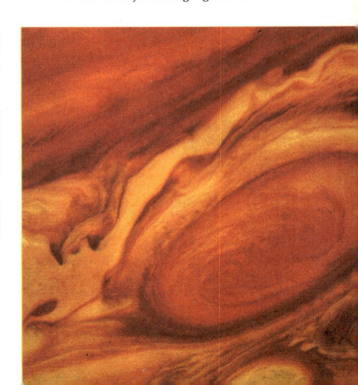

of the organism, such as the skeleton; in that case it will have been transformed into a different type of stone. Sometimes the body of the living thing will have dissolved but the ground will have preserved an impression (a cast) which will later have been filled up with other substances.

There are other ways in which fossils are formed. Fossils from organisms which existed between 3500 million and 800–700 million years ago are scarce; but fossil evidence of creatures living on Earth since then is very plentiful.

## How are species formed?

What exactly is a living species? It is possible to describe a number of common characteristics that a group of very similar individuals possesses. On the basis of such characteristics we can identify the species.

How does a species originate? The traditional answer is simple: all species originated together by the deliberate action of God. In the biblical account, the Creation lasted six days. From the moment that plants and animals were created, there were no further changes.

The first scientific classification of plants and animals was carried out by the Swedish scholar Carl von Linné (1707–78), better known as Linnaeus. He introduced *binomial nomenclature*, a system describing every living form with two Latin scientific names. The first, always starting with a capital letter, is the name of the genus (a subdivision of a family usually containing more than one species); the second, starting with a small letter, is that of the species.

This type of classification (systematics) is still used. Linnaeus declared that all the known species represented the many diverse forms that

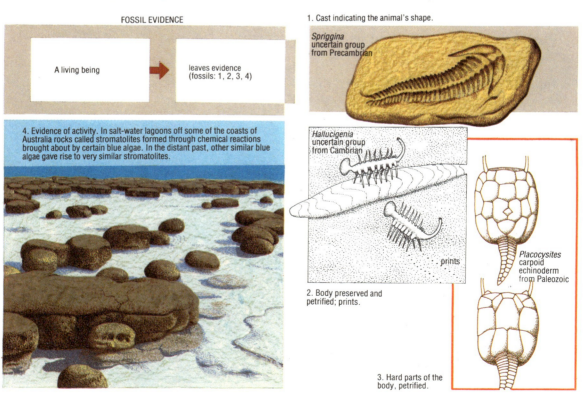

FOSSIL EVIDENCE

A living being → leaves evidence (fossils: 1, 2, 3, 4)

4. Evidence of activity. In salt-water lagoons off some of the coasts of Australia rocks called stromatolites formed through chemical reactions brought about by certain blue algae. In the distant past, other similar blue algae gave rise to very similar stromatolites.

1. Cast indicating the animal's shape.

*Spriggina* uncertain group from Precambrian

*Hallucigenia* uncertain group from Cambrian

prints

2. Body preserved and petrified; prints.

*Placocysites* carpoid echinoderm from Paleozoic

3. Hard parts of the body, petrified.

*Fossils are concrete evidence of the activities of living things in the past. For millions of years primitive blue algae have lived in an environment where there were no competitors (no other living things which could consume them). Undisturbed, the blue algae ejected vast quantities of calcium salts which today are as rocks (stromatoliths). Drawing on opposite page: the same kind of formations are sometimes found today in certain lakes where the strong salt content prevents any other organism surviving and where blue algae exist on their own, as they did long ago. In other cases clear marks or prints of animals have been preserved, or even skeletons and shells transformed into stone.*
*Right: A living one-celled foraminifer.*
*Below: Skeletons of one-celled fossils.*

PALEOZOIC RADIOLARIANS

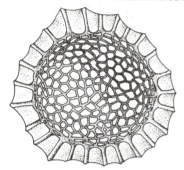 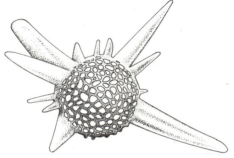 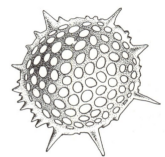

the Almighty created in the beginning. He said that nothing had changed since the time of Creation.

If that is how things are, how do we explain fossils? For a long time these objects were interpreted as strange examples of some mysterious activity of the Earth. Yet not all scholars agreed. Some, like Georges de Cuvier (1769–1832), maintained that fossils might be the remnants of animals which had lived in the past. Cuvier, rightly known as the 'father' of modern paleontology (talk or argument, and thus also science, of ancient beings), reconstructed the skeletons of certain animals which nobody had ever seen alive, for example, *Paleotherium* and *Megatherium* (described later in this book). To explain the disappearance of the most ancient animals, Cuvier suggested that there might have been major catastrophes, great enough to wipe out all the animals and plants of a given region or period. This theory was very different to the older, accepted theory that all species had existed unchanged from the Creation.

## The theory of evolution

Other scientists put forward a different interpretation. Species, in the course of time, had changed; there had been many gradual adaptations to the environment, so that animals and plants became as they are today. This is the basis of the theory of evolution published by Charles Darwin (1809–82) in 1858.

Any group of apparently similar living things actually shows slight variations; each individual is a little different from the next. The offspring, too, are not quite identical to their parents.

Certain individuals become better adapted than others to conditions of their environment. They share this environment as well with other living forms and, in particular, with other individuals of the same species. The individual who wins in contests with companions of the same species is also better adapted.

The best adapted individuals find it easier to reach the age of reproduction: they have offspring. These offspring will inherit some of their parents' useful characteristics and will perhaps acquire others yet more useful. Only the best adapted of these offspring will, in turn, manage to reproduce. This is the process of natural selection. As the characteristics useful for a given situation come to prevail, so there evolves a group of individuals slightly different from the parents. The process may, in time, give rise to a new species.

Darwin, for example, noticed that in the Galapagos Islands there were several different types of finch. Despite their variations, these birds all displayed a number of common characteristics. Darwin thought that these finches might be derived from a single original form, a common ancestor. He thought that the different species he saw were the result of a process of selection due mainly to the different environmental conditions in the islands. Isolation (the islands are separated by large areas of sea) had thus caused the appearance of these diverse characteristics. The same thing had happened to the giant tortoises there. Darwin maintained that the different species living in the Galapagos were descended from one original form. He was well aware of the procedures adopted by livestock breeders to obtain domestic species with chosen characteristics judged to be useful: sheep with abundant wool, hunting dogs, sheepdogs and the like. By cross-breeding individuals with 'useful' characteristics, it was possible to ensure that these characteristics would be a feature of the descendants. Here was an example of a selection determined by humans.

The same kind of phenomenon apparently occurs in nature over a far longer period. It is therefore possible that all similar living forms have common ancestors. If we imagine such a process taking place for an extremely long time, it is possible to believe that species that are slightly different may, in the remote past, have possessed a common ancestor. It is possible that by degrees, slowly and continuously, *all* living things came from *one* common ancestor. The systematic classification of living things thus came to possess new significance. It was no longer a mere exercise in filing, of drawing up an abstract catalogue: families, orders and classes indicated the links between species, links of parenthood, of descendance.

It is to Darwin that we owe our present-day understanding of living things and the story of this evolution (literally an 'unwinding', like a skein of wool).

Today we have available a large number of observations concerning the behaviour of animals, and we know that many patterns of behaviour are part of single species, inherited by each individual. It is possible in natural selection for species to select better adapted be-

haviour, producing an evolution of behaviour. Work done by ethologists (students of animal behaviour) confirms this extension of the theory of evolution.

*Opposite: A fossil crustacean,* Coleia mediterranea, *from the lower Jurassic, and, bottom, a present-day form, the shrimp* Stenopus hispidus.
*Below: The family tree of all the living beings of the animal kingdom. The comparative distances between the individual arrowed lines show roughly how closely related or far apart are the various groups. For example, the group of Vertebrata (a subdivision of the Chordata) and that of the Echinodermata are fairly close.*

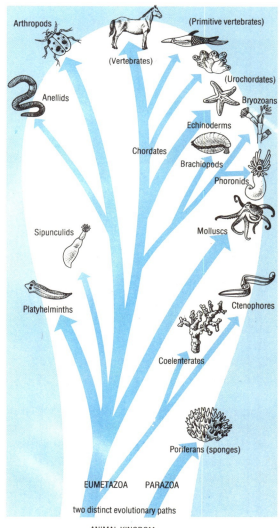

Arthropods
(Primitive vertebrates)
(Vertebrates)
Anellids
(Urochordates)
Bryozoans
Echinoderms
Chordates
Brachiopods
Phoronids
Sipunculids
Molluscs
Platyhelminths
Ctenophores
Coelenterates
Poriferans (sponges)
EUMETAZOA    PARAZOA
two distinct evolutionary paths
ANIMAL KINGDOM

# Cells galore

Today we are able to reconstruct, roughly, what must have happened in the long period that elapsed between the disappearance of the earliest living forms and the appearance of the earliest fossil documentation. This long phase is called the Archeozoic era ('of very ancient life'); sometimes, to indicate the final part of this era, the term Precambrian is used. It is a matter of hypotheses (supported only in some cases by fossil evidence), but there does seem to be a highly logical sequence.

1. Approximately 3500 million years ago, the first organisms absorb useful substances from the environment. They are forms similar to bacteria and are made up of a single cell (unicellular organisms).

2. About 2900 million years ago, organisms, perhaps similar to blue algae, appear. These are capable of 'using' energy from the Sun, in the form of light, and the water and carbon dioxide in the environment, to 'manufacture' useful substances. The process is called photosynthesis ('to put together by means of light'). It happens because the organisms (unicellular and still without a nucleus) contain the substance called chlorophyll (literally 'green leaf'). The useful substances manufactured are sugars. The sugars are broken down, by a process called metabolism, to obtain more energy and substances which form the body of the cell. One of the by-products of photosynthesis is oxygen gas, which is released into the atmosphere. Oxygen is partially used in this process, which is a form of respiration.

3. Organisms appear which are not able to photosynthesize and are thus incapable of manufacturing substances like sugars. They can 'eat' the photosynthetic organisms. Many of these organisms (still without a proper nucleus) use oxygen for their metabolism.

4. Perhaps through the link of various cells lacking a true nucleus, more complex unicellular organisms are formed to create one with a proper nucleus (eucaryotic cell).

5. More eucaryotic cells come together to give rise to multicellular ('with many cells') organisms. These cells have different tasks, but some of them are concerned with reproduction.

6. The main structural patterns of living things are by now outlined. There are multicellular organisms capable of photosynthesis (plants) and others which are not (animals).

7. All changes come about through the working of natural selection. This becomes much more active with the appearance of sexuality. Individuals no longer reproduce simply by dividing themselves, as has happened until now, but produce offspring which come from two different individuals who have mated. In the course of mating there is an exchange of information which increases considerably the variety of types and makes it more likely that they will adapt to a particular environment. In this way, the range of different living things becomes ever larger.

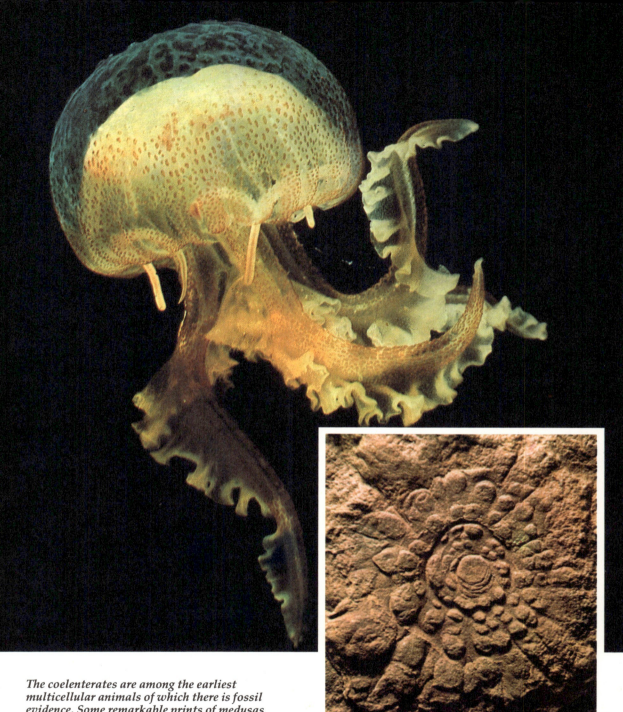

The coelenterates are among the earliest multicellular animals of which there is fossil evidence. Some remarkable prints of medusas (jellyfish) have been discovered in strata of the late Archeozoic (Precambrian, about 700 million years ago) from Ediacara – a site in southern Australia, not far from Adelaide. These animals had no rigid parts in their body. Evidently the medusas of Ediacara were thrown up on a sandy or muddy bank and were in due course covered by sand. In this way a mould of the animal was formed. The fossil in the inset, right, is described as *Mawsonites* (this being the name of the genus). The living medusa shown in the large photograph is *Pelagia* *noctiluca*. As its name indicates, it lives in the open sea (*pelagus* is Latin for 'sea') and which, according to the name of the species (*noctiluca*, from Latin 'night light') is luminous. This light is given off by particular substances in its body. The present-day group of Coelenterata contains more than 9000 species and includes in addition to the medusas, hydras, corals and sea-anemones.

19

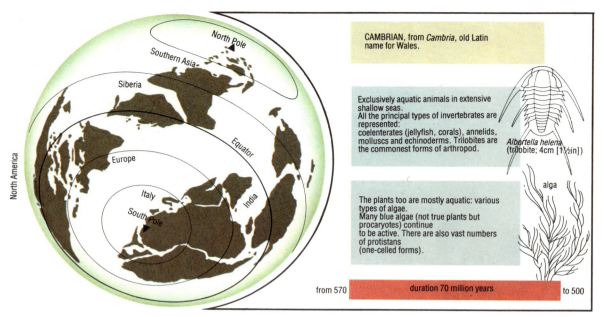

CAMBRIAN, from *Cambria*, old Latin name for Wales.

Exclusively aquatic animals in extensive shallow seas.
All the principal types of invertebrates are represented:
coelenterates (jellyfish, corals), annelids, molluscs and echinoderms. Trilobites are the commonest forms of arthropod.

*Albertella helena* (trilobite; 4cm [1½in])

alga

The plants too are mostly aquatic: various types of algae.
Many blue algae (not true plants but procaryotes) continue to be active. There are also vast numbers of protistans (one-celled forms).

from 570     duration 70 million years     to 500

# PALEOZOIC
# Cambrian

The Paleozoic era, which means 'of ancient life', began approximately 570 million years ago. The period that opened the era is called the Cambrian. At that point in the story of life, all the essential ingredients were present. In the seas were multicellular plant organisms, notably algae which were capable of photosynthesis and multicellular animals capable of eating the plants and feeding on one another.

The transition from unicellular organization, in which the cell is the whole individual, to multicellular organization, in which the cell is a part of the individual, occurred at different times. In the case of plants, it is likely that each major group of algae originated independently from one particular type of combination of single cells. Most experts believe that as far as the animals were concerned,

there were only two transitions. The first produced the sponges, animals in which the numerous cells are not organized. This means they do not form tissues with well-determined characteristics or true organs which are capable of performing a specific function. The second transition in animals was to the common stock of all other animals, the Eumetazoa.

The progress to multicellular organization involved only the eucaryotic cells, those with a defined nucleus. The procaryotic cells, those lacking a defined nucleus, remained forever in the unicellular state. The blue algae and the bacteria are examples of this and they still flourish today. Bacteria are 'feeding' procaryots (they are not photosynthesizers). As they feed they break down more complex organisms, that is, unicellular organisms with a true nucleus (protists) and multicellular organisms (both plants and animals). This breaking-down process makes simpler substances called molecules available again and these can be built up by photosynthesizing organisms, like blue algae and plants.

*Opposite: A diagram of the Cambrian period. The red band at the bottom shows the entire duration, in millions of years, of the Paleozoic era, of which the Cambrian was the first period.*
*Below: A fossil of a primitive annelid, from Burgess, British Columbia.*
*Bottom: A reconstruction of a seabed of the lower Cambrian. There are sponges, coelenterates similar to actinians, which are types of sea-anemone, and various annelids, which are similar to the marine worms sometimes used as bait by fishermen.*

# The shifting continents

Life began in the water and continued to develop in water up to about 450 million years ago.

In the long history of living things, the shape and position of the continents has been a matter of prime importance. This statement may sound surprising, for it implies that the continents move. This is indeed the case. Movement is very slow but the continents do move.

To explain this very simply we have to look at the structure of our planet. The Earth is more or less spherical. It

is made rather like an enormous onion: there are various strata or layers covering one another from the common centre towards the outside. At the centre is the core, made up of the metals iron and nickel in a fluid (inner core) and a solid (outer core) state. Then comes a thick mantle, the outermost part of which is made up of semi-fluid rocks. Over this is the crust, which literally floats, as it is made up of light rocks. The crust has raised zones and huge depressions: water (oceans) collects in the depressions, and the raised zones are the continents. The continents rest on bases known as plates. The plates move very slowly carrying the continents with them, which therefore 'drift'.

Continental drift is nowadays accepted as a fact, but for a long time the theory was disputed. People who adamantly refused to recognize that species change could hardly be expected to believe that anything of such an apparently solid nature as the Earth could also change. It is worth mentioning that in arguing this matter, geology, or study of the Earth, received strong support from paleontology. The discovery of virtually the same kinds of fossils in continents which are today separated by oceans proved that, in the remote past, those continents were linked and the same fauna and flora lived on them.

The continents themselves gave clear evidence of drifting movements. When the plates collide with one another, the edges are forced up and form mountains. Few traces remain of mountains formed like this, but they are unmistakable. They have folded layers, rather like a pile of newspapers flattened at the sides. These scattered traces can be dated, so we know *when* the continents collided.

nautiloid mollusc

The shape and development of these ancient mountains tell us, too, of the direction from which the continents came. In this way we can discover *where* they were originally. With the information available today, it is possible to reconstruct the activities of plates and continents over the past 1000 million years.

What was the shape and arrangement of the continents at the beginning of the Cambrian period? A single gigantic supercontinent from the Precambrian age had by now split up. A 'block' made up of what would be

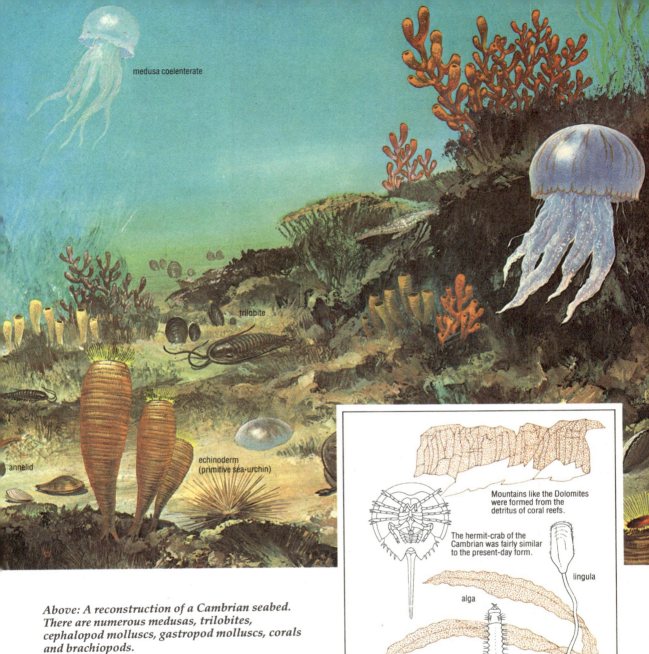

medusa coelenterate

trilobite

annelid

echinoderm
(primitive sea-urchin)

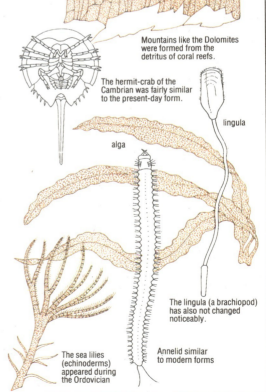

Mountains like the Dolomites
were formed from the
detritus of coral reefs.

The hermit-crab of the
Cambrian was fairly similar
to the present-day form.

lingula

alga

The lingula (a brachiopod)
has also not changed
noticeably.

The sea lilies
(echinoderms)
appeared during
the Ordovician

Annelid similar
to modern forms

*Above: A reconstruction of a Cambrian seabed.
There are numerous medusas, trilobites,
cephalopod molluscs, gastropod molluscs, corals
and brachiopods.*

*Right: A typical dolomitic formation. These
mountains are made up of the skeletons of corals
largely deposited in the Paleozoic era. The
creatures shown have survived from the Paleozoic
until the present day.*

Africa, South America and Antarctica, had coasts bordering the South
Pole. Connected to this continental
mass was the triangle of India, Australia and some parts of what would

later be southern Europe, that is, Italy, Yugoslavia and Greece. This huge southern land mass (Gondwana) was to maintain its form almost unaltered for some 300 million years. Other blocks detached themselves from it: one was made up of North America and Europe, and it was divided from Asia which was, in turn, cut in two by a stretch of sea.

# Cambrian animal life

The numerous coastal areas were notable for their comparatively shallow water. Fossils provide the best information about the creatures that lived in these zones. In some cases they are in an exceptional state of preservation. The Burgess fossils of British Columbia, for example, tell us about an entire fauna of small animals which clearly show how the main groups of Eumetazoa were already distinct and established. Among the Burgess fossils there are organisms similar to the annelid worms, that anticipate the arthropods, and others that resemble echinoderms and molluscs. There are medusas and sponges. There is even an animal which can be identified as a possible ancestor of all the chordates.

The arthropods are a vast group of animals, represented today by the insects, millipedes, spiders, crustaceans and other smaller groups. The annelids are well represented today by worms used as bait for fishing, by the lugworms of the genus *Arenicola*, by the earthworms and by the leeches. Present-day echinoderms include the sea stars and sea urchins, the sea lilies (crinoids) and the sea cucumbers (holothurians). Typical molluscs include the present-day octopuses, cuttlefish, mussels, oysters and snails.

The ancient forms of these types of

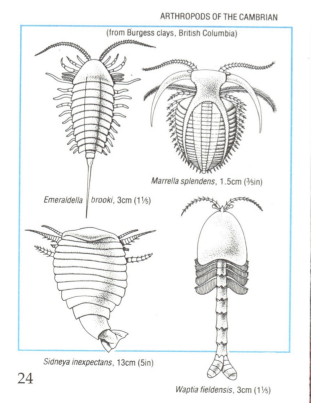

ARTHROPODS OF THE CAMBRIAN
(from Burgess clays, British Columbia)

*Marrella splendens*, 1.5cm (⅗in)

*Emeraldella brooki*, 3cm (1⅕)

*Sidneya inexpectans*, 13cm (5in)

*Waptia fieldensis*, 3cm (1⅕)

24

animal were different from those of today, but they had the same basic structures. The essential problem for animals has always been movement and, for multicellular animals, having a support for the soft parts of the body.

# Supporting the body

Certain animals make use of the natural support provided by water (Archimedes' principle); this is true of the medusas or jellyfish. Other animals have developed more or less rigid support structures, sometimes combined with appendages useful for movement. Such animals have, at a certain point, 'learned' how to extract salts of calcium, or silicon, from the water, transforming them into coverings of varying hardness. Others have 'discovered' how to synthesize certain proteins which can form rigid substances with calcium salts. This is why, from late Precambrian times onwards, there seems to have been an explosion of animal forms. Very few traces were left by the wholly soft animals that lived before then, where-

gastropod mollusc

nautiloid mollusc

gastropod molluscs

nautiloid molluscs

as the rigid skeletons of later forms have been preserved.

The bodies of the annelids and arthropods are arranged in a large number of more or less equal sections; all the structures (bristles, feet and breathing organs) are repeated. This is called metamerism. Even the oldest molluscs are metameric. Later, these animals developed most notably, a muscular foot divided, in the octopus and squid, into a number of arms. The molluscs later developed the shell, an interesting protective structure which sometimes became extremely complex, as with the ammonites.

The echinoderms display traces of metamerism only among the most ancient forms. Later they developed a star-like (five-pointed) body organization, adapted to life in the depths. Their skeleton is made of membrane bone (dermo-skeleton).

## The trilobites

The metameric body organization was particularly pronounced in the trilobites and similar animals. These were truly dominant elements of the Cambrian faunas.

The body of the trilobites was subdivided horizontally into three lobes; there was a head, a middle part and an end part. Each of the many segments had two feet and two gills, organs for absorbing oxygen from water and hence for breathing, on the underside. The head could be folded, and in almost all the thousand or so known species of trilobite, had compound eyes, formed of numerous simple eyes, as in modern insects. Food was moved towards the simple mouth opening by moving 'arms', as happens in present-day crustaceans. We know how the trilobites developed; there were different larval stages, as in insects and crustaceans. The adults, as they grew, had to change their hard covering from time to time, and it is mainly these remains of discarded parts that have been preserved and which enable us to study the trilobite body structure.

*The body of most animals has vertical symmetry. If you were to draw an imaginary line cutting the body into two parts, the left-hand side would be a mirror image of the right.*
*Below: Vertical symmetry in adult echinoderms is 'masked' by a star-shaped symmetry; however, the larvae, do have vertical symmetry.*
*Opposite: Living and fossil sea-stars and sea-urchins. These lived in Cambrian seas even though the earliest fossils only date from the following period, called the Ordovician.*

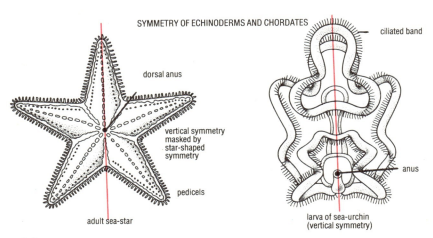

SYMMETRY OF ECHINODERMS AND CHORDATES

dorsal anus

vertical symmetry masked by star-shaped symmetry

pedicels

adult sea-star

ciliated band

anus

larva of sea-urchin (vertical symmetry)

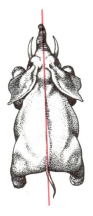

elephant (vertical symmetry)

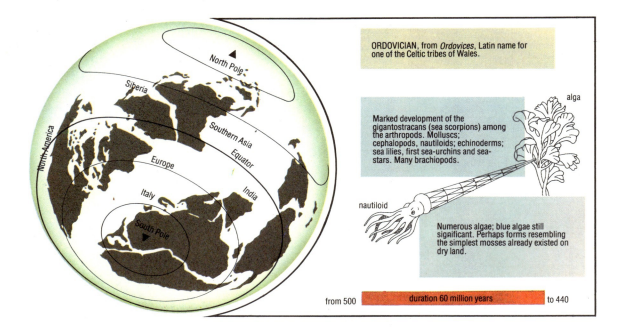

alga

Marked development of the gigantostracans (sea scorpions) among the arthropods. Molluscs; cephalopods, nautiloids; echinoderms; sea lilies, first sea-urchins and sea-stars. Many brachiopods.

nautiloid

Numerous algae; blue algae still significant. Perhaps forms resembling the simplest mosses already existed on dry land.

from 500 | duration 60 million years | to 440

# Ordovician

During the second period of the Paleozoic era, the Ordovician, the two blocks of the future Asia drew closer together. The zones that were to become Siberia and central Asia were on the Equator, which also ran through Canada. These areas enjoyed a fairly warm climate. The southern continental block moved north a little, and the South Pole was for a long time in the middle of the Sahara.

The presence of a huge continental land mass in a cold region helps to explain a phenomenon which has occurred on Earth on several occasions. This is known as glaciation. Snows and ice accumulate for thousands of years and form immense glaciers. This lowers the Earth's temperature and often leads to a drier climate as much of the continental water which might turn to rain is 'blocked' in the very thick glaciers.

There may also be a fall in the sea level and, in some cases, a 'wrinkling' of the crust beneath the weight of the glaciers. Some coasts may therefore be submerged.

Traces of glaciation are very clear. Rocks are literally eaten away, either smoothed by the slow advance of the glaciers or eroded by the rivers flowing down from them. Evidence of this can be seen in certain areas on the edges of the Sahara on rocks that date back to the Ordovician. It is also likely that the glaciations had a marked impact on living things. This may explain why at certain periods there are signs of fast-developing living forms, following periods when development seems to have been slow or even static.

For example, the explosion of new forms during the early Cambrian follows a Precambrian glaciation. This may, at least in part, be due to the fact that many areas near the coasts were again submerged to form shallow seas, and that the Earth's temperature was rising.

*Opposite: A diagram of the Ordovician period. The most striking feature in the map showing the appearance of the continental blocks, is the large concentration of land in the area of the South Pole. The Poles are the coldest regions of the planet; today there are huge amounts of snow and ice over the land masses. During the glacial periods the ice may have been several kilometres thick.*

*Characteristic traces of glaciers are rocks raised or eroded by the slow movement of the ice masses as they thawed and froze again and moraines.*
*Right: A typical moraine, heaped up the debris of rock that accumulated along the edges or at the front of a glacier.*
*Below: Pinnacles of eroded rock, probably the remains of an Ordovician glaciation. These rocks are in the Sahara desert.*

# The first giants

The numerous species of trilobites continued to dominate the seas. But other arthropods developed and soon established themselves. These were the gigantostracans or 'sea scorpions', notable principally for their exceptional size (over 2m (6·5ft) in length). They were animals fairly similar to crustaceans, with large paddle-like appendages for swimming and powerful chelae or claws at the front. The 'jaws' were of varying complexity. There was almost always a sturdy shield on the head. The eyes were usually multiple.

The molluscs, too, developed remarkably. In addition to forms resembling slugs (class Gastropoda, 'stomach-feet'), the nautiloids became widespread. These were animals of the class Cephalopoda ('head-feet'). They were similar to present-day squids but had very many arms and were protected by a long conical shell punctuated by a twisted cavity, like a gimlet. Some of these nautiloids had shells several yards long, often with a

29

partially spiral-shaped axis. The mouth opened between the arms. The nautiloids swam, unlike the gastropods who crawled on the ocean bed with their single large foot. Most of the nautiloid shell was full of gas given out by the animal, so it was used for floating, as well as protection.

*Below right: How a lake or river estuary during the Ordovician would have looked. The Gigantostraca, or 'sea scorpions', represented here by the genus Mixopterus, with specimens averaging 70cm (27½in) in length, were dominant in marine habitats and were already on their way to taking over inland waters as well. There may have been more powerful evolutionary stimuli in these surroundings, than in the sea, because the confined space would have meant the competition for food would have been stronger. The semi-transparent creatures are extremely primitive chordates similar to the present-day amphioxus. There are two specimens of Astrapsis on the seabed, these are primitive vertebrates without jaws. They lived during the middle Ordovician and were found in Colorado. All these creatures are collectively known as Heterostraca.*
*Below: The impressive gigantostracan of the genus Pterygotus.*

# The chordates

We come now to a group of animals from which all vertebrates are derived: the chordates. It is probable that certain prints found in the Cambrian Burgess strata belonged to these types of animal. They appear to have been quite similar to the amphioxus (*Branchiostoma lanceolatum*), which today lives on sandy sea beds. It is a small animal about 6cm (2¼ins) long, known as a lancelet because it resembles the point of a lance.

In order to solve the basic problem of movement, the combination of repeated parts (metamerism) and the semi-rigid internal structure of support, known as the notochord, would seem to be valuable. The metamerism permits the accordion-type movement of earthworms, whereby the segments swell and flatten by turns so that the body advances. The notochord favours a wriggling motion and so makes crawling possible and, more

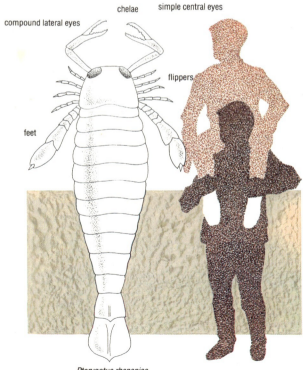

chelae

simple central eyes

compound lateral eyes

flippers

feet

*Pterygotus rhenaniae*
gigantostracan up to 2m (6½ft) long

primitive chordates (similar to amphioxus)

Mixopterus

importantly, swimming. The amphioxus and the earliest chordates share these characteristics.

We know for certain that the chordates closely resemble the echinoderms. The development of the larvae is similar and there are marked similarities in the protein structure of the two groups. Among the most ancient echinoderms are the carpoids or calcichordates, which have vertical and horizontal symmetry, rather than star-like symmetry. They have two arms as well as signs of metamerism in the 'tail' and in some 'gill' slits.

It is highly probable that, during the Precambrian, there was already a direct common ancestor of primitive forms of amphioxus and the carpoid-calcichordates. The basic structure of the amphioxus is retained in *all* chordates and also in vertebrates, at least during the first stages of development. It even holds true for ourselves in the earliest embryonic phase of life.

The first chordates were able to produce different types of rigid tissue. The principal ones were dentine which is the very hard main constituent of teeth; cartilage, which is relatively flexible, and bone. The animals thus developed a protective outer structure of plates made mainly of dentine and bony tissue, and internal cartilaginuous parts for supporting the gills and for protecting the nerve cord (vertebrae). The cartilaginous parts are usually metameric. The real supporting element for the entire body was the cord. The animals with these characteristics were the first vertebrates. They had no jaws but ate and breathed by absorbing water through a small opening, retaining food particles by means of a kind of filter or pharynx.

primitive chordates

Mixopterus

Astrapsis
(primitive vertebrate.)

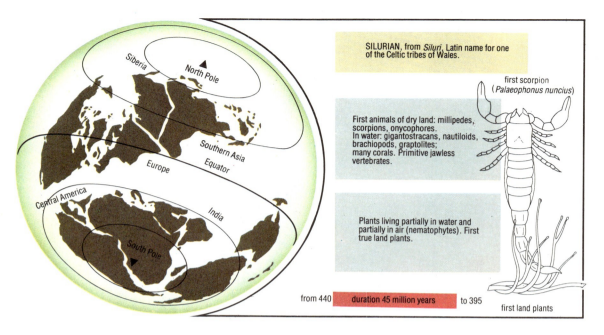

first scorpion (*Palaeophonus nuncius*)

First animals of dry land: millipedes, scorpions, onycophores. In water: gigantostracans, nautiloids, brachiopods, graptolites; many corals. Primitive jawless vertebrates.

Plants living partially in water and partially in air (nematophytes). First true land plants.

from 440     duration 45 million years     to 395

first land plants

# Silurian

The two sections of Asia joined together to form several mountain chains of which some traces remain. Europe approached the Asiatic block and the area that was to become the Urals began to be raised.

The shifts of Europe and North America resulted in various mountain ranges. Their remains are visible today in Scotland, Scandinavia and Nova Scotia.

The land mass of the southern continents (Gondwana) continued to move northwards. The South Pole was in part of southern Africa. The Ordovician glaciation had by now retreated. The climate was for a while a little warmer and in certain zones very dry conditions prevailed. There was now a phenomenon of immense importance, which signalled a dramatic leap forwards in the history of living things.

## From water to dry land

The great event of the Silurian was the gradual transfer of certain living forms from the water to the dry land. In describing this, we have to consider the important question of 'preadaptation'. We have seen that organisms adapt themselves to the conditions of their surroundings. In the many variants displayed by individuals of a certain group, there are some which may not appear to be an obvious advantage in that particular environment. However, seen with hindsight they maybe seen to be advantageous. This preparation for the future is preadaptation.

Algae that live in water find their support in the water itself-(Archimedes' principle). We all know that an alga or seaweed removed from the water turns flabby. This is naturally beneficial to those animals which normally feed on algae; they do not require powerful 'implements' to tear soft strips from these plants. However, certain algae may have developed the capacity to produce slightly stiffer tissues than was the norm. This capacity, which may have been of some use in water making the algae tougher and so less 'edible', represented a significant preadaptation for the move to dry land. The same kind of preadaptation happened to the arthropods. The hard exoskeleton of these animals had been developed as a protection against predators, but was also perfectly suitable as a support for the body out of the water. Arthropods and algae were thus ready to 'come ashore' on to dry land.

FIRST FOOD CHAINS OF DRY LAND

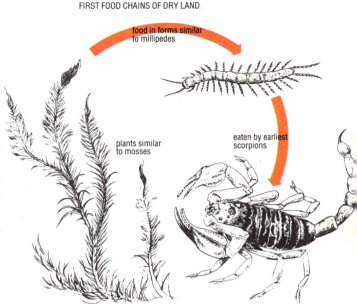

food in forms similar to millipedes

plants similar to mosses

eaten by earliest scorpions

*Opposite: A diagram of the Silurian period. Certain algae had long since acquired the capacity to produce fairly rigid tissues that gave them a supporting framework. When they were thrown accidentally on to banks or shores, these algae managed to survive and were the original plants of dry land.*

*Above: Very soon the plants were followed on to dry land by the animals. In the late Silurian there were already predatory land arthropods (scorpions) which certainly fed on herbivorous and omnivorous animals such as centipedes and millipedes.*

*Left: There is interesting evidence in these traces of* Baragwanathia longifolia, *from the late Silurian, that plants had by now followed a number of evolutionary paths, with diverse results.*
*Below: Plants developed simple tube-like organs which in due course became true vessels.*

FIRST PLANTS OF DRY LAND

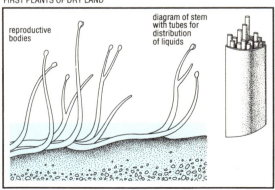

reproductive bodies

diagram of stem with tubes for distribution of liquids

# In search of light

As a result of tidal movements and strong waves, some algae were thrown into the spray zone and from there to the point where there was no more water. Preadaptation came into use. The algae became plants, discovering that there was plenty of light on dry land, more indeed than in water where, at a certain depth, it was very scarce. Perhaps some algae had already been driven to seek light on the coasts during the difficult time of the Ordovician glaciation. It is quite probable, too, that fairly simple vegetable organisms had attempted the great step in the Ordovician. They may have been plants similar to mosses. However, there are no traces of this.

The earliest land arthropods undoubtedly came later than these primordial mosses, and they were in turn followed by predatory arthropods. There are remains from the Silurian of certain scorpions, animals quite similar to modern scorpions but with short, stubby appendages.

In the second half of the Silurian, certain large plants, with a simple trunk still in the water, put long filaments, comparable to leaves, out of the water. These were the nematophytes or 'thread-plants'. These plants possessed surface cells which prevented excessive evaporation in the air, and simple vessel-like organs. We know, too, of land plants which did not yet have leaves and roots (*Cooksonia*). Finally, there is the fossil of a plant, *Baragwanathia longifolia*, from the late Silurian of Australia, which seems decidedly 'modern', with long needle-like elements similar to leaves. This plant had no direct descendants.

# Vanished skeletons

During the Silurian, the internal cartilaginous parts of the earliest vertebrates became more and more complex. They expanded so they could support side appendages adapted for swimming. The stiff outer covering or shell of certain animals began to get smaller, particularly around the tail, which thus became more mobile and more suitable for swimming, and only the head was covered. How can we be sure of the existence of an internal 'skeleton' which, since it was made of cartilage, decomposed and vanished? One clue is that the present-day lampreys and hagfishes are vertebrate animals without jaws (Agnatha), with a skeleton made of cartilage.

The first vertebrates with mobile appendages were the Cephalaspidea. They fed by filtering water that contained edible waste matter. Eating and breathing were a single operation: the 'used' water came out of a series of tiny holes and the food particles moved towards the intestine. These creatures have been compared to living tea-strainers.

*Opposite: A reconstruction of a Silurian seabed. The swimming creatures are two examples of Hemicyclaspis, jawless vertebrates of the Cephalaspidea. Some animals are able to create their own rigid structures of support and protection by emitting salts of calcium or silica that dissolve in the water. This accounts for the formation of the branches of corals, the 'under-the-skin' skeleton of the echinoderms, the external skeleton of the arthropods and the outer coverings of the first vertebrates. The cephalaspidians fed by absorbing water (rich in fragments of nutritious food) and filtering it through the pharynx. The water also supplied the animals with oxygen. Finally, the 'used' water was eliminated through a series of pores.*

HOW THEY FEED

teapot

strainer

tea

| food particles in water | filtering apparatus (pharynx) | → | food to be chemically transformed (metabolism) |

aperture to emit 'used' water

eye

mouth

front carapace

HOW THEY ARE PROTECTED

| calcium salts dissolved in water | capacity for precipitation | → | rigid framework (corals) |

rigid tissues (bony, cartilaginous, dentine)

| calcium salts and others | precipitation and various chemical processes | → |

eye

sensitive zone (with many nerve endings)

sea lilies

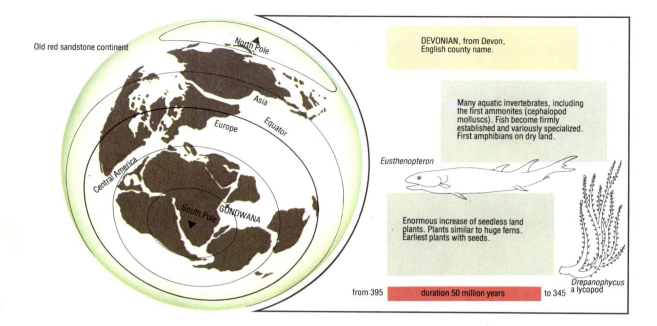

Old red sandstone continent

North Pole

Asia

Europe

Equator

Central America

South Pole

GONDWANA

DEVONIAN, from Devon,
English county name.

Many aquatic invertebrates, including
the first ammonites (cephalopod
molluscs). Fish become firmly
established and variously specialized.
First amphibians on dry land.

Eusthenopteron

Enormous increase of seedless land
plants. Plants similar to huge ferns.
Earliest plants with seeds.

Drepanophycus
a lycopod

from 395    duration 50 million years    to 345

# Devonian

Asia was by now a single block of land. Europe lay closer to it and the mountains of the Urals continued to grow. Gondwana shifted further north so that parts of Europe and North America were thrust up. These regions formed the basis of the Alps and the Appalachians. As the area between Europe and North America was compressed, various land masses which had been ocean beds, emerged. These areas were covered by reddish sandstone rocks. This new strip of land has been called the Old Red Sandstone Continent.

These ancient slabs of sandstone contain interesting fossils which tell us what happened at that time on the ocean floors.

Greenland was on the Equator; its surface was covered by lakes and swamps. The South Pole was approaching Antarctica, although it still formed part of Gondwana, corresponding to present-day southern Africa.

The climate of the southern continental block was fairly cold, but there were no true glaciations. Other continental areas were quite dry and warm, with hot and humid phases limited to the equatorial belt.

## Plants and sexuality

It is perhaps difficult to think of plants as having a sexual life; hard, for example, to realize that a plant's flowers are its genital organs. Linnaeus himself, when he proposed that his systematic classification of plants should be based essentially on the structure and functioning of their reproductive organs, risked being seen in some circles as something of a sex maniac! It has to be remembered that plants possess many other distinguishing features as well.

It may be useful to say something here about the reasons for sexuality

*Opposite: A diagram of the Devonian period. During the Devonian, the land plants, derived from the Silurian algae, developed interesting mechanisms for achieving sexual reproduction.*

*Right: A lycopod (club-moss) and several branches and sporangia (spore-cases) of an equisetum (horsetail). In the Paleozoic the Equisetales were sometimes enormous, up to 30m (98ft) in height. These may also have derived from the first Psilophytales. In the Devonian, primitive wingless insects similar to modern springtails (top photograph), and millipedes, scorpions and mites (bottom photograph) began to live on land.*

*Below: A reconstruction of some* Pseudosporochnus *plants, up to 3m (9ft) high, but lacking true roots and leaves. These belonged to the Psilophytales, and resemble the modern, rather insignificant* Psilotum *fern. In the background are several plants similar to club-mosses but rather larger than the present-day ones.*

sporangia (sexual organs) of equiseta

fertile branches of equiseta (horsetails)

present-day lycopod

reproductive organs

Pseudosporochnus (similar to a large Psilotum)

gigantic lycopods

absence of roots

and the various ways in which it can be accomplished. Sex offers the chance for each generation to obtain a mixture of the previous generation. It is likely that there will be a wide variety in the individuals created by the sexual act. This provides the opportunity for adaptations and evolutionary developments. Sex is therefore a highly important mechanism for preparing the 'material' which will be exposed to natural selection. An isolated cell, like a unicellular organism, can reproduce itself, without sex, by simple subdivision both of the cell and the nucleus. In a multicellular (eucaryotic) organism there may be specialized cells for reproduction; these cells will be produced by special organs. The sexual cells (gametes) make possible the exchange of genetic information by uniting and beginning the process that leads to the formation of a new individual. In the nucleus of each cell there is a fixed, determined number of chromosomes for every species. It might be assumed that the union of sexual cells would result in a doubling of the stock of chromosomes. This does not happen because the sexual cells develop with a number of halved chromosomes (haploid); only when they unite is the total number present in all the other (diploid) cells made.

Among animals there are few variations: the organs of the two sexes may be carried by the same individual

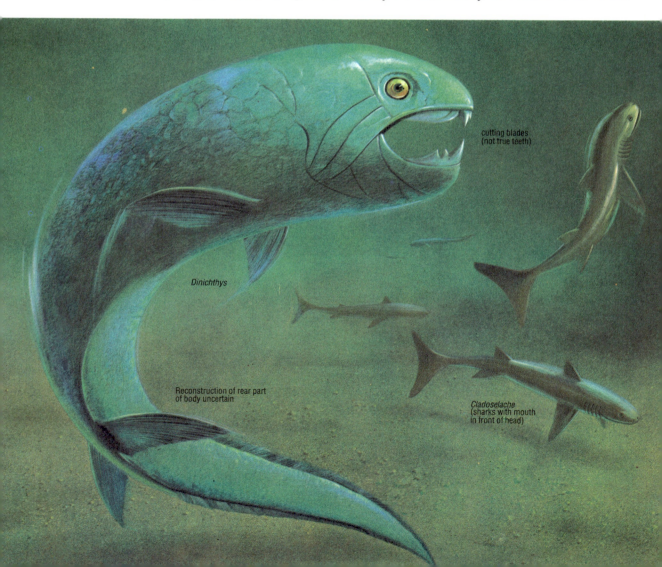

Dinichthys

cutting blades (not true teeth)

Reconstruction of rear part of body uncertain

Cladoselache (sharks with mouth in front of head)

(hermaphroditism, as in the earth-worm or the snail) or, more commonly, by distinct individuals, male and female.

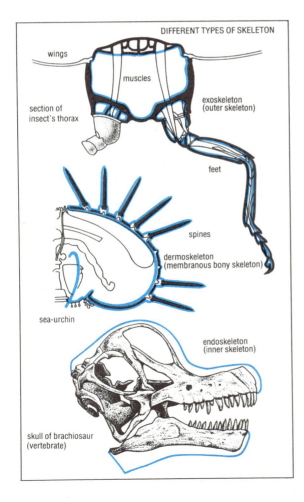

DIFFERENT TYPES OF SKELETON

wings

muscles

section of insect's thorax

exoskeleton (outer skeleton)

feet

spines

dermoskeleton (membranous bony skeleton)

sea-urchin

endoskeleton (inner skeleton)

skull of brachiosaur (vertebrate)

Plants tackle the problem in many ways. For example, in the case of certain green algae there are entire sexless (diploid) generations; provided there is from time to time a generation with sexual cells, the continuity of the species is assured. The vital problem for these living things has always been the need for an efficient cell structure to bear and protect the sexual organs and to allow the gametes to meet.

In water there are fewer difficulties; but on dry land it is necessary to 'invent' new strategies to make this possible, while preventing the gametes from drying out and becoming inactive. The algae, with their vast range of forms and sexual cycles, devised a variety of ways. Many of these methods were employed by land plants very successfully from the Devonian onwards. More and more areas were colonized, and some of the plants were gigantic.

# Invertebrates and vertebrates

The arthropods were soon rampant on dry land. In addition to scorpions, they included the first spiders, mites, millipedes and wingless insects.

In the oceans the gigantostracans were in decline, there were fewer trilobites, and tiny sea spiders (pantopods) appeared. Microscopic crustaceans known as ostracods and brachiopods, such as the daphnia or water fleas, were widespread. Both in sea water and in fresh water, these arthropods and various larvae were the principal animal parts of the plankton. The brachiopods, present since the Cambrian, were very widely distributed. Among the molluscs, the nautiloids were slightly in decline but the group of ammonites now emerged. These were cephalopods with a spirally twisted shell that contained several chambers. These animals were to remain on the Earth for more than 300 million years and were an essential element of the marine food chains.

We come now to the vertebrates. The Devonian has often been called the 'Age of Fishes'. The vertebrates that developed during the Ordovician and Silurian (which have deliberately never been described as 'fishes') now gave rise to animals possessing altogether new characteristics. The appearance of jaws, for example, was perhaps a feature of a number of groups and may have dated back to the late Silurian. The gills of the cephalaspids were supported by a series of cartilaginous gill arches. In time the anterior (front) arches were transformed into pincer-like jaws on which dentine elements developed; these were the teeth. Along the jaw, the other supporting parts of the anterior region remained separate. A true skull would form later.

There were several principal groups. The Acanthodii had the head protected by bony plates and possessed various triangular fins; they already looked like fishes (genus *Climatius*). The Placodermi, on the other hand, resembled the cephalaspids, looking like crabs with a tail, but they had a mouth with jaws (typical genera were *Pterichthys* and *Bothriolepis*). The Arthrodira were also placoderms, the head heavily protected, and the mouth, with serrated jaws but no true teeth, operating like a pair of shears. The body was tapered and forms such as *Dinichthys* were gigantic, up to 8m (28ft) long. The Arthrodira displayed some likenesses with the chimeras, pre-

Latimeria chalumnae (a coelocanth that has survived from the Devonian to the present day)

sent-day cartilaginous fishes. It has therefore been suggested that these placoderms should be considered to be ancestors of all the cartilaginous fishes. However, such a derivation may have happened even earlier, because in the late Devonian there were streamlined sharks (*Cladoselache*), with the mouth opening at the front end of the body instead of in the ventral region, as in present-day sharks.

The animals of these groups had an internal skeleton made of cartilage; but there is already a sign that the cartilaginous parts were being replaced by elements of bony tissue in some other animals. The change is seen in forms such as *Cheirolepis*, rightly taken to be the most ancient of the bony fishes, and in other very interesting fishes, the Sarcopterygii.

All these animals must have made a radical change in feeding habits: from consumers of waste matter and minute food particles they became hunters. They no longer strained their food; they trapped it and tore it apart.

Dipterus
(fossil dipnoans)

Left: As a result of changes in the environment and of competition from other fish one group of fleshy-finned fishes moved from the seabeds and inland waters to the ocean depths; these were the coelacanths, today represented by the celebrated Latimeria chalumnae, at the left of the drawing. Other fishes developed an expansion of the digestive tube which became a rudimentary lung. These were the Dipnoi or lungfishes. There are very few of them today but they were once very plentiful (at the right of the drawing is the genus Dipterus). They were able to withstand the drying-out of their environment by absorbing oxygen as well as air (through the lungs).

Bottom: A group of lungfishes (the Rhipidistia) grew very strong fins and were capable of surviving even on dry land, though near to water. The reconstruction shows Eusthenopteron.

Below: Some fishes of the Devonian developed fleshy fins supported by a collection of bones that resembled a limb.

EVOLUTION OF THE VERTEBRATE LIMB

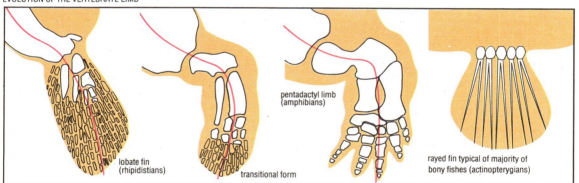

pentadactyl limb
(amphibians)

lobate fin
(rhipidistians)

transitional form

rayed fin typical of majority of
bony fishes (actinopterygians)

Eusthenopteron

# Fish on dry land

The water-inhabiting vertebrates of the Devonian prospered, and different groups almost certainly competed with one another. As a result, there must have been moves from seas to inland waters, and vice-versa. Judging from the wealth of living forms, we may take it that a number of evolutionary processes, more or less parallel, occurred in different environments.

The sarcopterygians developed, most notably, paired symmetrical fins, on either side of the body. These were stabilizers rather than paddles, for swimming was done mainly by movements of the tail. Each fin stemmed, like a fringe, from a fairly long bony support, looking like a foot without toes.

The sarcopterygians, which means 'fleshy fins' could withstand the drying up of a lagoon or a pond by making short journeys *out of the water*, from one pool to another. Yet it would be a mistake to think of these creatures as dedicated colonizers. Beverly Halstead points out rightly that emerging on to dry land was merely the last resort for them to survive *as fishes*. Some of these sarcopterygians were evidently not prepared to take the risk and migrated gradually to even deeper sea waters. One of them still survives today. This is the famous coelacanth (*Latimeria chalumnae*).

Other forms developed a kind of sac linked to the digestive tube, enabling them to take oxygen from the air. They also perfected their capacity to remain for long periods in the dry mud, thus surviving until the next abundant rainfall. Three such species still live today; these are the Dipnoi ('breathing twice', that is 'in two ways'). They actually possess gills and a rudimentary lung attached to the intestine. Clearly the sac linked to the tube was a preadaptation: in the bony fishes it was to become the swim bladder. This enables the fish to regulate its specific weight at various depths.

A third group of sarcopterygians, the Rhipidistia, responded to the challenge of the new environment by evolving a novel type of behaviour. They had openings (choanae) which linked the olfactory slits (nose) with the mouth (in other fishes the olfactory fossae had a dead end). This was obviously an advantage to an animal attempting to breathe while squatting, mouth closed, in the mud. The best known of these dipnoids was *Eusthenopteron*, 'with the very strong fin'.

# A double life

The animals of the genera *Ichthyostega*, *Elpistostega* and *Acanthostega*, found in strata of the upper Devonian, resembles the rhipidistians. These had a long tail and four feet, which were certainly webbed. The *Ichthyostega stensioi*, from the red sandstones of Greenland, was about 1m (3¼ft) long. The skull was similar to that of the rhipidistians, being formed of interlocking bones, the teeth were pointed and the legs were lateral. On land, the animal crawled on its belly, with wriggling movements. The head could perform limited movements up and down, so there was a trace of a neck. These animals were the first vertebrates to be partially land-dwelling: they were the first amphibians. Like the salamanders and present-day frogs, they certainly went through a larval (tadpole) stage with gills, this being spent entirely in the water. They led a 'double' life because at the start they lived as fishes and later as four-legged land animals (tetrapods).

*A reconstruction of Ichthyostega stensiöi, in a late Devonian environment. As the drawing of the skeleton shows, the animal had strong feet with five toes. These were pentadactylous limbs – the pattern that was to become basic for all land vertebrates. The scapular or pectoral girdle, connecting the 'arm' with the spinal column, was quite developed, whereas the pelvic girdle, connecting the hind limbs with the spine, was weaker. The skull was made up of numerous bony elements, as in the rhipidistians (Eusthenopteron and allied creatures).*

he tail has a characteristic sh-like fin

skull

top view

bottom view

Ichthyostega stensiöi

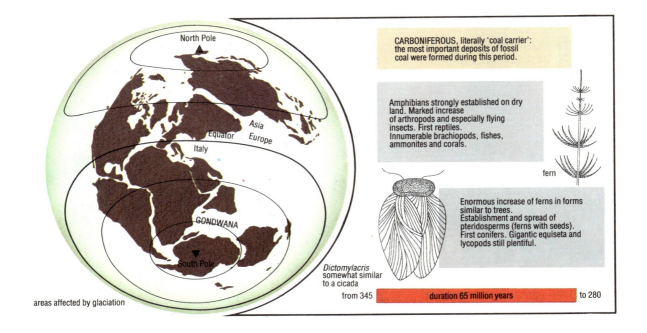

CARBONIFEROUS, literally 'coal carrier': the most important deposits of fossil coal were formed during this period.

Amphibians strongly established on dry land. Marked increase of arthropods and especially flying insects. First reptiles. Innumerable brachiopods, fishes, ammonites and corals.

fern

Enormous increase of ferns in forms similar to trees. Establishment and spread of pteridosperms (ferns with seeds). First conifers. Gigantic equiseta and lycopods still plentiful.

*Dictomylacris* somewhat similar to a cicada

from 345     duration 65 million years     to 280

areas affected by glaciation

# Carboniferous

The continental blocks were by now very close together, with Africa beginning to 'push' North America, raising the Appalachians, while Europe and Asia were joined, forming the Urals. The North Pole touched the extreme eastern tip of Asia and the South Pole was in mid-Atlantic. A good part of the emergent land surface thus lay in the belt between the tropics: the climatic conditions here were mainly mild and humid. Antarctica and adjoining areas were affected by a glaciation in which there were phases of varying severity.

Throughout the Carboniferous, the coastal areas and low-lying lands in general tended to rise and fall alternately; lagoons formed in estuaries and later dried up. Thus there were large deposits from the accumulation of sand and mud, sedimentary, sand-stone rocks. During the uplifted phases when the water retreated, plants and trees immediately invaded the land and formed forests. These were later submerged in a new phase and covered again by mud. Deprived of air, the vegetation, especially the trees began to decompose and decay. As a result of the pressure of the layers of sediment that continued to accumulate, these trees became carbonized, turning to coal. This process affected the hard, woody part of the trees which as a result of various and slow chemical reactions, loses its oxygen and practically all its hydrogen, thus becoming a fossil carbon. Research has shown that the major deposits of coal in the world today are found in areas which, during the Carboniferous, were in the equatorial belt. These areas were covered by immense forests, particularly in Europe and in North America.

It is worth referring to another common fuel nowadays used by man: petroleum. Deposits of petroleum are perhaps even older (Silurian-Devo-

44

nian). They would have come from complex chemical processes that broke down various organic substances, especially algae and aquatic animals, eliminating oxygen, nitrogen and other elements, leaving only carbon and hydrogen combined in such a way as to form hydrocarbons. The fuel, petroleum, is a mixture of hydrocarbons.

*Opposite: A diagram of the Carboniferous period, when the plant kingdom expanded enormously. Established plants were joined by more advanced plants like the arboreal (tree) ferns and ferns with seeds (Pteridospermae). These plants had fern-like fronds.*

*Below: The inset picture shows branches of* Sphaenopteris, *a fossil from Germany. They did not reproduce by spores, as true ferns do, but by seeds, produced by special sexual mechanisms. The pteridosperms must have resembled modern palms (lower photograph); but there is no relationship between these two types of plant.*

# From forests to coal

We are often led to imagine remote geological periods as the time of giants: scorpions 2m (6½ft) long, shells of 5 or 6m (16–17ft) and vertebrates measuring 10m (33ft) or more. The plants of the Carboniferous are surprising for their size, and for the fact that they belong to groups whose plants today are small. All living things, plants in particular, tend to grow large if they have no competition. Trees that are 30–40m (100–130ft) tall are quite commonplace today to the disadvantage of those plant seedlings whose stocks were dominant during the Paleozoic era. So if the huge trees of those times still exist, they are mere shrubs today.

The Lepidodendrales (*Lepidodendron*) with tufts of slender leaves measuring up to 1m (3ft), and *Sigillaria*, with plumes of leaves of about the same size were abundant in Carboniferous forests. They are related to the present-day lycopods or club-mosses. The huge Equisetales (*Calamites*), with a trunk 30m (100ft) high, nowadays represented by the horsetails, at most 1m (3ft) tall, and various treelike ferns were also widespread.

The appearance of 'ferns with seeds' (Pteridospermae) was a highly significant development. These were the first plants to evolve a part designed to protect and nourish a seed. This enabled the new individual to germinate only when conditions were favourable. Until then reproduction in land plants involved immediate development of the new plant, which had obvious disadvantages if the environment changed. Plants no longer needed to rely on a watery environment for reproduction. The water necessary for metabolism was absorbed by the roots which grew deeply into the ground. At the end of the Carboniferous the first conifers were growing. The seeded ferns became extinct about 200 million years ago.

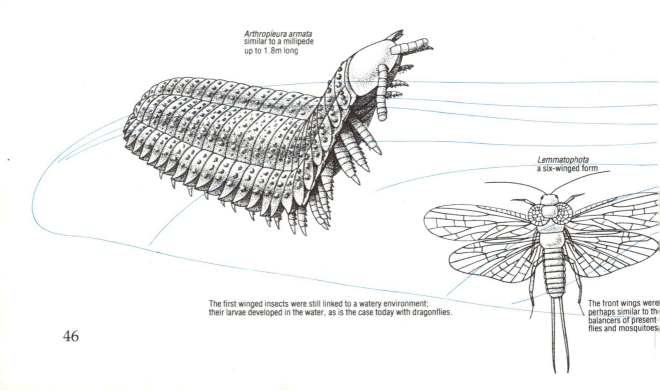

Arthropleura armata
similar to a millipede
up to 1.8m long

Lemmatophota
a six-winged form

The first winged insects were still linked to a watery environment; their larvae developed in the water, as is the case today with dragonflies.

The front wings were perhaps similar to the balancers of present flies and mosquitoes.

# The first wings

The tall foliage of the Carboniferous vegetation created an ideal environment for the arthropods – moisture, warmth and plenty of food, both in and out of the water. Some arthropods lived in water during the larval stage and in the air as adults. Some of the insects displayed an interesting development. On the back of the thorax, they had special growths which became articulated and which were moved by powerful muscles. They were the first wings on

*The Carboniferous forests were populated by hordes of insects and other arthropods: millipedes, spiders, scorpions and mites.*

*All insects have three pairs of legs at the front of the thorax. After the very earliest wingless insects, insects developed which had several pairs of growths at the back of the thorax. These growths became the wings. The first winged insects resembled dragonflies and, like them, had aquatic larvae.*

*Below: The wing of the Carboniferous 'dragonfly' Meganeura monyi, about 35cm (14in) long, actual size. The millipede Arthropleura was 180cm (70in) long.*

*Right: Several pairs of the modern dragonfly Lestes viridis. The females are laying eggs on the stem of a reed.*

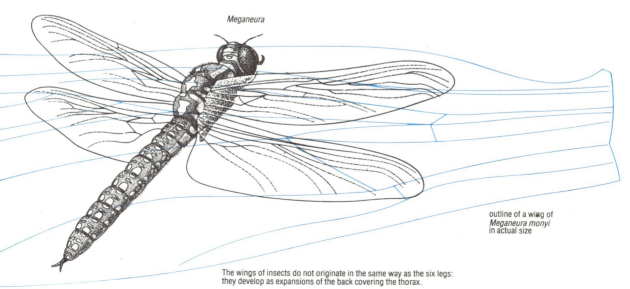

Meganeura

outline of a wing of
*Meganeura monyi*
in actual size

The wings of insects do not originate in the same way as the six legs: they develop as expansions of the back covering the thorax.

the planet Earth. Initially insects attempted to fly with four true wings and two small scales possibly used as stabilizers. Very soon the pattern of two pairs of wings was developed. There is a wealth of fossil documentation. One notable species was *Meganeura monyi*, similar to modern dragonflies. Other examples were various millipedes, among which the forms of the genus *Arthropleura* reached human size.

while others resembled crocodiles more closely. All these amphibians had teeth in which the dentine and enamel were folded. In cross-section the pattern is like a maze, and for this reason the animals have been called Labyrinthodontia, 'with labyrinth-type teeth'. Various rhipidist fishes

*The eggs of the Amphibia, in which the embryo is surrounded by a gelatinous covering (the photograph below shows the eggs of a frog) have to be laid in water. The larva which grows from the egg is the aquatic tadpole, and it has gills. Opposite is the larva of an amphibian of the late Carboniferous, genus Branchiosaurus. Amphibians several metres long known as labyrinthodonts (reconstructed at bottom) lived in the lagoons of the late Carboniferous. They had teeth with layers of dentine in closely packed folds which in cross-section (opposite, above) resemble a labyrinth.*

## Vertebrates with and without legs

Among the numerous amphibians living in Carboniferous forests, several evolutionary branches have been discovered. Some were rather like salamanders and present-day tritons,

equiseta

Dolichosoma
an amphibian with a snake-like body

Anthrachosaurus

section of a tooth of a labyrinthodont amphibian

The dentine is furrowed by complex grooves and seems to be folded repeatedly.

a typical labyrinth

Labrinth-type teeth already existed among various rhipidistian fishes.

gills

Skeleton and silhouette of *Branchiosaurus*, perhaps a large tadpole or a form in which the gills were also retained by the adults.

arboreal ferns

already had similar teeth.

It was not unusual for 'old' and 'new' amphibians to live alongside one another. *Diplovertebron*, of the late Carboniferous, an animal more than 1m (3ft) long had many skeletal elements of cartilage in the areas corresponding to 'wrist' and 'ankle' and the notochord was still present in adults.

There could be disadvantages in laying eggs with no shell in the water. A very large number of eggs had to be laid in order that some survived swamps that dried out and hungry predators. Yet once again we ought not to think in terms of a 'pioneering spirit' for the amphibians which were driven to colonize new environments were forced by the need to survive and to guarantee the survival of at least a few tadpole larvae during those critical periods when ponds and swamps dried up completely.

Some amphibians succeeded in laying eggs which could survive, without drying out, away from water: they were eggs with a shell. These amphibians, well adapted to withstand unfavourable conditions, were already reptiles. The remains of *Hylonomus*, one of the first representatives of the new class, date back 280 million years.

The tendency to exploit and improve the use of legs and feet contrasts with another trend, seen among various amphibians not belonging to the labyrinthodont group. These animals adopted a serpentine movement and in many cases there was an almost complete absence of limbs (Aistopoda, genus *Phlegetontia*).

As for sea-dwelling animals, the brachiopods and ammonites were very plentiful. The first belemnites appeared among the cephalopod molluscs. Bony and cartilaginous fishes dominated the food chains.

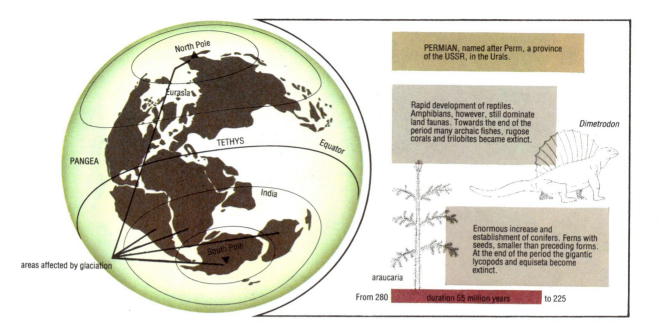

PERMIAN, named after Perm, a province of the USSR, in the Urals.

Rapid development of reptiles. Amphibians, however, still dominate land faunas. Towards the end of the period many archaic fishes, rugose corals and trilobites became extinct.

*Dimetrodon*

Enormous increase and establishment of conifers. Ferns with seeds, smaller than preceding forms. At the end of the period the gigantic lycopods and equiseta become extinct.

araucaria

From 280     duration 55 million years     to 225

areas affected by glaciation

# Permian

All the continental masses were joined together in a single supercontinent called Pangea ('the whole earth'). A number of seas, or long gulfs, cut into this enormous land block, one between India and Antarctica–Australia, another between north-east Asia and Canada. A third, along the line of the Equator, was the extensive Tethys Sea, named after the sea goddess. Sediments accumulated in this sea and subsequent plate movements formed the Alps and, later, the Himalayas. During the Permian the Urals emerged definitively.

The principal phenomenon of this period was the great glaciation which continued from the Carboniferous. Traces of glaciers indicate the maximum extent of the ice. Antarctica, southern Australia, India and a vast portion of Africa and South America were buried by ice.

The climate became drier but remained fairly hot in the equatorial belt and in the adjacent tropical zones. The insects continued to thrive, because they were able to tackle the problem of reproduction, the number of insects that had non-aquatic larvae increased because many swamps dried up.

Glaciation in the southern part of Pangea proceeded in a succession of waves, conditions slowly improving around the middle of the period. By the end of the Permian the extent of the glaciers was fairly limited.

## Climatic barriers

Living things were now able to move about on dry land without ever 'getting their feet wet'. This might suggest that during the Permian both plants and animals were distributed uniformly. Fossil remains indicate that different populations existed at

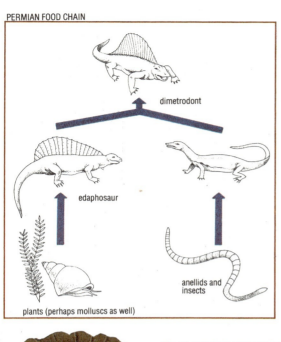

PERMIN FOOD CHAIN

dimetrodont

edaphosaur

anellids and insects

plants (perhaps molluscs as well)

*Opposite: A diagram of the Permian period. During the Permian, the reptiles adapted to the different climate and ecology in various parts of the Pangea supercontinent. In the northern part, where the climate was mainly dry, the pelicosaurs, with a 'sail' on their backs, were in their element. This skin formation, supported by very long extensions of the dorsal vertebrae, served as 'heat-exchangers', absorbing heat from the outside or dispersing it as the need arose. These animals could thus keep their temperature almost constant.*

*Left: A diagram of a Permian food chain.*
*Below: Edaphosaurus pogonias was a herbivore and also probably ate molluscs. Dimetrodon incisivus was a predatory carnivore.*

The sail on the back acted as a heat-exchanger.

*Edaphosaurus pogonias*

*Dimetrodon incisivus*

araucaria

different latitudes. The barriers to expansion were not stretches of ocean but differences of temperature and climate. In the southern part, especially, the existing glaciation caused particular adaptations which happened in several phases. This shows that the glaciers advanced and retreated alternately. In the northern regions other populations lived. In practice, Pangea was divided into three ecological regions: the northern, climatically not too cold but dry: the central belt, still with warm-humid conditions: and the southern zone, affected by glaciation. There was a wide southern distribution of pteridosperms and conifers. One fern with seeds, *Glossopteris*, is a kind of fossil guide. Its tongue-shaped leaves

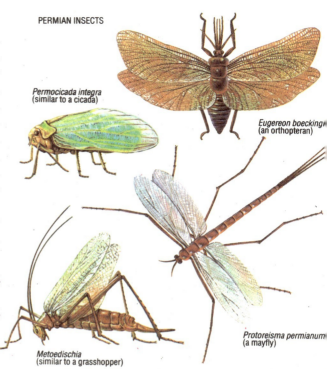

PERMIAN INSECTS

*Permocicada integra*
(similar to a cicada)

*Eugereon boecking*
(an orthopteran)

*Protoreisma permianum*
(a mayfly)

*Metoedischia*
(similar to a grasshopper)

*Lycaenops*
(predatory therapsid)

*Dicynodon turpior*
(omnivorous therapsid)

(the Greek name means 'tongue-leaf') have been found in the Permian strata of South America, Madagascar, Antarctica and Australia. The huge equisetes and tree-type lycopods were in decline but still plentiful in the equatorial zone. Environments that varied so much obviously accommodated a wide variety of plant and animal life.

# The egg with a shell

We know that *Hylonomus*, discovered in upper Carboniferous strata, may be regarded as a reptile. This opinion is based on the structure of its skeleton. The most important indication, however, has not yet been found. Carboniferous strata have not yet provided traces of any eggs with shell. The first egg fragments have appeared in Permian strata.

To describe how a reptile's egg is formed, we must first compare it with that of an amphibian. The amphibians lay eggs which are made up of a simple covering of gelatin around the embryo. Because there are very few nutritive substances available to the embryo, it must very quickly develop into a free-swimming larva or tadpole and look after its own food supply. Large numbers of eggs dry out. In the reptile egg the embryo develops in a 'private pool' which cannot dry out, because of a small sac filled with liquid, the amnion (from the Greek name for a special vessel in which the blood of the victim sacrificed to the gods was collected).

The embryo can obtain oxygen from the outside through another sac called the allantois (literally, in Greek, 'similar to a sausage'): this enables the embryo to eliminate its waste products. Food comes from a large yolk,

full of nutritive substances, connected to the embryo by the umbilical cord. All these organs are immersed in a larger sac containing liquid and surrounded by a membrane called the chorion. Finally, there is the outer protection furnished by the calcareous shell.

*Opposite: Some typical insects that lived during the Permian (above) and reconstructions of some therapsid reptiles (below). Among these mammal-like reptiles were powerful omnivores such as Dicynodon turpior and fierce predators like the gorgonopsidians (genus Lycaenops).*
*Below: Egg of an amphibian, fossil egg of a dinosaur and diagram of the type of egg laid by reptiles and birds.*

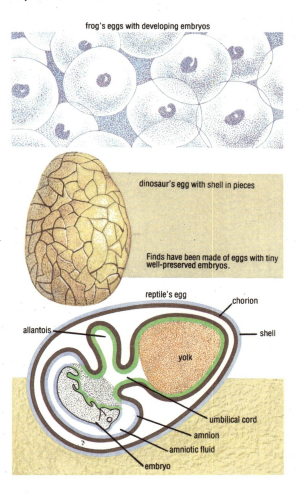

frog's eggs with developing embryos

dinosaur's egg with shell in pieces

Finds have been made of eggs with tiny well-preserved embryos.

reptile's egg

chorion

allantois

shell

yolk

umbilical cord

amnion

amniotic fluid

embryo

The shell is perforated by a very dense series of tiny holes. It is porous and allows air to filter through. The embryo can absorb oxygen and expel carbon dioxide. This gas reacts with the calcium carbonate of the shell to produce calcium bicarbonate. The shell is gradually used up and the calcium bicarbonate is dissolved in the blood, and is transferred to the developing skeleton of the embryo. The shell must be sufficiently thick to provide enough calcium to the skeleton but not too thick, so that air can get through and the baby can hatch.

In this perfectly protected environment, the embryo can complete its development. The creature that emerges will be a miniature copy of its parents. There are no tadpoles among the reptiles.

# The changing skull

How do we distinguish the skeleton of an amphibian from that of a primitive reptile? The legs of the reptiles are usually more robust and are often arranged at less of an angle; reptiles tend to hold their belly off the ground and do not crawl. But these distinctions can lead to errors. There are many reptiles which have continued to have legs that are inclined and not set vertically as they live close to ponds.

Let us look at the skull. Reptiles are more active in the search for food and especially in hunting. They have a skull that is better suited to seizing and chewing, and thus more solid and efficient than that of the amphibians. An essential feature of this pincers grip is the quadrate bone to which the mandible, or lower jaw, is attached. In amphibians the quadrate is inclined forwards, like the central stroke of a capital N. The reptile skull has the quadrate in a vertical position,

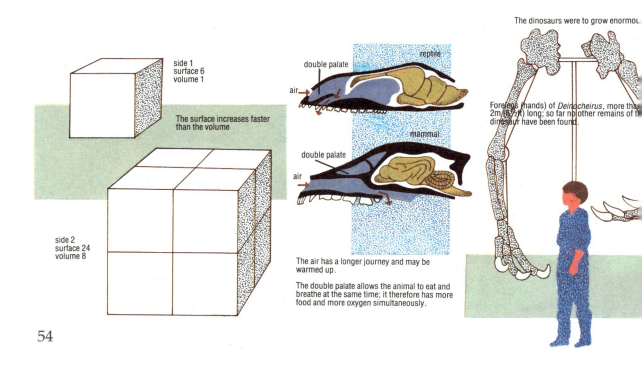

side 1
surface 6
volume 1

The surface increases faster than the volume

side 2
surface 24
volume 8

double palate

air

reptile

double palate

air

mammal

The air has a longer journey and may be warmed up.

The double palate allows the animal to eat and breathe at the same time; it therefore has more food and more oxygen simultaneously.

The dinosaurs were to grow enormou

Forelegs (hands) of *Deinocheirus*, more tha 2m (6½ft) long; so far no other remains of t dinosaur have been found.

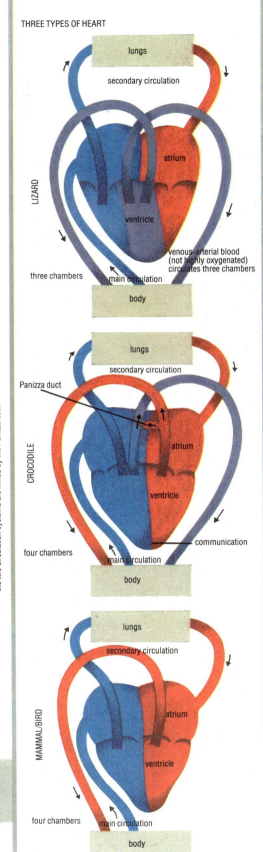

THREE TYPES OF HEART

LIZARD

lungs

secondary circulation

atrium

ventricle

venous-arterial blood
(not highly oxygenated)
circulates three chambers

three chambers

main circulation

body

CROCODILE

lungs

secondary circulation

Panizza duct

atrium

ventricle

four chambers

communication

main circulation

body

MAMMAL/BIRD

lungs

secondary circulation

atrium

ventricle

four chambers

main circulation

body

During the long periods that the crocodile spends under water there may be differences in pressure between the aerated and poorly oxygenated blood; so the two circulation systems are linked by the Panizza duct.

which ensures greater solidity. This has evolved either by straightening the oblique stroke of the N and moving it forwards so that it coincides with the letter's first vertical stroke, or by rotating it slightly so that it is shifted back to coincide with the second vertical stroke. Both these formations have evidently occurred in the course of vertebrate evolution.

In the first case the skull is shortened, in the second it is lengthened. The first arrangement, according to D.M. Watson, characterizes an evolutionary line leading to the present-day reptiles and the reptiles of the Mesozoic and to the birds. The second is typical of the mammal-like

*The reptiles, in the course of their evolution, by various methods and with various mechanisms have succeeded in maintaining their body at a constant (or almost constant) temperature, which varies according to the outside temperature. Illustrated here are some of the means: increase of body size, the secondary palate, a four-chambered heart, and perhaps viviparity (birth of living young) with special links of assistance between parents and babies in order to ensure rapid growth.*

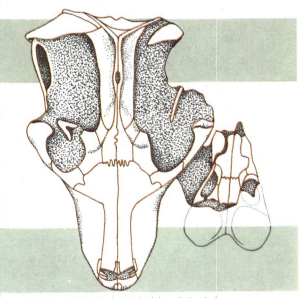

Skull of an adult (mother) and baby thrinaxodont, actual size. The comparative dimensions of the baby suggest that the paramammals gave birth to live young and that the mothers fed them with a substance (milk?) which encouraged rapid growth.

55

or mammalian reptiles, and of the true mammals. This shows that the evolutionary history of the mammals has been a very lengthy process and that its important prologue took place during the transitional phase of amphibians to reptiles. The events of the Permian suggest that the reptiles constituted a group of immense evolutionary potential; these creatures had already begun to show the basic features that were to be peculiar to the mammals. Recent research and information support this interesting viewpoint.

# Faster metabolism

To be an active hunter, to obtain food and to flee an enemy, an animal must have a rapid metabolism, that is it must be able to transform in a hurry the substances that its body needs. To speed up metabolism, a great deal of oxygen has to be continuously introduced into the body; it must also circulate efficiently through all the organs, carried by the blood. So the animal has to be able to breathe all the time, even when it is eating and the substances to be transformed are entering the body. For this to happen, the animal's mouth and the ducts that carry air within the lungs must be separated. This separation is absent in amphibians, but is present in reptiles and is increasingly efficient in the mammal-like types and in the true mammals.

To ensure the best distribution of oxygen-charged blood through the different parts of the body, it helps if the areas of the heart that pump oxygen-charged blood in the body are separated from those that remove the used blood for purification and oxy-

genation in the lungs. There is such a separation in the hearts of mammals and birds, yet the reptiles had already taken this step. In the heart of crocodiles, the two regions are separated. Perhaps certain reptiles of the past, the dinosaurs, for example, which are fairly closely related to the crocodiles, had a heart similar to the mammals' and thus enjoyed a rapid and efficient metabolism.

An animal must develop efficient systems of absorbing heat from its surroundings and of retaining what it has absorbed to produce its own heat energy by a rapid metabolic rate. Heat is exchanged through the body surface; the larger the surface the greater the amount of heat that can be absorbed and stored. The reptiles also followed this path, sometimes developing large and, in the case of the dinosaurs, truly gigantic bodies.

# Keeping cool and warming up

We are taught that in any geometrical solid, as the dimensions grow, the volume increases more rapidly than the surface. Big volume, big mass, big weight; for an animal that is too large, the difficulty in getting about outweighs the advantages of size. The reptiles exposed to changing temperatures resorted to various devices to make the best of their situation and to avoid any unpleasant consequences that might hamper their activities.

In the northern belt of Pangea the climate, during various phases of the Permian, was much like it is today in the deserts. Probably the intense heat of the day was followed by an extremely cold night. Some reptiles,

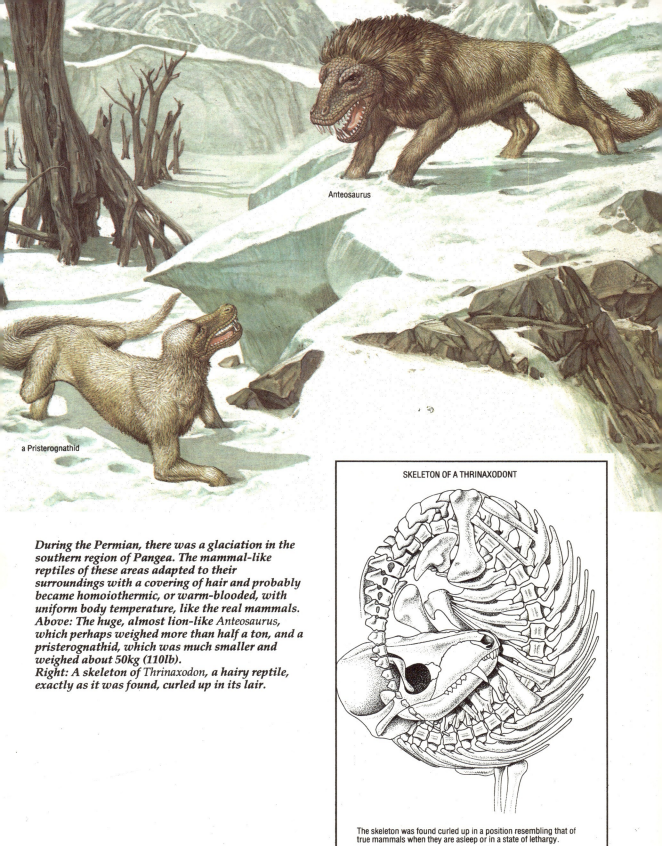

Anteosaurus

a Pristerognathid

**SKELETON OF A THRINAXODONT**

*During the Permian, there was a glaciation in the southern region of Pangea. The mammal-like reptiles of these areas adapted to their surroundings with a covering of hair and probably became homoiothermic, or warm-blooded, with uniform body temperature, like the real mammals.*
*Above: The huge, almost lion-like* Anteosaurus, *which perhaps weighed more than half a ton, and a pristerognathid, which was much smaller and weighed about 50kg (110lb).*
*Right: A skeleton of* Thrinaxodon, *a hairy reptile, exactly as it was found, curled up in its lair.*

The skeleton was found curled up in a position resembling that of true mammals when they are asleep or in a state of lethargy.

57

notably the pelicosaurs, the 'lizards with the axe', developed long extensions of the vertebrae of the back; these spines supported a large strip of skin, like a sail. It is believed that the skin may have been filled with many blood vessels, so that it could have exchanged heat between the animal's body and the environment: a broad expanse of surface with minimal increase of volume. The pelicosaurs, whose remains have been found in Europe and in North America, were able to lose heat when the surrounding temperature was too high or to warm up as soon as the first rays of the sun appeared. All they needed to do was to set the 'sail' parallel or perpendicular to the sun's rays.

Present-day reptiles are said to be 'cold-blooded' because they do not possess a physiological mechanism that maintains the body temperature at a constantly higher level than that of the outside surroundings. Modern reptiles are therefore known as poikilotherms ('different' or 'variable heat'). Vertebrates that can produce their own heat like mammals and birds are, in contrast, called homoiotherms ('similar' or 'constant heat'). The pelicosaurs were 'cold-blooded' but managed to maintain their temperature within certain limits, because of the 'sail'.

In the glacier region of southern Pangea the reptiles were able to keep their body temperature constant with hair. Hairy reptiles? The skulls of certain reptiles reveal series of tiny hollows which are like those in the facial bones of modern mammals with whiskers. Whiskers and hairs are therefore similar formations. It is thus very probable that the reptiles of cold regions had a coat or covering of fur, an effective form of insulation.

Study of the mammal-like reptiles (classified as therapsids) has recently led to some highly interesting theories, which we shall be discussing later. It is worth saying that some experts maintain that these animals should no longer be regarded as 'strange' reptiles but as very primitive mammals. L.B. Halstead has proposed giving them the new name of paramammals.

# Different kinds of teeth

The Permian reptiles displayed other striking adaptations that brought them close to being homoiothermic. A further evolutionary step towards mammals is shown in the development of different teeth: front teeth adapted for biting, like the incisors of the mammals; tusks, like the canines, and teeth for gnawing, like the premolars of modern carnivores, the carnassials. Such teeth are typical of predators. They have been found, among the pelicosaurs, in *Dimetrodon* and, among the therapsids, in *Lycaenops* and similar animals. The herbivores sometimes exhibit curious plates for chewing, with only two tusks in the jaw. These were possibly bigger in the males, as in *Lystrosaurus*, a reptile widely distributed in the southern part of Pangea, from Australia to Antarctica and from southern Africa to India.

The small aquatic reptiles known as mesosaurs had a very large number of equal-sized teeth similar to needles. These animals were fierce predators of fish and crustaceans in inland lagoons and in shallow coastal waters. The webbed feet and powerful tail which they had were perfect adaptations for swimming.

Left: **Remains of** Tridentinosaurus antiquus, **a Permian land reptile which was about 30cm (12in) long.**

Below: **The aquatic reptiles known as mesosaurs were common in inland waters and possibly in shallow coastal waters in the southern part of Pangea. They had needle-like teeth and preyed on fishes and very small crustaceans.**

Mesosaurus tenuidens

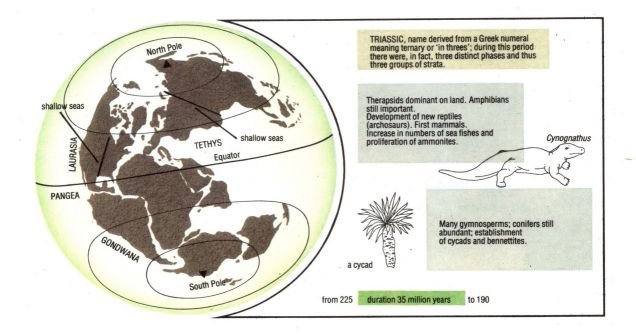

TRIASSIC, name derived from a Greek numeral meaning ternary or 'in threes'; during this period there were, in fact, three distinct phases and thus three groups of strata.

Therapsids dominant on land. Amphibians still important.
Development of new reptiles (archosaurs). First mammals.
Increase in numbers of sea fishes and proliferation of ammonites.

*Cynognathus*

Many gymnosperms; conifers still abundant; establishment of cycads and bennettites.

a cycad

from 225   duration 35 million years   to 190

# MESOZOIC
# Triassic

*Above: A diagram of the Triassic period. This was the time when there was a wide spread distribution of gymnosperms or plants that reproduce by seeds but which have no visible flowers. Nowadays the commonest gymnosperms are the conifers-pines, firs, sequoias, yews and junipers.*

*Opposite: The Triassic gymnosperms lived with plants that nowadays grow in oases because of the fairly arid climate. Among the conifers were many araucarians or monkey-puzzles, shown at left inset. Today they grow wild only in the southern hemisphere, but they are often cultivated elsewhere. Other common Triassic gymnosperms were the cycads and ginkgos, also cultivated today (middle and right inset).*
*The large photograph shows the famous petrified forest of Arizona, with trunks of Triassic gymnosperms which were buried under layers of mud or sand and were transformed, through the action of silica-rich waters, into hard rocks. The covering strata were subsequently eroded and today the trunks of 'stone' appear on the surface.*

The Triassic period opens the Mesozoic ('of middle life') or Secondary era.

Why has science decided to make a clear division, underlining the transition from the Permian to the Triassic, thus introducing a new geological era? Today we can say that although many new elements appeared in the Triassic, it was linked with the preceding period. In the past scholars concentrated only on a few phenomena, principally the disappearance of various groups of animals, interpreting them as signs of a new chapter in Earth's history.

Pangea still consisted of a single land block but the Tethys Sea had expanded so that the northern part of the land mass, Laurasia, was separated from the southern part, Gondwana. Various fractures had now opened up which would isolate the continents.

The climate was predominantly warm and dry. There were many desert zones but within them were vast oases.

# Continuity and discontinuity

There were not many sudden changes in the plant kingdom. The coniferous huge araucarias with typical scale-like leaves were still dominant. There was a marked increase in the number of Cycadales, which were gymnosperms, like the conifers. Today they are represented by a few genera, including *Cycas*, with several tropical species raised as bedding plants. *Cycas* has a characteristic stocky stem with the scars of fallen leaves. These are similar to palm leaves but much tougher, and the single leaflets have a finely serrated edge. The reproductive organs in the modern species are exposed; in the fossil species there were protective structures slightly resembling bristly petals.

During the Triassic, the ginkgos began to establish themselves. Today there is only one surviving species of these flowerless trees. Some forms of vegetation gradually disappeared. The Triassic saw the decline of the gigantic equisetes and of many of the pteridosperms.

In the animal kingdom the trilobites vanished completely from the seas. The dominant corals Rugosa or Tetracoralla, of the Paleozoic, were replaced by corals that are still plentiful in the seas today. There was enor-

*Skeleton and reconstruction of* Tanystrophaeus longobardicus, *a reptile belonging to the group of protorosaurs, close to the future lizards. This reptile was up to 4.5m (15ft) long, at least 3m (9ft) of which was neck. It fished without actually going into the water. The neck was formed of a few very long vertebrae, some of them 32cm (12½in) long and about 2cm (¾in) across.*

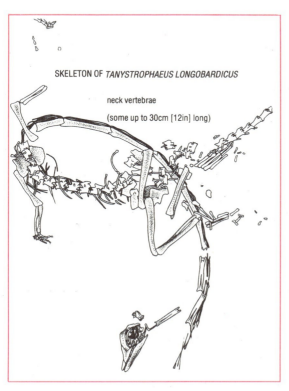

SKELETON OF *TANYSTROPHAEUS LONGOBARDICUS*

neck vertebrae
(some up to 30cm [12in] long)

Tanystrophaeus

mous development among the ammonites and also among the belemnites. These molluscs had a characteristic internal pointed shell, and possibly were similar in outward appearance to cuttlefish.

There is much evidence of sharks, based only on the discovery of their teeth, for their cartilaginous skeletons decomposed rapidly. These animals are proof that such a skeleton is an excellent supporting element in water. It also has the advantage of being light. The bony fishes, on the other hand, show that heavier bony body parts are stronger. The effect of their weight may be balanced by a swim bladder, which the shark or ray never possessed. The bony fishes were abundant in the Triassic but not yet dominant, as they are in the seas today. The brachiopods continued to progress; some have survived to this day. The sea lilies declined sharply but the sea urchins increased. Inland waters teemed with bony fishes, gastropod molluscs and crustaceans. And as we shall see, the reptiles had a strong impact on all these animal communities.

# Amphibians: giants in trouble

During the Triassic the number of reptiles increased triumphing over all other animals. They were a vast range of types. Meanwhile the amphibians were still flourishing. Some of the biggest of all the labyrinthodont amphibians date from the Triassic. Certain animals of the genera *Mastodonsaurus*, *Capitosaurus* and *Trematosaurus* were up to 5m (16½ft) long, with the skull alone measuring more than

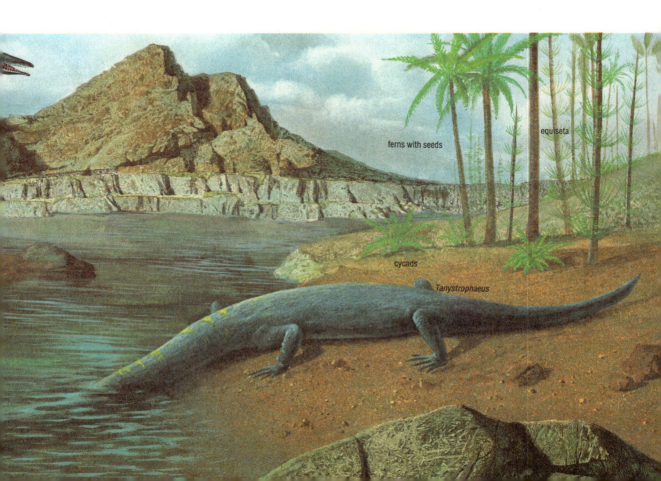

ferns with seeds

equiseta

cycads

*Tanystrophaeus*

1.5m (5ft). Although the labyrinthodonts were gigantic, they did not depart from the basic pattern, resembling colossal salamanders with a disproportionately big head and a large tail adapted for movement in water. The limbs were feeble and always set with the uppermost part horizontal or slightly at an angle, so that out of the water they were extremely clumsy and slow. New forms of amphibians which emerged at the beginning of the Triassic were very different. These animals developed the capacity to jump using only their hind legs. This was a new movement for vertebrates. Among the first jumping amphibians was *Triadobatrachus massinoti*, a small 'toad–frog' of the early Triassic, with fairly short hind legs. These amphibians are abundant today in lakes, ponds and all wet surroundings.

The labyrinthodont amphibians existed fairly well in the tropical region during the Permian, with many forms of varying sizes. The giants of the Triassic frequented inland waters, especially lagoons and ponds of oases.

Throughout the period, but particularly during the second part, movements of Pangea caused frequent variations in the land level, with much flooding. The numerous lakes and inland seas which were formed provided favourable habitats for reptiles capable of remarkable adaptations.

Excavations of large heaps of labyrinthodont fossils of the same species indicate that in many instances many of these amphibians were killed when a lake or pool dried up very rapidly.

# Expert swimmers

Many reptiles were well adapted for swimming. This was because of the mobility of the tail and the flexibility of the limbs, which were articulated at 'shoulder' and 'hip'. The scapular and pelvic girdles, connecting the limbs and the spine, became very strong, and the vertical setting of the limbs became more pronounced. Finally, many reptiles developed powerful hind limbs designed for swimming.

By gradually adapting themselves to life out of water the reptiles evolved a standard pattern of four strong, almost equal limbs, like present-day lizards and crocodiles, or two powerful hind limbs, from which many two-legged reptiles were to evolve.

# In and around water

The association with water, and especially with the sea, continued to be a powerful evolutionary stimulus for the reptiles.

The ichthyosaurs, reptiles adapted for swimming in the open sea, hunters of fishes and ammonites, appeared. The placodonts flourished. Their characteristic front teeth were possibly designed to prise bivalve molluscs from rocks, and their flat teeth for grinding hard materials, including shells. The notosaurs also flourished. They had a snakelike neck and feet with toes that were distinct but webbed like a duck's. It is probable that the notosaurs spent much of their time on cliffs, diving into the water to catch fish: they lived much like the present-day walruses. Long-necked reptiles lived on the beaches

*Right: A well preserved fossil of* Paralepidotus ornatus, *a bony fish of the Triassic, close to the Holostei group, which today has very few types. Fishes and molluscs were a rich source of food, and many reptiles evolved capable of using this resource.*

*Below: A reconstruction of* Mixosaurus carnalius, *an icthyosaur of the middle Triassic, 1–2m (3–6½ft) long. The limbs of these reptiles were transformed into fins which were probably used as depthfinders and stabilizers. The tail was the propeller. At the bottom is a specimen of the genus* Placodus.

Mixosaurus carnalius

Mixosaurus carnalius

Placodus

at the edge of lagoons and inland seas. They could fish without swimming, by merely dipping their head under water. One curious member of this group was *Tanystrophaeus longobardicus*, which had an almost rigid neck of exceptionally long vertebrae.

There were also reptiles which already bore a strong resemblance to modern crocodiles and huge water lizards with webbed feet (genus *Askeptosaurus*).

# On dry land

The direct ancestors of true lizards (genus *Prolacerta*) emerged on dry land during the Triassic. In the early part of the period this environment was still dominated by the therapsids or paramammals. *Lystrosaurus* and other similar forms roamed the areas covered by vegetation near the swamps. Their habits resembled those of the hippopotamuses of today.

One predatory therapsid was *Cynognathus*, a kind of small dog almost 2m (6½ft) long, with five strongly clawed toes on each foot, a leathery nose, external ears with auricles, whiskers on the muzzle and powerful teeth with tusk-like canines. Not all the paramammals were large; some were small, like *Thrinaxodon*, but all were active predators. From the remains of several young specimens, we may deduce that there was a change of teeth with the 'milk' teeth dropping out and being replaced, as in true mammals. The arrangement of the ribs indicates that these animals already had a diaphragm, the flat muscle which, in mammals, separates the cavity containing the heart and lungs from the one containing the intestines.

During the second half of the Triassic, the small paramammals lived alongside the equally small and earliest true mammals.

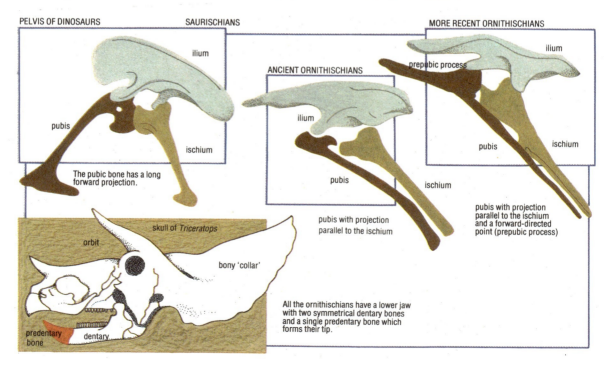

PELVIS OF DINOSAURS  SAURISCHIANS

ilium

pubis

ischium

The pubic bone has a long forward projection.

ANCIENT ORNITHISCHIANS

ilium

pubis

ischium

pubis with projection parallel to the ischium

MORE RECENT ORNITHISCHIANS

prepubic process

ilium

pubis

ischium

pubis with projection parallel to the ischium and a forward-directed point (prepubic process)

skull of *Triceratops*

orbit

bony 'collar'

predentary bone

dentary

All the ornithischians have a lower jaw with two symmetrical dentary bones and a single predentary bone which forms their tip.

Cynognathus crateronotus

Euparkeria

At the beginning of the Triassic, the land was still dominated by the therapsids or 'mammal-like reptiles'; but the evolutionary story of the archosaurs, the group of reptiles which included the dinosaurs, was about to begin.
Above: A reconstruction of Cynognathus crateronotus, a therapsid almost 2m (6½ft) long, and some archosaurs of the genus Euparkeria, maximum length 90cm (35in).

Right: A skeleton of Euparkeria compared with that of another archosaur, Hypsilophodon (up to 1.5m [4½ft] long), In both skulls the opening in front of the eye orbit, typical of all the archosaurs, can be seen. The pelvis of Euparkeria is like a saurischian, whereas Hypsilophodon's is of the ornithischian type.

Opposite: A diagram of various types of pelvis which make it possible to distinguish the saurischian from the ornithischian archosaurs. There is also an ornithischian skull with the predental bone, characteristic of all the animals of this group.

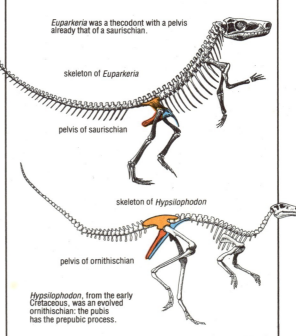

Euparkeria was a thecodont with a pelvis already that of a saurischian.

skeleton of Euparkeria

pelvis of saurischian

skeleton of Hypsilophodon

pelvis of ornithischian

Hypsilophodon, from the early Cretaceous, was an evolved ornithischian: the pubis has the prepubic process.

# The ruling lizards

Among the active land reptiles of the Triassic, one that is of particular interest was a creature just under 1m (3ft) long and fairly agile. It walked on its hind legs, which were stronger than the forelimbs, balancing the weight of the front part of its body with the long muscular tail which it held raised from the ground. This was *Euparkeria*. Probably it was the successor to the first descendants of the most ancient reptiles, such as *Hylonomus*, so it already had a long history. Its skull was fairly big with strong jaws but the bony structure was lightened by large empty openings. There was a cavity between the orbit containing the eyes and the nostril, and it may be that this cavity contained a 'salt' gland. Present-day reptiles and birds which live in arid areas have a similar gland; it gets rid of excess salt accumulated in the body.

Today only crocodiles have this type of skull, but in the past it was a characteristic of all the huge reptiles known collectively as archosaurs ('ruling lizards') and, in particular, the dinosaurs.

The enormous group of archosaurs may be subdivided into five groups. The first was the thecodonts, relatively primitive forms of modest size. *Euparkeria* was one of the more highly evolved thecodonts, with various characteristics anticipating the true dinosaurs. A second group was the crocodiles, the only archosaurs to survive. A third was the pterosaurs, flying reptiles which we shall speak of later. Finally came the two groups of dinosaurs.

The reason for two groups of these last reptiles is that the archosaurs exhibited two different types of pelvis which make it possible to distinguish two lines of evolution.

In the saurischian, or 'lizard-hipped', dinosaurs the pelvic bone known as the pubis projects for-

*Euparkeria **is included in the relatively primitive group of thecodont archosaurs although it has a saurischian pelvis.** Ornithosuchus **(below) and** Saltoposuchus longipes **(opposite), 90cm (35in) long also belong to this group. Both were predators of the late Triassic. The huge predatory surischian dinosaurs known as carnosaurs came from reptiles similar to** Ornithosuchus. **The first true saurischians were the coelurosaurs, predatory animals, typified by** Coelophysis **(below) of the late Triassic, of average size but very slender.***

ANCIENT ORNITHISCHIANS

Coelophysis

Ornithosuchus

Saltoposuchus

The plateosaur could probably get around both as a quadruped and a biped. Standing on the hind legs only, it could reach the fronds of the tallest trees.

The outline of the skeleton shows the typical saurischian pelvis.

fern with seed

cycad

wards: this is found in the majority of reptiles living today.

In the ornithischian ('bird-hipped') dinosaurs the pubis is turned towards the rear and is elongated. In later animals the bone itself has a kind of forward-directed point. All the ornithischians have a special predental bone at the tip of the mandible and are mainly herbivorous. The pelvis of the ornithischians, as the name suggests, resembles a modern bird's, but this does not mean there is a direct relationship. We shall be discussing the evolution of birds and we shall see how these vertebrates were descended from forms of saurischian dinosaurs.

*The first gigantic saurischians were herbivores: the abundance of plant food encouraged the development of ever bigger animals. Plateosaurus, from the late Triassic, had large forelimbs, which were shorter and less powerful than the hind legs. It was thus a biped which could, if necessary, move about on four legs. Some specimens of plateosaur were 9m (29½ft) long. These animals probably lived in herds, as many herbivores do today. In their search for food they move from one feeding ground to another. During the Triassic this meant going from one oasis to another. Perhaps the animals were sometimes surprised by adverse weather conditions. This would explain the large heaps of skeletons, all of the same species, found in 'plateosaur graveyards' in parts of Europe.*
*Top: A reconstruction of plateosaurs on the move towards areas with more food.*
*Above: The two positions possible for a plateosaur.*

Plateosaurus

Plateosaurus

# Lizard-hips

A few thecodonts already had a lizard-like pelvis. This group showed the evolutionary tendency that was to lead to many typical forms of saurischians. For example, *Ornithosuchus*, 3.6m (12ft) long, is a good model of what were later to be the huge carnivorous saurischian dinosaurs, the carnosaurs.

Already classifiable as saurischians were the coelurosaurs, measuring 2m (6½ft) or a little more, agile, slender and two-footed. These animals were swift predators and were able to live with the largest of the paramammals

and the even more massive and probably slower carnosaurs. Certainly there was little serious competition for food, considering the very wide range of prey available.

The saurischians began to be aware of the vast quantity of plant food and many of them developed into herbivores of considerable size. Abandoning the bipedal pattern, they once more discovered the advantages of walking on all four legs, retaining the ability to raise themselves on their hind legs only. One of the first gigantic, herbivorous saurischians was *Plateosaurus*, normally 6m (19½ft) long but sometimes up to 9m (29½ft). These were probably the first reptiles

71

to be able to maintain an almost constant body temperature because of their enormous mass.

After the 'sails' of the Permian pelicosaurs and following the homoiothermic experiments of the hairy paramammals, this was to be the third way of keeping warm that the reptiles evolved.

The dry climate of the Triassic must have created problems for the herbivores. The drying up of an oasis could compel the plateosaurs to move to other vegetated areas and the journey of the herd across the desert often ended disastrously. This would explain the presence of 'plateosaur graveyards' with numerous skeletons of animals that had apparently all died together and been buried by the sands.

Towards the end of the Triassic the first ornithischians appeared. We know of *Fabrosaurus*, 1m (3¼ft) long, and the curious *Heterodontosaurus*, which had various kinds of teeth including tusk-like canines, suggesting a carnivorous diet. The tusks were probably used in defence and in duels between rival males.

# Dawn of the future

The discovery of a small paramammal called *Thrinaxodon* at the beginning of the Triassic has provided fascinating evidence of the transition into true mammals. Some excavated skeletons were curled up in a position typical of a mammal, indicating that the animals had rolled themselves up in their fur to keep warm. No modern reptile behaves in this way. In one case the remains of an adult, possibly a mother were found closely attached to those of a baby. The skull of the baby, apparently just born, was bigger, in proportion to that of the adult, than is usual for the skull of a baby reptile. The proportions were the same as are found among new-born babies and adults of mammal species. Some people maintain that animals such as *Thrinaxodon* must have given birth to live young and fed them with a substance similar to milk, produced by special glands. The development of the young would have been quicker if they had a metabolism improved by food that was easy to digest. Mammal's milk is just such a food. So why should this not apply to the more highly evolved of the paramammals?

Towards the end of the Triassic, *Thrinaxodon* and the other paramammals vanished. They were replaced by small hairy animals, wholly homoiothermic, which were probably better adapted and more efficient than their reptilian predecessors. These were the first true mammals.

*Morganucodon* is a typical example measuring about 10cm (4in). It must have looked much like a present-day insectivore. Its teeth were of various shapes and sizes, with small tusk-like canines and premolars suitable for crushing hard substances. Remains of *Morganucodon* have been found in England, China and South Africa.

These earliest mammals learned to inhabit all possible environments as they could live in the cold. They hid in the smallest cracks and perhaps burrowed in the ground. They learned how to be active at night when small reptiles and amphibians were forced to rest. At sunset the morganucodonts started hunting insects, spiders, millipedes, small amphibians and reptiles numbed by the cold. They may also have fed on seeds and roots.

Morganucodon

SKULL OF MORGANUCODONT

dentition of morganucodont (*Eozostrodon*)

mandible 2.25cm (9/10in) long

During the Triassic, especially near the end of the period, the smallest mammal-like reptiles were replaced in the same environments by the first true mammals. Very soon these animals adapted to an active life during the evening and night, avoiding competition with the reptiles, active by day.
Above: A reconstruction of Morganucodon.
Left: Upper and lower jaw of a morganucodont (Eozostrodon). The mammals of the Triassic, predators and perhaps omnivores, were very like present-day insectivores.

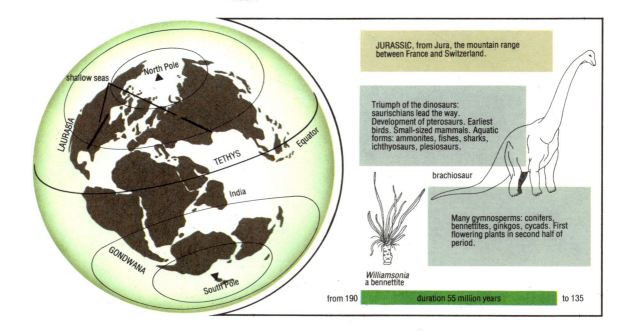

JURASSIC, from Jura, the mountain range between France and Switzerland.

Triumph of the dinosaurs: saurischians lead the way. Development of pterosaurs. Earliest birds. Small-sized mammals. Aquatic forms: ammonites, fishes, sharks, ichthyosaurs, plesiosaurs.

brachiosaur

Many gymnosperms: conifers, bennettites, ginkgos, cycads. First flowering plants in second half of period.

*Williamsonia* a bennettite

from 190 — duration 55 million years — to 135

# Jurassic

The Jurassic period, midway through the Mesozoic, was notable for its relatively stable climate. The break-up of the supercontinent Pangea caused significant changes in the shapes of the existing land masses. The majority still lay in a broad belt which did not include the South Pole and which scarcely touched the North Pole. There were no phases of intense cold during the Jurassic and there were probably heavy and frequent periods of rain. This was ideal for the growth of vegetation, and therefore for the herbivores. This was the time when the largest plant-eaters lived on the Earth.

## Continents on the move

During the Jurassic the North American plate broke away from Gondwana, and the North Atlantic began to fill the space between North America and Africa. The split between America and Eurasia also occurred during this period. Vast seas of shallow water formed, from north to south, in North America and, in Eurasia, between Europe and Asia.

Antarctica, Australia and South America were detached from Africa. Towards the end of the period, the South Atlantic was already evident. The plate movements thrust up the Andes and the Rocky Mountains. A rotation of the land later to become Spain and Portugal formed the Bay of Biscay and the Pyrenees.

Later in the period India, breaking away from East Africa, began drifting north, still staying south of the Equator. On all continents there were extensive areas of lakes and swamps.

conifers

*Williamsonia sewardiana*

cycad

## REPRODUCTION OF A FERN

prothallium

Among ferns growing on wet ground, the prothallium develops from the spores: in this are formed the sexual organs whose male and female cells create a new, asexual plant (sporophyte) when they unite.

The fern we all know is the sporophyte.

stamens with pollen (♂)

ovaries with ovules (♀)

The entire plant is an asexual support to the flowers.

In flowering plants the sexual cells are produced on the plant itself within the parts of the flower.

The reproduction of the fern is linked to a watery environment. In plants with seeds the seed may remain dormant for some time and then originate a new plant exactly like the one that has produced it.

*Opposite: A diagram of the Jurassic period.*
*Above: Specimens of ginkgos, cycads and bennettites, all gymnosperms that were still abundant and widely distributed in the Triassic. The first angiosperms, plants with visible flowers, also appeared.*
*Left: In both the gymnosperms and angiosperms union of the sexual cells occurs in parts that no longer develop on wet ground but which form on the plant itself. A tree is actually an enormous support, sexually neutral, which bears flowers with sexual organs.*

75

# Jurassic plants

Ferns and horsetails, some of them very large, even gigantic, covered the river banks and lake shores. The conifers and cycads expanded their range to form forests. So, too, did the Ginkgoales, an enormous group, nowadays represented by only one species, *Ginkgo biloba*. It was to explain the extraordinary survival of this plant that Darwin invented the term 'living fossil', later applied to many other plant and animal forms. Today the ginkgo or maidenhair tree grows in botanical gardens. It is strange to think that those leaves that provide shade may once have been browsed by dinosaurs. The reproductive method of the maidenhair is similar to the conifers, so it is classified among the gymnosperms, in which the seeds are exposed. It also has features in common with the flowering trees or angiosperms, where the seed is enclosed in a seed vessel. Each maidenhair tree bears organs of one sex only; pollen is carried to the female organs by the wind, and a large seed, enclosed in a reddish pulp, is formed. Little red balls with stalks, resembling cherries, appear among the double-fanned leaves, which are like larger versions of the fronds of the maidenhair fern. The ginkgo is transitional midway between the old and new trees.

Other trees of the Jurassic forests with intermediate features of known groups were the Bennettitales, now totally extinct but seen in many well-preserved fossils. They had a woody trunk covered by a kind of shell formed from the bases of fallen leaves, similar to palms. The leaves, resembling the fronds of ferns, were grouped in tufts at the end of the trunk, which could be quite tall – up

bony fishes

to 4m (13ft) in the very common genus *Williamsonia*. The organs of both sexes were contained in vessels similar to the flowers of the angiosperms. They had neither petals nor sepals, but a series of feathery leaflets. It is likely that pollination of these trees was by wind and by insects and other arthropods, which were very plentiful in the forests, scrubland and steppes throughout the Jurassic.

During the second half of the period the first angiosperms appeared. For the first time flowers bloomed on dry land. By now trees and other plants were wholly independent of water for reproductive purposes. For this reason they formed ever closer relationships with the animal kingdom, and especially with the insects.

Geosaurus

Geosaurus

ammonite

ichthyosaurs

# Life in the seas

With the emergence of intercontinental oceans and inland seas, the Jurassic provided ideal conditions for marine animals. There were many molluscs and innumerable cephalopods: belemnites and, above all, ammonites, but also types similar to octopuses and squids. The many cartilaginous fishes included sharks and rays. The bony fishes, too, were expanding their range everywhere, and were common even in inland waters. All these animals were a valuable food source for the reptiles, and there was an enormous increase in the numbers of predatory reptiles.

The three principal groups of reptiles adapted to life in the seas were the plesiosaurs, the ichthyosaurs and the crocodiles. The last group made a

*Above: The shell of an ammonite from the English Jurassic, diameter about 13cm (5in).*
*Top: A reconstruction of some Jurassic marine reptiles. Geosaurus was an archosaur of the crocodile group, perfectly adapted for swimming, its toes were all linked to form efficient flippers. Its tail had two muscular expansions which looked like a forked fin. These marine crocodiles preyed on fishes and ammonites, which were very plentiful in Mesozoic seas.*

particular impact towards the end of the period, for example, *Geosaurus*, up to 4m (13ft) long, and *Steneosaurus*, up to 9m (29½ft). The limbs of the Jurassic marine crocodiles were similar to flippers but the skeletons retain the structure of distinct fingers, with a normal number of phalanges. Among the plesiosaurs and especially among the ichthyosaurs, the phalanges were very numerous so that the fingers grew close together,

forming a sort of mosaic of small bones as support for the flippers. The flippers of the ichthyosaurs were less mobile than those of the plesiosaurs because of the formation of the upper parts of the limbs. It is probable that the ichthyosaurs swam with the tail alone, using the fins as rudders for direction and depth. The plesiosaurs, on the other hand, used the fins as paddles. Certainly the ichthyosaurs were able to submerge without difficulty and could therefore hunt at great depths. Study of the limb structure of the plesiosaurs indicates that these animals were unable to raise their limbs above the shoulder, and so they could only swim near the surface. This is the explanation for the length and extreme flexibility of the neck. This was their real fishing instrument; when they were as close as possible to the prey, they would dive and stretch the neck taut for the kill.

## Fishing techniques

The ichthyosaurs were active in the open sea and plesiosaurs were active close to the shores. The plesiosaurs probably fed mainly on fishes, whereas the ichthyosaurs caught bony and cartilaginous fishes and cephalopods. Sometimes the different species would appear to have concentrated on one or the other only. The dentition of the ichthyosaurs varied; some had a long mouth with sharp teeth, ideal for grabbing fast-moving fishes, while others had a broad mouth with flat teeth, better suited for cracking shells. In some specimens the stomach contents are still visible; they are either the remains of fishes or of cephalopods. Curious pellets, consisting of numerous tiny hooks have also been found. These hooklets are similar in every way to those found in the suckers on the arms of present-day cephalopods. In one fossil of a young ichthyosaur about 478,000 hooks were discovered. We can estimate that it must have caught about 1600 cephalopods. These remains accumulated in the stomach, like fragments of sea shells, and were vomited up from time to time, as happens today with sperm whales that prey on squids.

The plesiosaurs had to come ashore to lay their eggs. They were probably as clumsy on beaches and cliffs as present-day turtles and walruses are. The ichthyosaurs were perfectly adapted to life in the ocean and were viviparous, that is, gave birth to live young. This has been verified by examining a number of unusual fossils: skeletons of females in whose

*Opposite: A fossil of the ichthyosaur* Stenopterygius quadriscissus. *The soft parts of the body are clearly seen as well as the skeleton. Experts have been able to make reliable reconstructions of these creatures from fossil finds. For a long time such reconstructions were incorrect. It was believed that the downwards bending of the spinal column was due to fractures: nobody suspected that actually the tail itself had two lobes and that only the lower one was supported by a skeleton. There was no indication, either, of the existence of the fleshy dorsal fin.*

abdomen fully developed embryos have been preserved. There is also a fossil of a female that evidently died in the course of giving birth. Embryos of young ichthyosaurs generally appear wrapped around themselves; but in certain specimens skeletons of babies in fragmentary shape have been found. It provides evidence of ichthyosaurs' cannibalism. This is common among many viviparous

aquatic animals; the common aquarium guppy and various sharks often devour newborn young.

In the second half of the Jurassic different types of plesiosaur evolved. These were the pliosaurs with a short neck and a large, elongated skull. These animals could also move their fins upwards, so that they could propel and submerge the body. The pliosaurs were most widely distributed at the beginning of the next period (Cretaceous).

# The biggest of all

The Sauropoda are undoubtedly among the best-known dinosaurs. They emerged near the end of the Triassic and descended from a group of herbivores that included *Plateosaurus* and *Melanosaurus*. Although they are familiar, we do not fully know how these animals lived.

Why did such gigantic forms develop? There are a number of logical replies. A large mass was an efficient means of maintaining the animal's temperature at an almost constant level. Sheer size discouraged predators. There was an abundance of plant food, which often required a lengthy process of digestion, because it was very tough. The digestive system of the herbivores meant that large quantities of chewed-up food was stored in enormous stomachs. Perhaps the sauropods were simply immense systems of transport for a huge digestive system, vast stomachs supported by four legs.

How did the sauropods move? What environment did they live in? The bones of their legs were practically solid, unlike the hollow bones of the majority of vertebrates, so they must have worked as columns to support the huge weight of the body. The hind legs in *Diplodocus* had five toes with claws on the three inner ones. The two outer toes were encased in a thick, hard pad, similar to the feet of present-day elephants. The first toe of the forefeet also had a fairly large claw. Traces of the feet have been preserved quite clearly in petrified mud. Some are depressions, as big as the wheel of a bus. They show that the animals moved around in groups. In other cases the prints, always of several individuals, are curious. Now and then only the marks of the front feet can be seen. Ruling out the likelihood that these animals could jump or balance, the conclusion must be that, some of these creatures lived in shallow water and only occasionally trod the bottom, like hippopotamuses.

The formation of the vertebrae shows that the tail region was massive, that the trunk was lighter and hollow, and that the neck was long, yet hollow and almost fragile. The generally accepted reconstruction of the sauropod shows it with the back emerging from the water, the neck floating and the tail dangling, almost like an anchor. Alternatively, in some forms, for example, *Brachiosaurus*, the long neck and hind legs, longer than the forelegs, suggests an elephant–giraffe type of reconstruction; with column-like legs for dry ground, and an extremely long neck for browsing on plant shoots.

The teeth of some sauropods like *Diplodocus* were comparatively few and peg-like, suitable for chewing soft water plants and algae. In other species like *Camarasaurus* and *Brachiosaurus* the teeth were more numerous, better set and more pointed, adapted for eating tough leaves and possibly bark and roots. Rounded stones have been found among the bones of some sauropods; the animals probably swallowed these stones to help the grinding of food and digestion, just as hens swallow pebbles today for the same reason.

An argument against the hippopotamus theory is that the animal might have risked being crushed by the weight of water and would not have been able to immerse its head to browse on the bottom. The elephant–giraffe hypothesis is contradicted by evidence of the foot-prints. Probably there was no such thing as a single 'model'; different species led different lives, not even competing with one another. We know that in certain areas several distinct forms of sauropod lived together peaceably.

The discovery of the cub of a *Camarasaurus*, only measuring about 5m (16½ft), the adult was more than

*The heads of four of the best-known sauropods are shown below. The silhouette in white of an adult Camarasaurus can be compared with the reconstruction of a baby, whose body is more stocky, with a short neck. The two silhouettes in colour, the smaller of which is a brachiosaur, give some idea of the size of the 'supersaur', a sauropod known so far only from several vertebrae and a shoulderblade.*

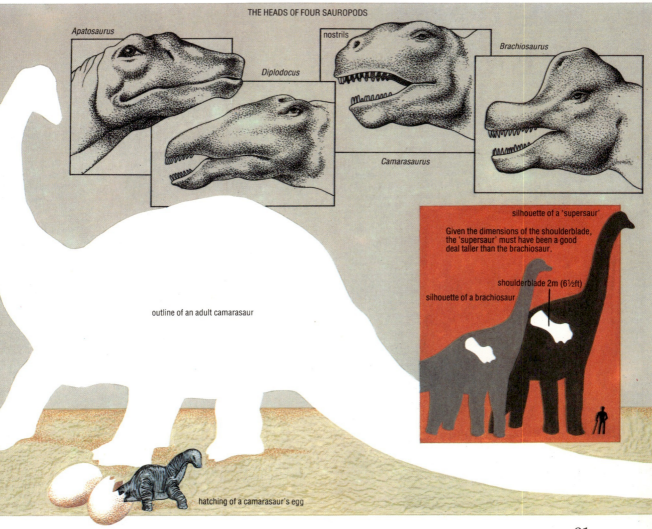

THE HEADS OF FOUR SAUROPODS

Apatosaurus

Diplodocus

nostrils

Brachiosaurus

Camarasaurus

outline of an adult camarasaur

silhouette of a 'supersaur'

Given the dimensions of the shoulderblade, the 'supersaur' must have been a good deal taller than the brachiosaur.

shoulderblade 2m (6½ft)

silhouette of a brachiosaur

hatching of a camarasaur's egg

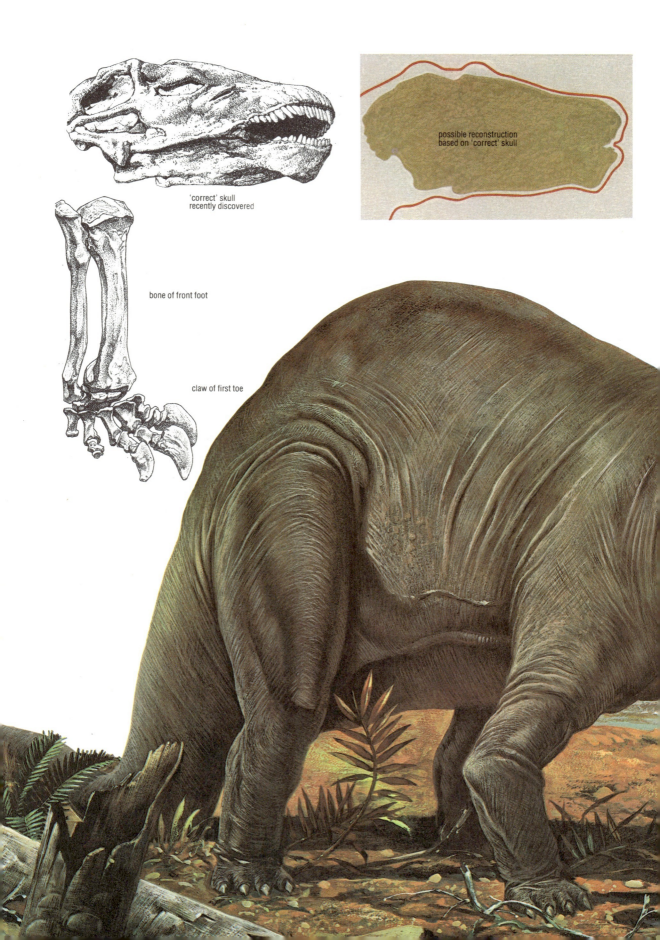

'correct' skull
recently discovered

possible reconstruction
based on 'correct' skull

bone of front foot

claw of first toe

*Apatosaurus, better known as* Brontosaurus, *is one of the most popular dinosaurs. The reconstructions that are usually made (below) are not accurate because the head of the animal is really that of* Camarasaurus. *Recently the true head of this giant was discovered. The skull on the opposite page is published here in a popular book of science for the first time. It is rather like that of* Diplodocus. *On the right of the skull is an outlined reconstruction of the head, and below it is a detail of the skeleton of the foreleg.*

Apatosaurs (brontosaurs) reconstructed with 'traditional' head.

16m (52ft), shows that the young animal had a proportionately shorter neck and tail than the adult, while the head was proportionately bigger. The youngsters probably would have had a faster rate of metabolism than the adults to achieve rapid growth. It may be that they were warm blooded and gradually tended to become cold blooded when their increase in size meant they had to cope with the problem of maintaining a constant body temperature.

As if to underline the controversy that has always surrounded the sauropods and their way of life, the huge creatures have not even been left alone as reconstructed museum specimens. The head of all the reconstructed skeletons of *Apatosaurus*, better known by its former name of *Brontosaurus*, is now known to be wrong. In the skeleton discovered by Othniel C. Marsh at Como Bluff, Wyoming (USA), in 1879, the skull bones were missing. Marsh completed his remarkable find with a reconstruction based essentially on fragments of a *Camarasaurus* skull. The mistake was eventually spotted, to the embarrassment of the experts. The true head, similar to that of *Diplodocus*, was recently discovered by John McIntosh and David Berman in a dusty heap of bones that had never been re-examined. Pittsburgh and Chicago museums were prompt to arrange a 'decapitation' and to make the necessary substitution, preparing casts for despatch to other museums all over the world. The 'new' skull, with peg-like teeth, is better adapted to the theory of *Apatosaurus* as an eater of soft plants and thus perhaps a habitual occupant of swamps and shallow lakes.

Ornitholestes

*Throughout the Jurassic the coelurosaurs, small predatory saurischian dinosaurs, were well represented. These animals were bipedal, usually with short forelegs but with well developed 'hands', with three or four fingers, which were ideal for seizing and grasping prey. The tail, long and sometimes stiff, helped to balance the weight of the rest of the body when the animal was running.*
*Left: A reconstruction of Ornitholestes, which was up to 2m (6½ft) long. There were three large toes on the hind feet and a fourth directed backwards. All the toes had claws.*
*Below: The skull of Ornitholestes exhibits the typical dentition of a carnivore, with all the teeth fairly similar.*

skull 15cm (6in) long

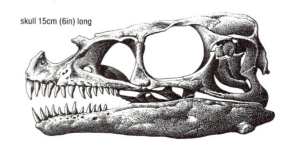

# Predators large and small

The dry land teemed with insects, spiders and millipedes, hunted by the earliest lizards. Many types of the group were now represented solely by the tuatara, another living fossil, and by other small vertebrates. These were, in their turn, hunted by Coelurosaurs, medium-sized reptiles descended from those living in the Triassic.

The coelurosaurs were slender, agile animals which moved about rapidly on two legs. Lizards are very difficult to catch, so the coelurosaurs must have been just as fast as their prey. Some experts think this speed is due to the ability to expend considerable energy, and hence to a high rate of metabolism. It is possible, that the agile coelurosaurs were warm-blooded. *Ornitholestes* was 2m (6½ft) long but when upright was hardly bigger than a baby; and *Compsognathus* was smaller than a chicken.

The huge predatory two-legged dinosaurs known as carnosaurs were descended from *Ornithosuchus* and related forms. At the beginning of the Jurassic we know of *Dilophosaurus*, 6m (19½ft) long; and near the end of the period there are *Ceratosaurus*, *Allosaurus* and *Megalosaurus*. In certain genera the skull is adorned with crests and bony projections.

*Megalosaurus* was the first dinosaur to be discovered and have its remains described. The description given by Robert Plot in 1677 in his *Natural History of Oxfordshire* (where the find was made) was rather misleading; so much so that in 1765 R. Brooks named a fragment of the tip of the animal's huge femur *Scrotum humanum*. The resemblance of this fragment to the

*Right: A reconstruction of another late Jurassic coelurosaur,* Compsognathus longipes. *This animal was 60cm (23½ft) overall, its head measuring about 8cm (3in).*
*Below: The skull of* Compsognathus *shows one opening in front of the eye socket and two behind it. There is also a cavity, to lighten the weight, in the lower jaw. The hind legs of* Compsognathus *were very like those of a running bird. Several series of prints, definitely left by these little dinosaurs, were originally thought to be those of primitive birds. This saurischian is quite close to the first birds in its skeletal structure.*

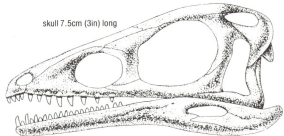

skull 7.5cm (3in) long

Compsognathus

scrotum or sac containing the testicles of a man suggested to him that this was the petrified remnant of a gigantic antediluvian from before the Flood. A correct description was only provided in 1824.

We possess extremely interesting evidence about the life of the allosaurs. From certain series of prints in mud which was later petrified, it is assumed that these carnosaurs up to 10–12m (33–39ft) long hunted in packs, just like wolves and lionesses. Because there is strength in numbers, they could even attack sauropods which could defend themselves against single predators. The skeleton of one apatosaur shows vertebrae with teeth marks of an allosaur, even the tail of the huge herbivore was damaged. The carnivore had evidently approached and attacked from the rear, seizing its prey by the tail. Hardly a cat and mouse situation, however, unless we imagine a cat biting the tail of a creature as big as a calf. Among the sauropod's bones were a few broken teeth of an allosaur, suggesting that the herbivore had not given up to the carnivore without a struggle.

How were these hunts carried out? Presumably there woud have been a chase. The largest living saurian or lizard, the Komodo dragon (*Varanus komodoensis*) is up to 3m (10ft) long and weighs up to 135kg (300lb). It is not a very speedy animal and does not deliver sudden lightning attacks. It frequently feeds on carrion. It is a cold-blooded creature which has survived by living in a hot climate. Crocodiles are bigger still but can only move about swiftly in water; on land they are slow and awkward. So what are we to think of an animal which is ten or a hundred times heavier? The footprints indicate that the animals

Diplodocus

Allosaurus

took fairly long strides and that they must thus have moved fairly fast. This would use a considerable amount of energy. Would it all have been obtained from the environment and retained in the large size of the body, or would it have been produced?

Let us return to the theory of a high rate of metabolism linked with warm-bloodedness.

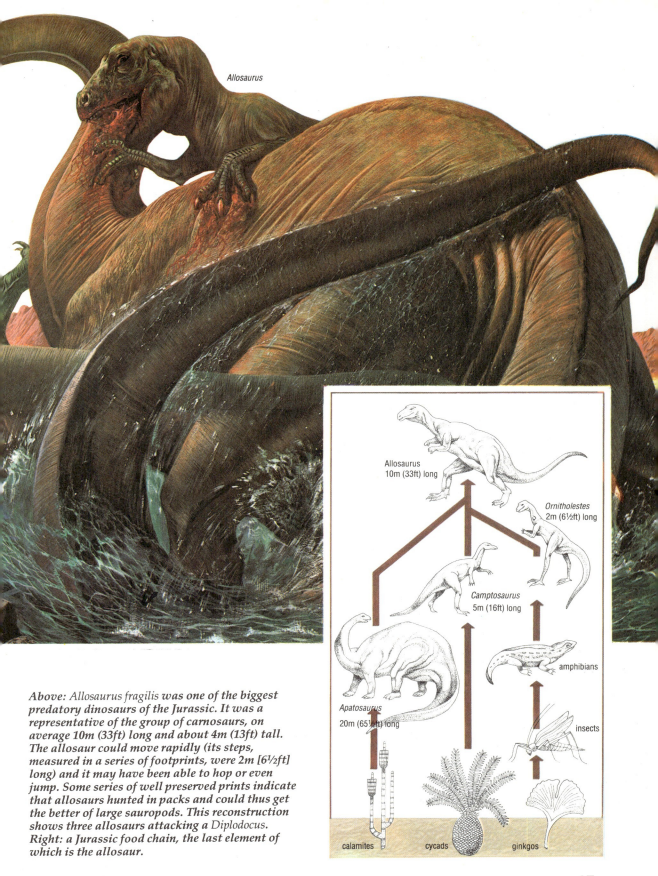

*Above:* Allosaurus fragilis *was one of the biggest predatory dinosaurs of the Jurassic. It was a representative of the group of carnosaurs, on average 10m (33ft) long and about 4m (13ft) tall. The allosaur could move rapidly (its steps, measured in a series of footprints, were 2m [6½ft] long) and it may have been able to hop or even jump. Some series of well preserved prints indicate that allosaurs hunted in packs and could thus get the better of large sauropods. This reconstruction shows three allosaurs attacking a* Diplodocus. *Right: a Jurassic food chain, the last element of which is the allosaur.*

Allosaurus
10m (33ft) long

*Ornitholestes*
2m (6½ft) long

*Camptosaurus*
5m (16ft) long

amphibians

*Apatosaurus*
20m (65½ft) long

insects

calamites

cycads

ginkgos

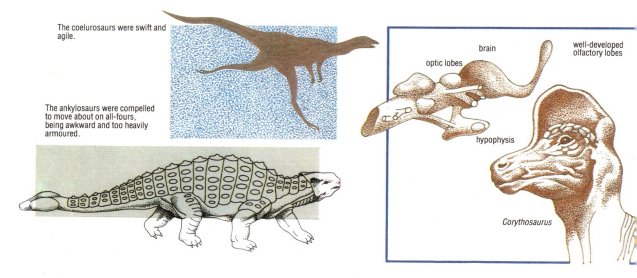

The coelurosaurs were swift and agile.

The ankylosaurs were compelled to move about on all-fours, being awkward and too heavily armoured.

optic lobes

brain

well-developed olfactory lobes

hypophysis

Corythosaurus

# Warm-blooded dinosaurs?

By revising the old, traditional ideas about dinosaurs, we now possess a mass of fascinating information which enables us to understand these creatures much better. At one time they were merely regarded as mysterious giants, veritable monsters. But nowadays we realize that they were astonishingly varied in their adaptation to the environment, as is shown by the vast range of species known to exist. The possibility of their being warm-blooded almost makes them seem our relatives. Enquiry can now be extended to other fields of research so that we can understand not only what they looked like but how they lived. Students of ethology or behaviour compare these creatures of the past with modern animals. Those concerned with ecology try to reconstruct the primitive environments and to examine the relationships between the various species. Despite this scientific exposure the dinosaurs still remain as awe-inspiring and fascinating as ever. Once they tended to be dismissed as lumbering giants whose sheer bulk doomed them to extinc-

tion, but now attitudes are changing. The fact that these reptiles survived for some 160 million years means they are one of nature's major evolutionary successes.

The relationship between predator and prey has given rise to many ingenious devices and stratgems. We have already mentioned the advantage of increased body size as a defence. Other defences include the development of armour. spines and prickles. When we speak of weapons there is only a thin line between defence and offence. Spiny tails and clawed fingers and toes certainly enable many potential victims to deter their would-be assailants. Flight has always been another route to safety. Many dinosaurs, especially those of small and average size, developed two footed movement, agility and swift reflexes. Others relied on their sense of smell. Perhaps the carnosaurs literally stank of flesh, as present-day wild cats do, so that their prey learned to scent them from a distance. Some herbivorous dinosaurs have complex parts on the skull which have been considered as enlargements of the nasal passages, thus increasing the surfaces designed to pick up odours.

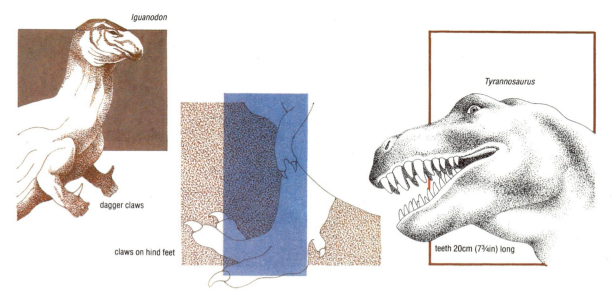

Iguanodon

dagger claws

claws on hind feet

Tyrannosaurus

teeth 20cm (7¾in) long

How did the hunters cope with the different defences of their victims? We have seen that some resorted to teamwork when the prey was too big. Such behaviour indicates that these animals had quick reflexes, that they could plan a strategy, that they possessed a measure of 'intelligence'. Obviously the predators could also use offensive weapons: long, sharp teeth, enormous jaws with powerful muscles, and terrible claws capable of gripping, slashing and ripping the victim apart.

The numerical relationship between predators and prey also reveals some interesting facts. The bones found in a particular encounter can tell us which were the principal species involved and also how many individuals there were in each species or group. From this we can deduce the comparative numbers of predators and victims. Let us consider some statistics that apply to modern animals in the wild. A lion or a cheetah will consume a weight of prey equal to its own every 7–10 days. A Komodo dragon takes 60 days to do the same. It is clear, therefore, that a warm-blooded predator, with high metabolism, needs to

*In the course of their long and triumphant evolutionary journey, the dinosaurs, both predators and prey, developed interesting mechanisms of offence and defence. The herbivores acquired armour, sensitive organs of smell, very large bodies and various defensive organs. The predators developed increasingly efficient claws and sharp teeth. There were many agile and swift-moving types. Dinosaurs led a very active life and it is believed today that they used up a great deal of energy which they produced themselves by a high rate of metabolism.*

catch more animals than does a cold-blooded predator. So for a given quantity of prey, there would have to be a greater number of cold-blooded than warm-blooded predators. Thus if in a particular assembly of fossils there seem to be a few predators present, the conclusion would be that the latter were warm-blooded. Of course we have to be sure that the fossil remains truly represent the proportions applicable to animals living in the remote past; and there may be doubts about this. Yet they do provide a clue that enables us to make a comparison, not with the present but with another phase of the past. Let us look at the proportional numbers of remains dating from the lower Permian. Scientists have counted about seven dimetrodonts as against ten reptiles preying on them. In the Jurassic, when there were hordes of allosaurs and other carnosaurs, the ratio becomes one predator to every nine prey animals. So here is strong support for the theory in favour of warm-blooded dinosaurs.

Further clues can be deduced from the bones and how they are formed. Scientists examining sections of dinosaur bones under the microscope have noted many small holes corresponding to dense networks of blood vessels: there are also large numbers of Haversian canals, in which important chemical changes occur. The sections appear fairly similar to those of modern mammal bones. The many blood vessels are signs of warm bloodedness; and the numerous Haversian canals indicate high metabolism. But this is not absolute proof. Various present-day cold-blooded reptiles have bony structures of this type, while some warm-blooded mammals do not have these features. Even so, the clues cannot be ignored. To be absolutely precise we should perhaps say that the dinosaurs had a tendency to be warm-blooded, having developed a measure of homoiothermy and exhibiting a fairly high rate of metabolism. This can also be inferred from their fairly active life style. In many cases this was related to their huge body size. It must also be remembered that the surrounding temperature was quite mild and perhaps without great seasonal contrasts.

Why did the dinosaurs develop this trend towards homoiothermy? It is a reasonable question which we have in a sense answered, that like rapid metabolism it has many advantages. But perhaps there is an even simpler reply which takes history into ac-count. The dinosaurs had this tendency because they were descended from animals that were *already* warm-blooded. Alongside the mammal-like reptiles of the late Permian, there may also have been other reptiles which were adapted to produce energy with great efficiency. This capacity would not have been lost and was passed on to the dinosaurs, which made use of it to a greater or lesser degree. The cold climate which prevailed during the late Permian, mainly because of the different positions of the continents, may partly explain why the reptiles developed the ability to keep warm.

# The mysterious stegosaur

The dinosaur belonging to the genus *Stegosaurus* is familiar to us. The species described in 1877 was *Stegosaurus stenops*. Reconstructions of this creature have led to many misinterpretations and arguments. This animal embodies many of the developments that occurred in the course of dinosaur evolution. The stegosaur was an ornithischian, had a large body (up to 15m [49ft] long, with a weight of 1.8t [2tons]), and had nails on the feet that were similar to hooves. Its offensive weapons were two pairs of long spines on the tail;

*Opposite: A traditional reconstruction of Stegosaurus stenops. Nowadays various authors suggest that the dorsal plates of this ornithischian dinosaur did not stand up straight from the back and that they had the double function of defending the animal and of serving as heat-exchangers, like the sails of the Permian pelicosaurs. At the top, in two colours, are the two possible arrangements. On the left is a detail of the tail skeleton, and on the right an artist's impression of a young stegosaur; the babies were born without plates.*

four bony points

flattened plates on back

vertical plates

a baby with undeveloped plates

skeleton of tail

Stegosaurus stenops

and it also had a series of huge plates, some of them a metre (3ft) long, along its back. For years experts tried to work out the reasons for these curious plates on the creature's back – a difficult task since the spine offered no clues as to their likely position. Discovery of the skeleton of a young stegosaur, however, helped partially to resolve the mystery. The animal was clearly born *without* plates; these grew later as formations of the skin of the back. Not being an integral part of the skeleton, they were not connected to the spine. How were they arranged? In pairs, alternately, vertically, or flat, resting against the sides of the body? The plates were cut carefully into sections and examined under the microscope; there were numerous signs of blood vessels. So is it now possible to give an overall explanation which would also allow an attempt to make a correct reconstruction? Maybe. The plates served both as a protective element and as a heat exchanger. They were probably arranged alternately because this positioning allows better exposure to the air and thus a greater dispersion or greater absorption of heat. Perhaps the young, with their higher metabolism, did not need a heat exchanger. Or would this have been necessary to the adults because, being homoiothermic, they risked getting *too* hot during their active life?

The stegosaur is one of those dinosaurs with a very obvious cavity at the base of the spinal column, just before the beginning of the tail. This is the legendary 'second brain'. It has been said, fancifully and quite incorrectly that the stegosaur 'thought better with its backside' than it did with its head, because the cavity in question was ten times bigger than the cranial cavity. In fact it contained a nerve nodule connected with the workings of the tail and the powerful hind legs, as well as a special system of glands designed to supply energy more efficiently as and when needed.

What did *Stegosaurus* eat? Its teeth and jaws were pretty weak. But could a diet consisting only of soft vegetation have been sufficient? Many scholars maintain that the animal must have needed to consume food with a higher energy content, such as small prey and scraps of carrion; an omnivorous diet. This indicates that the rigid division between herbivores and carnivores was becoming less clearcut. The dinosaurs, like every living creature, obviously tried to exploit all the opportunities that were offered by their environment.

# The first mammals

We have mentioned that any available food was eaten by lizards, by relations of the tuatara and by other small vertebrates. By now these vertebrates were mammals.

The transition from parammals to true mammals had already happened by the end of the Triassic. The mammals now began to play their modest role in a drama still dominated by the reptiles and, in particular, the dinosaurs.

The dentition of the Jurassic mammals, notably the Pantotheria and, at a later stage, the Triconodonta shows that they fed on insects and that they were also scavengers, mopping up the remnants left by the carnosaurs and coelurosaurs. They perhaps supplemented their diet with tough plants and even seeds. This was a range of food similar to modern insectivores and rodents. The small or tiny

*Below: The skull of* Triconodon, *a mammal of the late Jurassic. The upper and lower jaws are quite long and there are specialized teeth of the four types characteristic of all mammals: incisors, canines (long and protruding), premolars and molars.*

*Bottom: A reconstruction of* Triconodon *which as an adult grew to the size of a cat. In one well-preserved specimen there are 56 teeth. The molars have three typical conical ridges.*

Jurassic mammals, the largest of them scarcely bigger than a mouse, played quite an important ecological role. They were active mainly at dusk or during the night, but they already occupied ecological niches in areas where they could dig burrows that could be used by day. There are few remains of these busy little animals, although plenty of their teeth have been recovered.

SKULL OF TRICONODONT

teeth

from above

from side

baby *Triconodon*

*Triconodon*

# Life in the air

The insects had for a long time been lords of the air. In the late Triassic and then in the Jurassic, certain vertebrates also attempted to master this environment. The reason was to get food. Even the smallest insects are potential prey; and the air allows them the opportunity of a new form of attack. Plummeting down from the sky is by far the best way of taking a land animal by surprise or even of catching a fish.

One small reptile of the late Triassic, *Podopteryx mirabilis*, some 20cm (8in) long, was equipped with hairy membranes both between hind legs and tail and also between the short forelegs, the sides and the thighs of the hind legs. It resembled a small living kite, broadest in the tail region. *Podopteryx* launched itself from trees either to glide down on its undoubtedly tiny prey or to flee its enemies. All the Pterosauria are descended from creatures similar to *Podopteryx*.

The body structure of the pterosaurs stayed more or less the same for about 130 million years. There were many species, distinguished mainly by the form of skull and, above all, by the dentition. The 'wing' was always a membrane of skin stretching from the sides of the body to the tip of the enormously long fourth finger of the forelimb. The skull was very fragile. In some cases the petrified internal impressions of the space occupied by the brain have been preserved. From these it has been deduced that the brain of these animals was fairly big and that the part associated with vision was particularly well developed. The eye orbits are large, so the pterosaurs must have been able to see very well. The parts of the brain relating to the coordination of movements are also well developed. It is likely that the pterosaurs could glide, come to a sudden stop, circle and perform other manoeuvres with speed and agility. *Dimorphodon* which lived in the early Jurassic, has a wingspan of 70cm (27½in). The skull is large and the teeth are peg-like at the front of the mouth but smaller and stronger towards the rear. Perhaps there was a pouch below the jaw as in pelicans. In *Ctenochasma* the lower jaw is studded with very fine points resembling the whale-bone of baleen whales. In *Rhamphorhynchus* the teeth are bare and similar to daggers. It is probable that the majority of these animals hunted fishes and other marine creatures; some of them perhaps caught insects. The discovery in 1971 of a very well preserved pterosaur specimen in Kazakhstan in the USSR threw light on one problem which had been argued for years. Dating from the upper Jurassic, the Kazakhstan animal was given the name *Sordes pilosus* ('hairy devil'). This pterosaur was the size of a pigeon, had teeth and a dense covering of fur over the entire body, including the wings. Other skeletons had already led experts to suspect that these creatures were hairy, and this was definitive proof. The only explanation for this characteristic is that it was developed to store the body heat produced by the animal itself. Pterosaurs were thus homoiotherms, and this why they were able to lead such an active life.

Additional evidence that *Pterosaurus* was excellently adapted for flying is that its bones were extremely light as they were largely hollow. The old description of these creatures as 'flying reptiles' hardly seems acceptable nowadays. Could these hairy,

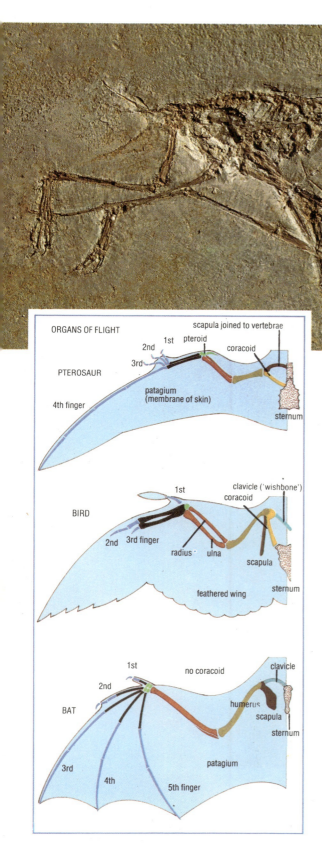

ORGANS OF FLIGHT

PTEROSAUR

scapula joined to vertebrae
1st pteroid
2nd
3rd
coracoid
4th finger
patagium
(membrane of skin)
sternum

BIRD

1st
clavicle ('wishbone')
coracoid
2nd 3rd finger
radius ulna
scapula
feathered wing
sternum

BAT

1st
no coracoid
clavicle
2nd
humerus
scapula
sternum
3rd
4th
5th finger
patagium

*Left: The structure of the flight organ of pterosaurs, birds and bats (mammals of the order Chiroptera). As can be seen, pterosaurs did not have any clavicles (collar bones), which form the typical 'wishbone' in birds. The large strip of skin (patagium) making the wing was supported by the whole arm and especially the enormously long fourth finger.*
*Above: A fossil of* Pterodactylus antiquus, *about 15cm (6in) long. The pterosaurs, too, were archosaurs. In the specimen illustrated here the opening in front of the eye orbit is cleary visible.*

warm-blooded vertebrates, with bones that weighed very little, really have been reptiles? Even the name pterosaur ('flying lizard') appears inadequate, but it can be kept for historical reasons and to avoid confusion that might arise from the introduction of a new one. Remains of pterosaurs come from almost all marine and swamp sites where Jurassic fossils have been found, for as we have seen, the animals were well adapted for fishing. But could it be that there were also land pterosaurs, hunters rather than fishers? Very probably, for as we shall see, finds attributed to the next period, the Cretaceous, appear to indicate the presence of pterosaurs on dry land as well. Moreover, it is logical that the fragile remains of flying animals should only have been preserved as a result of their falling into the mud, near swamps, or of being washed up on beaches by the waves and quickly covered by sand. The pterosaurs' reputation for being prevalently aquatic is probably because their bones have only been discovered at such sites.

# Archaeopteryx: the first bird

At the beginning of the Triassic the remains were found of a reptile called *Longisquama insignis* which was roughly the size of *Podopteryx*. This animal was probably capable of making short gliding flights, but its support was two lateral 'fans' made of very long flexible scales lying on top of one another. These scales, set into the forelimbs, are not unlike feathers, and are considered to represent the

lozenge-shaped 'rudder' of skin

*Right: A reconstruction of some rhamphorhynchids and pterodactyls in flight. The pterosaurs in general had a covering of hair and were probably homoiothermic.*
*Below: The five flight stage of* Rhamphorhynchus gemmingi *(measuring about 50cm [19½in], including tail). The tail, covered by a strip of skin similar to a small kite, acted as a balance and perhaps as a rudder.*

FLIGHT OF *RHAMPHORHYNCHUS*

*Pterodactylus*

*Rhamphorhynchus*

first 'experiments' which eventually led to the development of true feathers and thus to the evolution of birds.

The Jurassic limestone rock of Bavaria has provided scientists with dramatic evidence of this evolutionary step forward. In 1861, and at intervals over a period of 90 years, five more or less complete skeletons were found of an animal with teeth, a long tail, well developed forelimbs, with three fingers, and the hind legs, with four toes, of a runner. The skeleton resembles, in size as well, a coelurosaur, for example, *Compsognathus*. But there is one important and different characteristic: the bones show recognizable traces of a series of feathers on the front legs and the tail. A feathered reptile or a bird? The animal was named *Archaeopteryx lithographica* and is generally regarded as the first bird.

The pelvis is that of a bird yet it does not seem possible that it was related to the ornithischian dinosaurs. Perhaps this creature was really a coelurosaur adapted for living in woods. Maybe it ran and made short leaps, supporting itself with its 'wings'; or it may have climbed trees with the aid of its separate toes and clawed forefingers and taken off in a glide. Among trees, feathers would have been more useful then the membrane of a pterosaur. The membrane might be damaged by striking a branch, whereas feathers would absorb such a blow and expand to clear an obstacle. A covering of feathers was also an invaluable asset to homoiothermy. A further point of interest is the number of feathers of *Archaeopteryx*. There were 10 primaries and 14 secondaries on either wing, just as in modern birds.

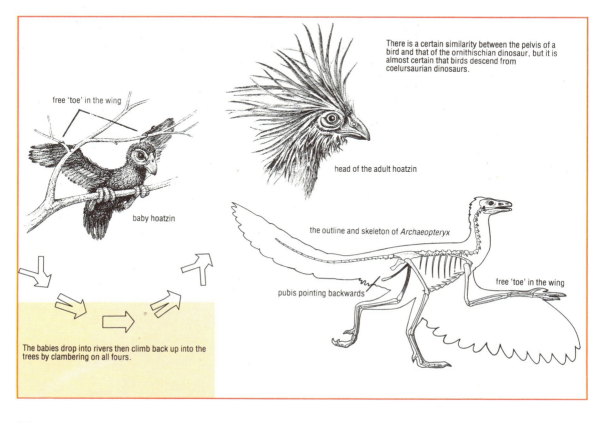

free 'toe' in the wing

baby hoatzin

The babies drop into rivers then climb back up into the trees by clambering on all fours.

There is a certain similarity between the pelvis of a bird and that of the ornithischian dinosaur, but it is almost certain that birds descend from coelursaurian dinosaurs.

head of the adult hoatzin

the outline and skeleton of *Archaeopteryx*

pubis pointing backwards

free 'toe' in the wing

*Opposite: The hoatzin (*Opisthocomus hoazin*), a bird which lives today in the Brazilian forests and has habits possibly similar to those of* Archaeopteryx. *Baby hoatzins are the only birds with free toes and with claws on the front foot. They use these to climb about in trees from which they often dive into the water.*

*Left: The skeleton of* Archaeopteryx lithographica, *kept at the British Museum of Natural History, London.*

*Below: On the basis of five skeletons it is possible to make reasonably confident reconstructions of* Archaeopteryx.

Archaeopteryx lithographica

iguanodont

Dinosaurs dominant on land, with ornithischians especially plentiful. ...ichthyosaurs abundant. Mosasaurus well established. End of period sees ...

established. The dicotyledons are

(among the latter the most common prairie grasses).

magnolia

SAURISCHIANS

*Coelophysis*

*Allosaurus*

theropods

*Scelidosaurus*

ORNITHISCHIANS

*Fabrosaurus*

ornithopods

The Cretaceous period lasted 70 million years and brought the Mesozoic ... Earth's history the supercontinents were finally split up. The plates forming the present-day continents separated. Only Antarctica and Australia still remained, at least partially, attached to South America. India approached the Equator and by the end of the period passed beyond it. Madagascar, too, detached itself from Africa. The Atlantic was by now quite big and continued to expand. The pieces of land that are nowadays Italy and the Balkan peninsula approached

vast areas of shallow seas. The

They still divided Europe from Asia

and the western part of Asia from Siberia and the Far East. They also divided Africa into a western portion and a much bigger part comprising what are now the eastern, the western and the southern regions of the continent.

*Opposite: A diagram of the Cretaceous period. It was at this time that the dinosaurs established themselves securely in all environments, showing an increasing range of specializations. At the end of the period the giants and many other forms became extinct. The only archosaurs to have survived are the crocodiles.*
*Below: The evolution of the principal groups of dinosaurs. Other archosaurs (pterosaurs) are shown but crocodiles are omitted. As is evident, differentiation of the various groups of ornithischians occurred after that of the saurischians.*

# Flowers and insects

The vegetable kingdom was beginning to take on an ever more modern appearance. Flowering plants or angiosperms, grew everywhere, mainly as trees but also as shrubs. The conifers were still well represented even in areas where they no longer grow. They included sequoias, monkey puzzles, pines, firs and cypresses. Alongside them grew flowering species; the scent of resin blended more and more with the perfume of the flowers whose colours now dotted the landscape. The most primitive angiosperms are the magnolia group. The flower of these trees

Brachiosaurus

Pteranodon

Quetzalcoatlus

birds

carnosaurs
Spinosaurus

coelurosaurs
Ornithomimus

carnosaurs
Tyrannosaurus

rmoured
inosaurs

Stegosaurus

Polacanthus

Parasaurolophus

Iguanodon

hadrosaurs

Triceratops

ceratopsians

Jurassic

Cretaceous

and shrubs has a typical cone structure with the petals and sepals arranged in a conical spiral (rather like the peel of an orange when removed from the top in one piece). This arrangement is similar to that of pine cones and the cones of other coniferous trees.

There was a continual and ever growing exchange of goodwill between flowering plants and insects. The insects carried pollen, sucked nectar and other sugary substances. The plants developed their own defences, of spines, sharp leaves and poisons, against excess plundering by the insects. In the second half of the Cretaceous the angiosperm monocotyledons, which had leaves with parallel veining, became more widespread. Grasses established themselves in many areas. These plants contained a large amount of silica in their tissues, and were very hard, like the stem of a spike of wheat or of a bamboo. The seeds of these plants were very numerous and quite rich in nutritive substances. They provided plenty of food for the insects and their larvae and for many mammals.

Throughout the Mesozoic, the termites perfected their capacity to feed on wood. At the same time they built up complex social organizations. Similar patterns of social life were evolved by insects resembling bees and by the ants.

# Decline of the dinosaurs

The movements of the continental masses led to the 'birth' of many mountains and to intense volcanic activity. Snow fell in areas which had previously enjoyed a warm climate; and elsewhere the sun was obscured by the ashes of an eruption. Thus food was sometimes hard to find.

Pteranodon

The living things of the Cretaceous were affected by two vital conditions: isolation of certain areas of dry land and the instability of the environment. The consequence was a spectacular proliferation of species, particularly among the dinosaurs. Yet this intense activity takes on more sinister repercussions when we remember that the Cretaceous also witnessed the disappearance of the legendary ruling reptiles. It was like a luxuriant autumn, full of fruits and generous in harvests, but which is inevitably followed by winter.

Elasmosaurus
a plesiosaur

Kronosaurus
a pliosaur

Pteranodon

Tylosaurus dyspelor
a mosasaur

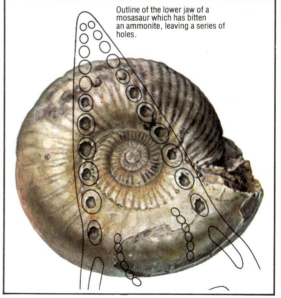

Outline of the lower jaw of a mosasaur which has bitten an ammonite, leaving a series of holes.

*Top: A reconstruction of some of the reptiles of the Cretaceous living in shallow sea waters and along the coasts. The long-necked plesiosaurs and the short-necked pliosaurs, with long upper and lower jaws were already well established in the Jurassic. These animals were not archosaurs and belonged to the group of sauropterygians. The pterosaurs gliding overhead are* Pteranodon ingens, *with a wingspan of up to 8m (26ft).*

*Above: The skeleton and a miniature reconstruction of* Tylosaurus proriger, *a mosasaur up to 6m (19½ft) long. This was a new reptile related to the present-day monitors.*

*Right: The fossil of an ammonite, with a diameter of 26cm (10in) which had been killed by a mosasaur. The holes left by the teeth make it possible to reconstruct the dentition of the predator.*

We shall come back to the mystery of the disappearance of so many apparently well established species. For the time being we shall simply note that the numerous environmental changes caused a series of adaptations among animals which, in many cases, could not be reversed. Dramatic alterations in the conditions of the various environments may have led to crises that threatened the survival of some species. Among the principal victims were the dinosaurs.

*The ammonites were cephalopod molluscs which were quite important elements of the marine food chain throughout the Mesozoic. The living animal occupied only the last and outermost chamber of the shell. This, in addition to being a protective structure in which the animal could shut itself up completely, was an organ for floating.*
*Below: The three principal types of ammonite shell, distinguished by the arrangement of the septa dividing the chambers, revealed on the outside by complex lines of insertion. The ammonites fed on plankton, small invertebrates and fishes, and were in their turn preyed on by marine reptiles, larger fishes and birds.*
*Opposite: A reconstruction of two Cretaceous birds:* Hesperornis regalis, *1.2m (4ft) in length, with atrophied wings, and* Ichthyornis victor, *20cm (8in) tall, a flier.*

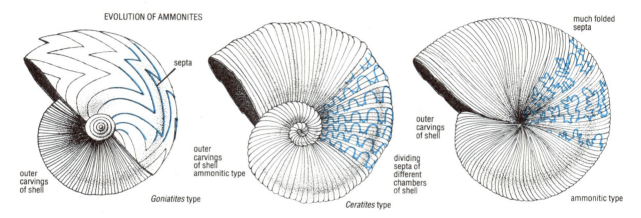

EVOLUTION OF AMMONITES

septa

outer carvings of shell

*Goniatites* type

outer carvings of shell ammonitic type

dividing septa of different chambers of shell

*Ceratites* type

much folded septa

outer carvings of shell

ammonitic type

# Seas everywhere

With the progressive splitting up of the continents, the seas naturally extended for immense distances. But the continental shifts isolated inland seas and coastal areas; and there were many local examples of evolution and survival.

The Cretaceous seas were inhabited by the last plesiosaurs *Elasmosaurus*, up to 15m (49ft) long, including a 7m (23ft) neck, and by many pliosaurs, some of them gigantic, like *Kronosaurus*, 13m (42½ft) long, with a 3m (10ft) skull. There was also a vast range of bony fishes. The ichthyosaurs, now in decline, contained some rather specialized forms: *Ophthalmosaurus*, for instance, had no

teeth in its mouth, apparently swallowing its prey whole. The eyes of this creature were protected by a ring of bony plates, a typical adaptation to variations of pressure under water. There were also huge turtles, such as *Archelon ischyros*, over 4m (13ft) in length which were fairly similar to modern types.

The Cretaceous saw the development and rapid spread of mosasaurs. They are considered to be the ancestors of the present-day monitors, and were descended from lizards adapted to life in water. The biggest specimens were close to 15m (49ft) long. The mosasaurs must have looked much like legendary sea serpents with an enormous mouth and large conical teeth, a back adorned with

Ichthyornis victor

Hesperornis regalis

crests or series of triangular plates, and a long, tapering tall. Their eyes were surrounded by bony rings. Among the best known forms are *Tylosaurus* and *Mosasaurus*. Georges Cuvier takes the credit for having recognized the fossil of *Mosasaurus* as a marine lizard. It was discovered in 1780 near Maastricht, in West Germany, close to Aquisgrana, on the Meuse. It is not known whether the mosasaurs gave birth to live young.

Other creatures of marine habitats were the pterosaurs, *Pteranodon ingens*, toothless, with a sac-like mouth similar to the beak of a pelican and a wingspan of almost 8m (24ft); birds with undeveloped wings, *Hesperornis regalis*, specialized swimmers and fishers close to shore; and flying,

fishing birds *Ichthyornis victor*. None of these predators needed to compete for food, since fishes and molluscs were plentiful. It is likely, however, that the mosasaurs, pterosaurs and birds did frequent the same environments, for their bones have often appeared in the same strata. One such find led to a famous misunderstanding of *Ichthyornis*. The skeleton in question was discovered without a head, but with the small head of a mosasaur among the other bones. For years there were reconstructions of a bird with a beak and teeth. It is probable that *Ichthyornis* had a beak without teeth.

The ammonites were very plentiful in the marine habitats of the Jurassic and the Cretaceous. The shell of these cephalopod molluscs, which possibly resembled the present-day *Nautilus* cephalopods, show closely packed series of grooves with rather complicated patterns; some of these look like the indented borders of oak leaves.

These squiggly patterns are actually the outward marks of the walls dividing the various chambers of the shell. The living animal occupied only the last chamber on the very outside. Why do the walls appear so twisted? Evidently the folded shape gave additional strength to the shell, so that its outer walls could be thinner and lighter which is an obvious advantage for the animal inside. A comparison can be made with a piece of paper which, if folded in two can at most support the weight of a pencil; but if the paper is pleated like an accordion, it will bear the weight of a book. The ammonite managed to vary its total specific weight and so was able to float at any depth. It did this by pressing its soft body against the pleated wall and regulating the quantity of air contained in the shell. Perhaps if the wall had not been pleated, the manoeuvre would have been less efficient and less rapid. We can imagine an ichthyosaur or a mosasaur hurling itself on its prey with great sweeps of the tail, but we can also imagine the ammonite sinking swiftly to safety, leaving the predator open-mouthed and cheated.

# Life in the swamps

The movements of the continents led to frequent variations in land levels. Lakes might be transformed into swamps or a river might be diverted to form a broad estuary where slow-flowing fresh water would mingle with salt sea water. These swampy areas were ideal places for new forms of dinosaurs to develop and to encourage the continuous, though relatively slow, evolution of the crocodiles. During the Cretaceous, while marine crocodiles were still active near the coasts, others which were like the alligators and true crocodiles of today appeared in swamps. Their size distinguished these creatures from our modern forms. *Deinosuchus* was up to 18m (59ft) long, with a head of 1.8m (6ft). Giant crocodiles continued to flourish throughout the next period as well. A 15m (49ft) gavial, *Rhamphosuchus indicus*, was recorded in India in strata of the late Cenozoic.

The Cretaceous swamps were breeding grounds, too, for the first snakes. All the legless reptiles which subsequently established themselves on dry land were descended from aquatic types which had only the tiniest legs which they used for swimming. Both the frogs and the toads greatly increased their range.

*Opposite, above: A reconstruction of a late Cretaceous swamp. The crocodiles belong to the genus* Deinosuchus. *Some specimens of this genus were 18m (59ft) long. These crocodiles were not very different from the present-day Nile crocodile, which may grow to a length of 7m (23ft). There were also small and tiny types.*
*Opposite, below: The fossil skull of a dwarf crocodile which measured barely 1m (3ft) overall.*

Deinosuchus

Anatosaurus

# Iguanodon: a mine disaster

Of all the many astonishing finds of dinosaur bones, none was more spectacular than the discovery made in 1878 in a coal mine at Bernissart, near Mons, in Belgium. In one single stratum the remains of 29 large animals were found, apparently all of the same genus. The animal had already been partially known since 1822. But the Bernissart find revealed for the first time an entire group of animals from the distant past. Today eleven of the skeletons are on display in a room of the Natural History Museum in Brussels. The genus is *Iguanodon*, two species of which have been distinguished: *I. bernissartensis* and also *I. mantelli*.

The iguanodonts were bipedal and stood 5m (16½ft) high; they were up to 11m (36ft) long, *I. mantelli*, with four fewer vetebrae in the spinal column than *I. bernissartensis*, was slightly smaller. They were ornithis-chians of the Ornithopoda group, which emerged in the late Jurassic with forms of the *Camptosaurus* type. The camptosaurs already had specialized teeth for grinding plants. In the front part of the mouth they had a horny beak in the lower jaw which rubbed against a horny thickening of the tip of the upper jaw. This was similar to present-day cattle where the incisor teeth make contact with a similar thickening of the upper jaw, which does not have incisors. The grinding teeth of iguanodonts often showed signs of wear; they were gradually replaced by new teeth when the others fell out. This is what happens with the molars of present-day elephants.

How did the iguanodonts live? Certainly in groups, perhaps in wooded areas on the fringes of swamps. The camptosaurs were able to move about either on four legs or on two hind legs; and they probably browsed vegetation on the ground. The iguanodonts always stood on their hind legs and must therefore

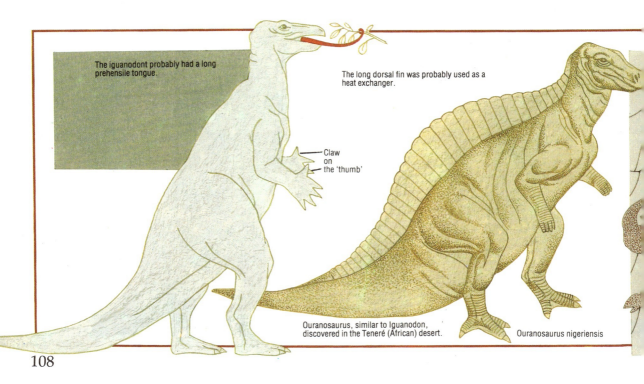

The iguanodont probably had a long prehensile tongue.

Claw on the 'thumb'

The long dorsal fin was probably used as a heat exchanger.

Ouranosaurus, similar to Iguanodon, discovered in the Teneré (African) desert.

Ouranosaurus nigeriensis

An unexpected natural disaster could have caused the iguanodonts of Bernissart into mad flight which caused them *all* to fall into a deep crevasse.

Above: The iguanodont skeletons of the Brussels Museum of Natural History.
Left: An iguanodont browsing leaves with its long prehensile tongue. Scholars claim that the animal had a tongue similar to various present-day saurians. In the centre is a type related to the iguanodonts, *Ouranosaurus,* with a dorsal sail. The sketch on the right illustrates the theory that the iguanodonts of Bernissart hurled themselves into a crevasse because of some natural catastrophe. This may explain why these animals of the early Cretaceous were found in a coal mine. The 20 skeletons were found in a shaft reaching down to strata of the Carboniferous.

have browsed on high leaves and shoots. They probably had a long, prehensile tongue for reaching and tearing off branches. They had three toes on the hind feet and five fingers on the forefeet, all with hoof-like nails, except for the thumb, which had a large horny claw, like a dagger. This claw would have been useful against predators and possibly against rival males of its own species in duels for winning females. The nails may also have been used as tools for splitting bark and trunks. The vertebrae of the powerful tail were stiffened by a series of tendons. The tail acted as counterweight to the front part of the body. Many other large and small bipedal dinosaurs used the tail in the same way.

Another interesting dinosaur, related to *Iguanodon*, was *Ouranosaurus*. Its remains were discovered in 1971 in the Teneré desert, between the Sahara and Nigeria. This ornithopod was notable for the enlarged outgrowths of the vertebrae which had to support a crest right along the back. This was an adaptation to a hot climate and may have enabled the animal to disperse heat. It was the same device as the pelicosaurs used. But the dinosaurs, perhaps homoiothermic, used it to keep cool rather than to stay warm.

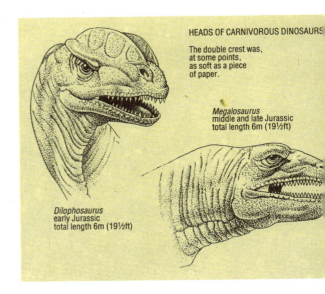

HEADS OF CARNIVOROUS DINOSAURS

The double crest was, at some points, as soft as a piece of paper.

*Megalosaurus* middle and late Jurassic total length 6m (19½ft)

*Dilophosaurus* early Jurassic total length 6m (19½ft)

*Above: The heads of four predatory dinosaurs. The crests of* Dilophosaurus, *were supported by bony formations as soft as a piece of paper. They were probably a feature of the males only and were a distinctive mark of the species.*
*Opposite: Spinosaurus, a predator of the carnosaur group, and the sauropod Dicreaosaurus. The spinosaur had a dorsal sail supported by the vertebrae. These animals were quite active with a high metabolism producing energy, so they risked dying of heat if they were unable to cool themselves with this 'sail' (lower inset).*

# Devices old and new

Throughout the Cretaceous both plants and animals used forms that had been successful in the past. They also perfected new mechanisms for survival.

The flower of the magnolia, as we have seen, was an entirely new version of the old pine cone. Similarly, the thin stems of the grasses, monocotyledonous angiosperms, were modelled upon the very long, slender 'needles' of the pines. In dense forest, leaves of this type did not deprive one another of sunlight; and now at ground level such stems could grow upwards without casting too much shade on plants below. As protection against greedy herbivores, many plants had already grown tough leaves; others now chose a new method. Instead of getting rid of certain substances produced by their metabolism, they transformed them into poisons.

Ceratosaurus
late Jurassic
total length 6m (19½ft)

Deinonychus

Dicraeosaurus

Spinosaurus

dispersal by means of sail

too much heat

| probable homoiothermy | much activity | hot environment |

One carnosaur of the middle Cretaceous, *Spinosaurus*, 12m (39ft) long, had a crest like that of *Ouaranosaurus*, although it was slightly shorter and did not reach the tail. Its function was probably to disperse heat.

The huge sauropods continued to model themselves on earlier forms, without any striking innovations. *Alamosaurus*, from the North American late Cretaceous, was very similar to *Apatosaurus*.

The pattern of plates seen in *Stegosaurus* had no imitators among the ornithischians but a large group of 'armoured' animals called Ankylosauria did emerge. These creatures had plates, spines and tails resembling the lances of medieval knights. These provided excellent protection for the back and were in some cases formidable offensive weapons. Skeletons of ankylosaurs have often been found lying belly-upward in the mud which buried and preserved them. It was assumed that they were attacked by predators who rolled them over on their back because their bellies were unprotected by plates or spines. The carnivores could then disembowel their helpless victims. It is now believed that the herbivorous ankylosaurs, who were all quite big, about 5–6m (16–20ft) long, died of natural causes. Their corpses were carried away by water and, because of fermentation of the stomach contents, would have floated on the surface, eventually turning upside-down. In due course the bodies were stranded

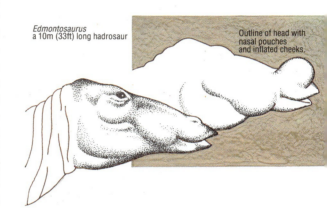

*Edmontosaurus* a 10m (33ft) long hadrosaur

Outline of head with nasal pouches and inflated cheeks.

*Polacanthus*

*Left: The head of* Edmontosaurus, *a duck-billed dinosaur measuring up to 10m (33ft) long, which is thought to have been able to inflate the sacs corresponding to nostrils. Like other allied forms, it had muscular cheeks for storing the vegetable food that was ground up by the powerful set of teeth. The drawing on the right shows the likely shape of the huge pterosaur* Quetzalcoatlus, *known only by a few bones. The long vertebrae of the neck, the parts of the arm and parts of the fourth finger suggest that the creature was a kind of 'flying giraffe' with a wingspan of about 16m (52ft). Opposite and below: A reconstruction of two ankylosaurs,* Polacanthus, *4m (13ft) long, from the lower Cretaceous, and* Palaeoscincus, *up to 6m (20ft) long, from the upper Cretaceous.*

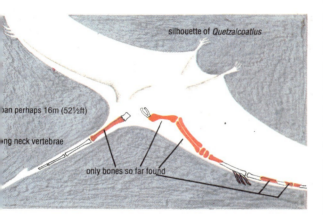

silhouette of *Quetzalcoatlus*

an perhaps 16m (52½ft)

ng neck vertebrae

only bones so far found

and then buried by mud in that position.

There is evidence in the late Cretaceous of the pterosaurs adapting to environments far from water. This suggests that it may have happened before then. In 1971 the fragmentary remains of a pterosaur with a wingspan that must have been 16m (52½ft) were found in Texas. This sets a new record of the biggest animal, so far as we know, that ever flew. The name chosen for this Texan pterosaur is *Quetzalcoatlus*, a Latin form of the name of the Aztec god, the 'plumed serpent'. Several extremely long vertebrae, belonging to this creature, have made it possible to reconstruct a giraffe-pterosaur, which still awaits official confirmation. The zone where the skeleton was found contained no lakes or rivers during the Cretaceous. Perhaps *Quetzalcoatlus*, like a modern vulture, fed on the carrion of land animals, spotting the carcases from a height, circling slowly on air currents just as these scavengers and other birds of prey do today.

*Palaeoscincus*

# Collars and horns

In the middle and late Cretaceous a very interesting group of ornithischians evolved. They were all descended from an ornithopod of the mid-Cretaceous found in Mongolia. This animal, about 2m (6½ft) long, had a strong, parrot-like beak, and is called *Psittacosaurus* ('parrot-lizard'). It had the build of a bipedal dinosaur, but its fairly long forelegs meant it

*Bottom: A reconstruction of two adult Protoceratops intent on saving their nest, dug in the sand, from the raiding activities of small egg-stealing dinosaurs of the genus Oviraptor. The scene is imaginary but we know that the herbivorous protoceratopsians had to contend with small carnivores such as these. At one site the skeleton of one such predator (Velociraptor) was found closely joined, in a death embrace, to the skeleton of Protoceratops, after the two animals had killed each other.*

*Below: A young protoceratopsians hatching from the egg. This reconstruction is based upon the discovery of some nests with eggs that were broken open and others that still contained embryos.*

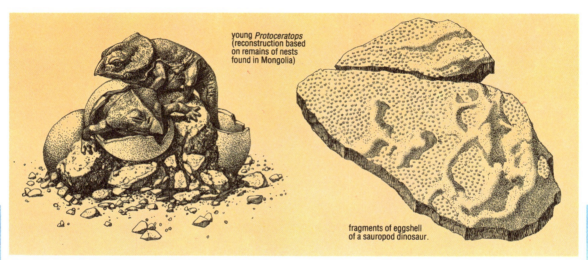

young *Protoceratops* (reconstruction based on remains of nests found in Mongolia)

fragments of eggshell of a sauropod dinosaur.

Protoceratops

Oviraptor

could walk on four legs. Its descendants of the late Cretaceous were all quadrupeds. These dinosaurs are collectively known as Ceratopsia. The feature common to all ornithischians, the predentary bone of the mandible or lower jaw, is very marked in the ceratopsians. The bony formations at the tip of the mandible slot under those at the tip of the upper jaw, forming what looks like a huge beak. The grinding teeth are placed a good way behind the beak and are very sturdy. They look like molars and possibly have two roots, which is a quite exceptional feature for a reptile. The ceratopsians certainly fed on plants which they tore off with the beak and ground up with their teeth. But what types of plant would they have eaten?

During the late Cretaceous one group of monocotyledonous angiosperms called the palms suddenly grew large. It seems very probable that these trees formed the main element of the diet of the ceratopsians. It may be that the animals soon came to realize, that the palms contained a nutritious sugary sap which was good to drink.

The first true ceratopsian was *Protoceratops*. Its remains have been found in Mongolia. *Protoceratops* was 2m (6½ft) long with a massive bulk. Its skull already displays another characteristic of the whole group: a huge 'collar' formed by an expansion of the bones of the skull. Its function has been interpreted in various ways: a defensive device, a recognition feature, and so on. But it is logical to assume that it had something to do with the animal's specialized diet of tough plants. The ceratopsians must have had huge, strong jaws for the beak and grinding teeth to work efficiently and also extremely powerful muscles for chewing. Such muscles would have been fimly attached to the front part of the collar. Furthermore, the entire head was certainly very heavy; so there must have been other powerful muscles in the neck set in the rear part of the collar. As the size of the animals' skulls and bodies increased, so too did the collars. Yet this contraption surely had a defensive purpose as well. The neck is a notoriously weak point in all animals, and predators go for it at once. However, the ceratopsians also had long horny bones on various parts of the head, especially on the forehead, as defensive weapons. The skin often consisted of plates or other bony outgrowths.

We know about the earliest stages of ceratopsian development because some nests of *Protoceratops* have been discovered in Mongolia. The eggs

Triceratops

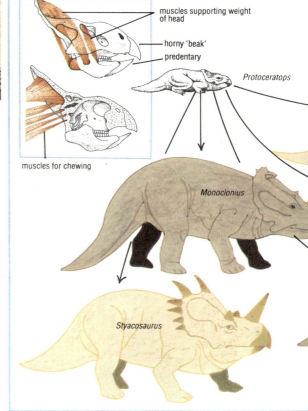

muscles supporting weight of head

horny 'beak'

predentary

Protoceratops

muscles for chewing

Monoclonius

Styacosaurus

*Above: A reconstruction of three* Triceratops *charging.*
*Right: The evolution of the ceratopsians, showing some of the most typical genera. These forms derived from* Protoceratops, *about 2m (6½ft) long. The only bipedal form was* Leptoceratops. *The small inset at left shows the arrangement of the principal muscles associated with the skull, jaw and neck of* Protoceratops.

were laid in sandy depressions, like those of modern crocodiles. Some of the eggs that were found contained embryos that had apparently died before they developed.

Many of the later ceratopsians come from North American sites. These dinosaurs had two main areas of distribution, one in central-eastern Asia and the other in North America. In all, 20 genera have so far been described. The most famous species is *Triceratops prorsus*, described by Marsh in 1889. Probably these animals, up to 11m (36ft) long and weighing up to 8t (7 tons), behaved much like modern rhinoceroses; they browsed systematically on palms but if they were disturbed or feared an attack by some predator, they turned and charged, either forcing the enemy to flee or doing it damage. The frontal horns of *Triceratops* were up to 1m (3ft) long. The real enemies of the ceratopsians were the small 'egg-stealing' dinosaurs such as *Oviraptor* or the mammals with the same habits. In the comparatively arid zones in which they lived there was not much food and the small predators were skilled in raiding nests. This is just a theory, but it seems reasonable.

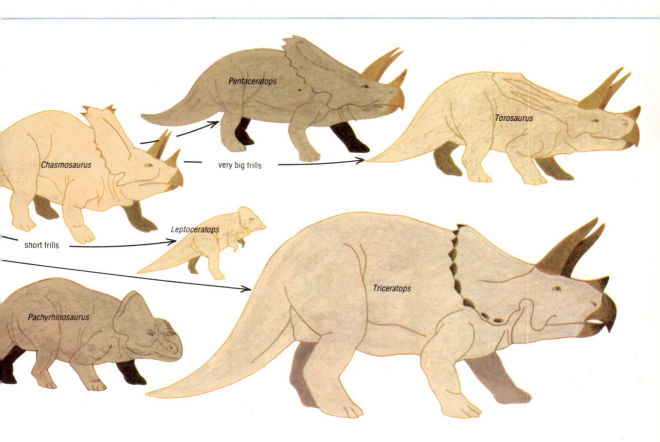

Pentaceratops

Torosaurus

Chasmosaurus

very big frills

Leptoceratops

short frills

Triceratops

Pachyrhinosaurus

# Hard heads

In the late Cretaceous the group of ornithischian ornithopods, earlier represented by the renowned *Iguanodon*, got a new lease of life. They developed specializations which make it possible for small and very similar groups to be distinguished from one another. In one such minor group the bones of the skull were enormously thick. In the genus *Stegoceras* (3m [10ft] long) the 'dome' protecting the brain, little bigger than

a hen's egg, was 5cm (2in) thick. It consisted of solid, compact bones. These skulls have shown exceptional resistance to the wear and tear of time. Many have been preserved virtually intact. So we know the different versions of 'hard-headed' dinosaurs that then existed. The dentition tells us that, like all ornithopods, they were plant-eaters. The hard head may have been a defence against carnivores. But why was it restricted to the head? Earlier scholars thought that it might be due to some malformation, disease or disorder. It seems odd that such a disorder could have occurred in so many animals of different species and sizes. Furthermore, the thickening of the skull was often accompanied by outgrowths on the nasal bones, small collars on the neck and reinforcements around the eyes. It is now believed that this strange skull formation may have had something to do with the animals' behaviour. The development of domes

*Opposite: Mating rituals of dinosaurs (genus* Camptosaurus *from the late Jurassic). The reconstruction is based upon observations of the behaviour of various present-day saurians and the discovery of marks of 'love-bites' on the neck vertebrae of some herbivorous dinosaurs.*
*Below: An imaginary reconstruction of a duel between two male* Stegoceras *for the conquest of females. These ornithischian ornithopods formed part of a group noted for extraordinarily thick skull-bones. The inset shows an outline of the skull of* Pachycephalosaurus.

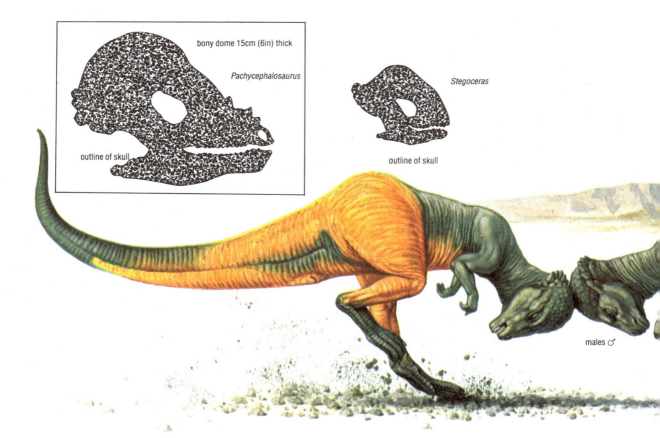

bony dome 15cm (6in) thick

*Pachycephalosaurus*

outline of skull

*Stegoceras*

outline of skull

males ♂

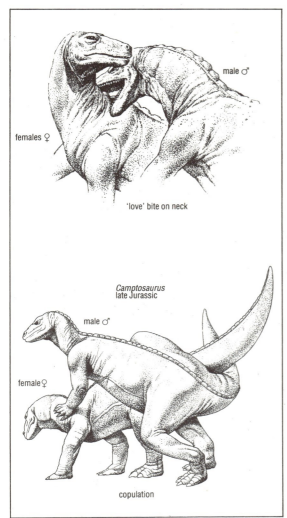

females ♀

male ♂

'love' bite on neck

Camptosaurus
late Jurassic

male ♂

female ♀

copulation

could be associated with problems of sex: it would have been a useful feature for males in their duels for possession of the females. Ethologists who study the behaviour of present-day reptiles have confirmed that challenges and duels are common among saurians (the group comprising lizards, geckos and monitors). It seems likely that *Stegoceras* and its relations such as *Pachycephalosaurus*, 8m (26ft) long and with skull bones over 15cm (6in) thick, should fight one another and even resort to butting, like rams and ibex. Another fact about the sexual life of dinosaurs is that the males had no external sex organs, they must have had a penis similar to that of crocodiles, snakes and lizards. This would be an organ which could be extended at the moment of copulation and which was normally withdrawn into a pouch of the single opening that was the outlet of the intestine and the urogenital apparatus. In order to copulate and

female ♀

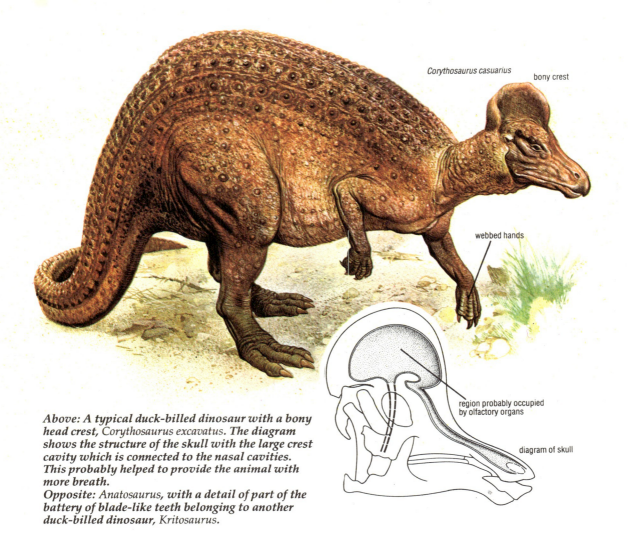

Corythosaurus casuarius

bony crest

webbed hands

region probably occupied
by olfactory organs

diagram of skull

*Above: A typical duck-billed dinosaur with a bony head crest, Corythosaurus excavatus. The diagram shows the structure of the skull with the large crest cavity which is connected to the nasal cavities. This probably helped to provide the animal with more breath.*
*Opposite: Anatosaurus, with a detail of part of the battery of blade-like teeth belonging to another duck-billed dinosaur, Kritosaurus.*

transfer sperm, the male dinosaur had to bring his opening into contact with that of his partner by mounting her, which could be a difficult operation considering the dimensions of limbs, belly and tail. Today many saurians (such as those of the genus *Anolis*) bite the female on the neck during copulation, this serving both to hold her tight and to stimulate her. The neck bones of certain herbivorous dinosaurs bear scratches which could not have been caused by the bites of predators. The marks correspond to those which could have been made by the beaks and teeth of plant-eating dinosaurs, perhaps by animals of the same species.

## Duck bills and crests

It may be that the duck-billed dinosaurs were descended from *Batrachosaurus*, of the Mongolian lower Cretaceous. The group had a very large number of genera and species. Towards the end of the period, these ornithischians inhabited every continent. South America was reached by a land link in the Central American region.

Collectively known as Hadrosauridae, these dinosaurs grew to a considerable size. The genus *Anatosaurus* was 9m (29½ft) long and probably weighed over 3t (2¾ tons).

The front part of their lower jaw was flat, broad and rounded, and was covered by horn. The upper jaw had a predentary bone of the same form which fitted beneath the lower jaw. The predentary also had a horny covering. This was quite different from the parrot-like beak of the ceratopsians. There was an extremely efficient grinding mechanism in the innermost part of the mouth. A tightly packed series of plate-like teeth were inserted in each half of the upper jaw and in the corresponding halves of the lower jaw.

We also have detailed information about the soft body parts of the hadrosaurs because several examples have been found in an exceptional state of preservation. The animals had muscular, dilatable cheeks which exerted repeated pressure on the mass of food ground up by the batteries of teeth. In this way the animals could cope with any vegetable substance, however tough.

The forefeet with four toes, two of them with a small claw, were

battery of teeth
of a hadrosaur

The skin of some hadrosaurs, in states of exceptional preservation, display dense 'mosaics' of scales, like that of certain modern lizards, which are brightly coloured: From this it may be deduced that the duck-billed dinosaurs, and possibly all the dinosaurs, were very colourful.

webbed; but we do not know whether the hind feet, which were very large and with three clawed toes, were similarly webbed.

How did the hadrosaurs live? The webbed feet suggest an adaptation for swimming or at least life in water; remains of their diets show that most of their food consisted of forest plants. The evidence is contradictory. The fact that the remains of adults and young have never been found on the same sites suggests that the female hadrosaurs may have laid their eggs around swamps, and that the babies and youngsters spent much of their time here. They could keep at a safe distance from predators. Later, as adults, their size made them more vulnerable to attack; so they abandoned the swamps and began roaming forests and dry shrubland areas.

In addition to the normal duckbilled mouth, many hadrosaurs developed strange helmets or crests. These head growths were connected with the animals' sense of smell and helped members of the same species to recognize one another.

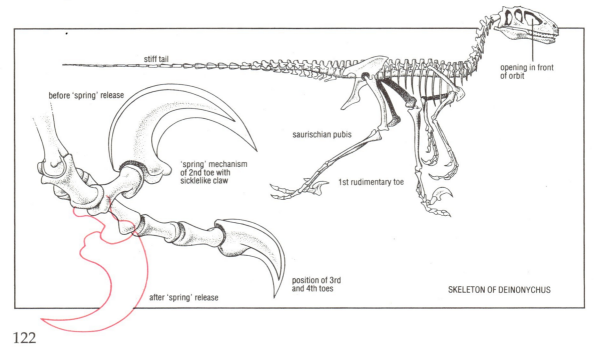

stiff tail

before 'spring' release

'spring' mechanism of 2nd toe with sicklelike claw

after 'spring' release

position of 3rd and 4th toes

saurischian pubis

1st rudimentary toe

opening in front of orbit

SKELETON OF DEINONYCHUS

*Opposite: The skeleton and foot of* Deinonychus, *a small coelurosaur 2.4m (7¾ft) long. The tail consists of vertebrae with a bony extension which keeps it very stiff. The second toe of the hind foot has a hooked claw with a kind of spring mechanism.*
*Above: The site near Billings, Montana, USA, where the remains of* Deinonychus *were found.*

## Clawed killers

The predators of the late Cretaceous roamed far and wide. Some carnivores were huge, others smaller but no less dangerous. The coelurosaurs used their speed to attack massive herbivores, but many of them were omnivores, feeding on eggs and probably supplementing their diet with plant food. Among these fleet-footed predators, all of average size, were *Ornithomimus, Oviraptor, Velociraptor* and *Deinonychus.*

The hind feet of *Deinonychus* (terrible claw) had four toes, all with

123

claws. The first toe was very small but the second was a fearful weapon, for its claw was sickle-shaped, enormous and lethally sharp. When the animal walked on its third and fourth toes it tucked up this killer claw to prevent wear and tear, in the same way as the cassowary, the large present-day Australian running bird. Face to face with its victim, *Deinonychus* reared up on one leg and struck a flailing blow with the sickle-claw of the other foot. This could be fatal. During such an attack the animal balanced its body with its long tail, stiffened by bony parts which slotted into one another and were connected to the vertebrae. The three toes of the front feet also had sharp talons and were obviously used with the other claws and the teeth to finish off the victim.

## Tracks of the tyrant lizard

Probably the best-known and most popular of all dinosaurs is *Tyrannosaurus rex*, two specimens of which were found in Montana (USA) in 1902 and described three years later by Henry Fairfield Osborn. The name comes from the Greek word *tyrannos*, tyrant, meaning absolute ruler, and has helped to consolidate its image as a cruel, terrifying monster – villain or hero of many a science-fiction fantasy, comic strip of film cartoon. To reinforce this daunting reputation there are reconstructions of its skull and skeleton in natural history museums. It was a massive creature which measured 15m (49ft) and weighed around 10t (9 tons). The skull was flat and long, and the jaws contained 60 huge, jagged teeth. Yet the tyrant lizard shared its world with other equally massive dinosaurs,

such as *Albertosaurus*, from Canada (a genus which may include animals previously classified under the genus *Gorgosaurus*), and *Tarbosaurus bataar* from Mongolia (a region where further skeletons of *Tyrannosaurus* have also been found).

What did the tyrant lizard eat? Meat, obviously, but what kind and how much? Considering its size and weight, it would have needed to consume half a 20t (18 ton) sauropod or three 3t (2¾ ton) hadrosaurs at one meal. But how long would it have taken *Tyrannosaurus* to get through such a quantity of food? Comparing its bulk with that of a cold-blooded animal such as a crocodile or a Komodo dragon, we may conclude that a meal like this would have lasted it for months. But if we think of *Tyrannosaurus* as an animal of high metabolism, we must assume that it would have needed more frequent meals and thus more victims. We do not have much useful information on the ratio of predator to prey, because very few skeletons of our tyrant have been found. Anyway, it is hard to envisage the predator in mad pursuit of a gigantic herbivore, killing its victim, gorging until it is full and then settling down for a very long period of digestion. Surely a sluggish,

*Opposite: The skeleton of* Tyrannosaurus rex *at the New York Museum of Natural History. In the upper inset are the terminal parts of the hind and front limbs of this gigantic carnosaur. The short forelimbs, with only two fingers but with strong shoulder muscles, were probably used for taking a firm grip on the ground when the animal, with difficulty, raised itself from the flat resting position to the normal standing position. In the lower inset are the various stages of this 'gymnastic' operation.*

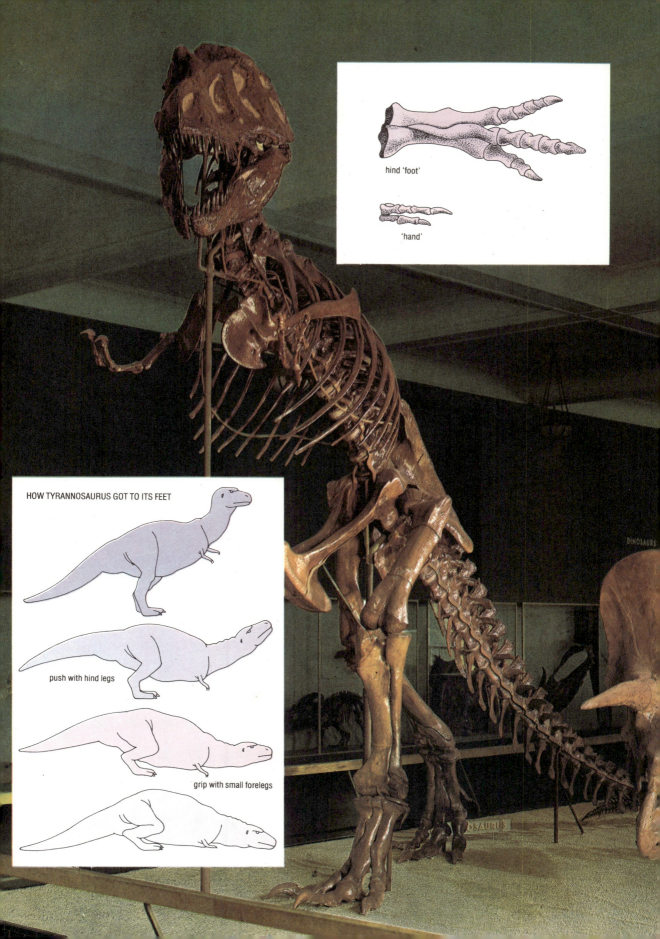

hind 'foot'

'hand'

HOW TYRANNOSAURUS GOT TO ITS FEET

push with hind legs

grip with small forelegs

?

=

Was it a predator, like a tiger?

?

=

Was it a scavenger, like a hyena?

1

Tyrannosaurus **was undoubtedly a carnivore, as is evident from its dentition. But because the huge body dimensions may have given it a rather clumsy gait, some authors believe that the enormous carnosaur fed on carrion (see diagram above). The reconstruction shows two tyrannnosaurs fighting for possession of the carcase of an anatosaur. As the right part of the diagram indicates, a homoiothermic (constant-temperature) predator requires a bigger quantity of meat.**

Tyrannosaurus rex

Anatosaurus

If we regard it as a homoiotherm, with a constant
temperature, it would have consumed a weight of meat equal
to its own weight within a relatively short time (several days):
weight of a tyrannosaur (10t [11 tons])3= weight of 3
hadrosaurs; so the diet could have consisted of 1 hadrosaur
every 3 or 4 days.

If we regard it as a poikilotherm, with a variable temperature,
its own equivalent weight in meat might have been enough
for several weeks; 3 hadrosaurs or ½ sauropod each month.

Tyrannosaurus rex

drowsy *Tyrannosaurus* would have been easy prey, while sleeping off its meal, for *Triceratops* or even for one of the fierce little carnivores like *Deinonychus*. It seems much more logical to think of the tyrant lizard as an eater of carrion: like an enormous vulture, it would consume a quantity of meat at intervals whenever it happened to come across a suitable carcase. Perhaps it only killed small animals, stunning its victims by lashing out with its huge, powerful clawed feet.

Footprints of *Tyrannosaurus* have been discovered and these have shown that the creature took relatively short steps of about 2 metres (6ft). Maybe it walked like an enormous goose, waddling along and swinging its tail as counterweight to body and head.

The tiny forelimbs pose another mystery. Why are they so small and why are only two toes equipped with fairly strong claws? Such arms could not even reach the mouth. Yet detailed study of the bones has shown that they were attached in the shoulder region to strong muscles. This suggests that the arms must have been used for planting firmly on the ground and supporting the body as the animal clambered with difficulty on to its feet after its period of rest.

It is worth mentioning that in 1965 a discovery was made in upper Cretaceous strata of the Gobi Desert, in Mongolia, of the forelimbs and shoulder-blades of an animal that was clearly a predatory dinosaur. A proportional comparison with *Tyrannosaurus*, suggests that the bones must have belonged to a creature of at least 30m (98½ft) in length. It is possible that the animal looked more like a vastly bigger version of *Deinonychus*. The name given to the

creature, was *Deinocheirus* (terrible hands). An interesting theory has been advanced concerning these hands. As a result of the greatly increased development and distribution of social insects, it is suggested that dinosaurs may have evolved with claws especially adapted for ripping open nests, just like present-day giant anteaters. Could the 'terrible hands' indicate the existence of anteater-dinosaurs? This would provide further proof of the huge adaptability of these reptiles.

# Parental care

Relationships between old and young, parents and children may help to explain why certain animals adopted certain forms, serving as a model for others. The egg is important in establishing a relationship between the body of the mother and the embryo or developing child. The eggs of reptiles and birds isolate the embryo from the mother's body. When the embryo develops either in close contact with the mother's body, as in marsupial mammals, or actually inside it, as in placental mammals, the relationship is different. The offspring are much better protected, but there are other factors concerned with behaviour, which affect such relationships. These patterns of behaviour can often be observed in some species although not in others belonging to the same animal group.

Let us look at the amphibians. Present-day frogs lay eggs in the water; fertilization generally occurs as the eggs themselves are expelled from the mother's body. In one species, the Surinam toad (*Pipa pipa*), the fertilized eggs are made to stick to the mother's back. Skin grows around them and the tadpoles develop. The baby toads emerge when they have already gone through the larva-tadpole stage. This toad has devised the same kind of protection as is provided by mammalian mothers.

Another example is the female crocodile who lays her eggs in a hole in the sand, covers them with rotting vegetation and another layer of sand. When the baby crocodiles emerge, the mother at once carries them one by one in her mouth and places them in the water where they can swim. This is more like the typical behaviour of birds and of mammals.

*Below: A reconstruction of* Tarbosaurus bataar, *found in Mongolia. The face of this carnosaur had a swelling over the nasal bones. The forelimbs had two fingers, as in the case of the tyrannosaur. The length from head to tip of tail was 12m (39ft) (the tyrannosaur measured, on average, 15m (49ft)).*

Tarbosaurus bataar

Did the animals of the past already display complex behaviour patterns such as these? If so, were they useful for the animals' evolution? Probably, yes. We know that many animals 'learn' from their parents and from others of their kind various patterns of behaviour. Would the dinosaurs and also the more primitive reptiles not have done the same? It is hard to believe that the allosaurs did not learn to hunt in packs; or that baby trinassodonts, suckled by their mother, would not somehow have been protected in a burrow. The need to share out food may have led to the setting up of a hierarchy. The great development of reptiles during the Mesozoic suggests that much of the behaviour that we see among modern birds and mammals may have been 'practised' by the dinosaurs and other reptiles.

## Mammals on the march

From the Triassic to the Cretaceous, small mammals had been increasing. Towards the end of the Cretaceous, certain groups were tending to become specialized. We know of animals similar to the opossum, insectivores and primates. The small animals which for millions of years had been active by night began to venture out.

The forests, with their dense undergrowth of shrubs, were very inviting. The animals were furry which protected them and was an efficient means of insulation. The light-and-shade conditions of the forests and undergrowth were ideal for their progress.

Mammals eat virtually every kind of food. Their young are nourished on mother's milk and so grow very quickly.

*Opposite: A reconstruction of some Paleocene mammals.*
*At the top is Planetetherium, at the bottom Taeniolabis and the smaller Ptilodus.*
*Below: The different links that exist, in various animal groups, between parents and young. Patterns of behaviour, especially those relating to parental care, are very important factors in defining different lines of evolution. The protection baby mammals receive from their parents gives them a number of advantages.*

| | amphibians | re |
|---|---|---|
| links with mother's body | | egg with calcareous shell |
| nest | sometimes nests of foam or mud nests in sand or rotting grass | burrows among small species |
| capacity at birth | free larvae | young already active |
| after birth | as a rule independent of parents | rare examples of parental care |

When the dinosaurs met difficulties in hostile environments, the mammals stepped in and replaced them.

## Why did the dinosaurs become extinct?

The Mesozoic drew to a close and a new era, the Cenozoic ('of recent life') or Tertiary opened.

When we speak of an era 'closing' or 'opening', these are simply geological expressions to denote a transition, a change in the Earth's strata. This implies a change in the fossil

*Planetetherium*

| | | marsupials | placentals |
|---|---|---|---|
| ...ds | | | |
| ...egg with ...calcareous shell | | short gestation (without placenta) | long gestation (with placenta) |
| ...very elaborate nests | | teaching, learning | rare burrows, in small species |
| ...active young (nidifugous) | | young totally inept (almost embryos) | young often active and sometimes inept |
| ...or inept young (nidicolous) | | parental care protection in pouch | marked parental care, teaching, learning |

turtles

*Taeniolabis*

*Ptilodus*

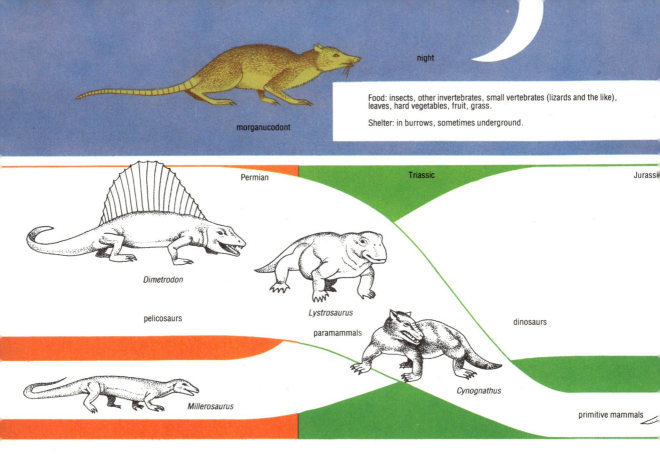

night

Food: insects, other invertebrates, small vertebrates (lizards and the like), leaves, hard vegetables, fruit, grass.

Shelter: in burrows, sometimes underground.

morganucodont

Permian

Triassic

Jurassic

Dimetrodon

pelicosaurs

Lystrosaurus

paramammals

dinosaurs

Cynognathus

Millerosaurus

primitive mammals

evidence. In the strata that succeed the Cretaceous there is no further trace of the vertebrate groups of saurischians, ornithischians, pterosaurs, mosasaurs, pliosaurs and ichthyosaurs. The invertebrate ammonites and belemnites vanish completely. The great mystery is the fall of the giants, the disappearance of the ruling reptiles. This also affected pterosaurs and marine species. So is there a single cause to explain the extinction of living forms in land, sea and air? There must have been a number of causes.

It is impossible to be sure how rapidly everything happened. We cannot say that at one moment the dinosaurs were present and that the next moment they were gone.

Everything suggests that their decline must have lasted at least ten million years, during which some quite exceptional things may have happened.

*At the end of the Cretaceous there was a major change. The gigantic reptiles were replaced by birds and small mammals. The mammals who had been noctural took over from the reptiles, which had been diurnal, occupying their various ecological niches (top). The lower diagram illustrates how the two principal evolutionary paths alternated and intermingled.*

## Decline of the dinosaurs

Some herbivorous dinosaurs increased during the final part of the Cretaceous. But towards the end of the period something seems to have checked their progress.

Certain strata of the upper Cretaceous of North America have been named after famous deposits discovered there. Three successive phases are Belly River, Edmonton and Lance. As many as 29 genera of duck-billed dinosaurs have been found in the Belly River strata, as against 7 in the Lance. There were 16

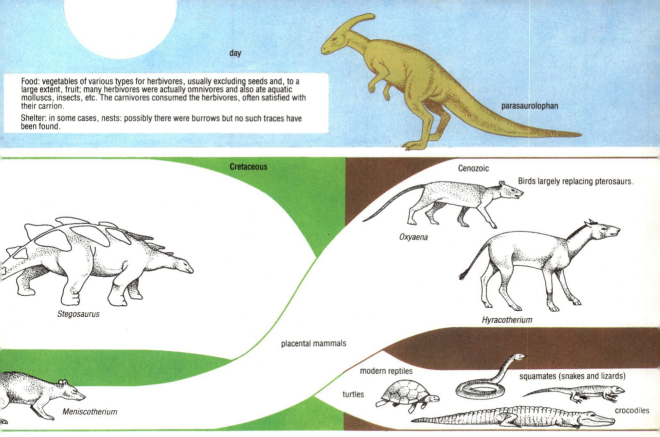

day

Food: vegetables of various types for herbivores, usually excluding seeds and, to a large extent, fruit; many herbivores were actually omnivores and also ate aquatic molluscs, insects, etc. The carnivores consumed the herbivores, often satisfied with their carrion.

Shelter: in some cases, nests: possibly there were burrows but no such traces have been found.

parasaurolophan

Cretaceous

Cenozoic

Birds largely replacing pterosaurs.

Oxyaena

Stegosaurus

Hyracotherium

placental mammals

modern reptiles

squamates (snakes and lizards)

turtles

Meniscotherium

crocodiles

ceratopsian genera in the Belly River strata, 7 in the Lance. Fossils of predators showed more consistency: 15 genera for Belly River, 14 for Lance. The Lance strata, furthermore, revealed a large number of *Triceratops* specimens. There was no sign of old genera being replaced by new ones only a thinning out. The decrease among the herbivores suggests that something was beginning to go wrong with their food supply. The carnivores still had plenty to eat and continued their activities.

The dinosaurs were particularly well equipped to feed on the flowering plants. Evidently the plants went through a crisis and this had repercussions on the herbivores.

In studying the transition from the Mesozoic to the Cenozoic, scientists have often paid too much attention to the world of animals, and failed to focus on the plant kingdom. Many

plants also disappeared, and around the end of the Cretaceous there is a striking reduction in the amount of fossilized pollen in the various strata. Plant life in general was going through a difficult period. Why was this?

During the late Mesozoic, mountains rose over areas that had been flat. Volcanoes were continuously erupting. The majority of shallow continental seas dried up, leaving swamps and prairies. This led to the disappearance of environments inhabited by the marine mosasaurs, ammonites and pliosaurs. More importantly, it did away with the sea barriers. The animals of dry land found wide open spaces for migration. Competition among animals confined to relatively limited areas had stimulated the evolutionary process, more space and less rivalry slowed it down. The mountains represented an im-

133

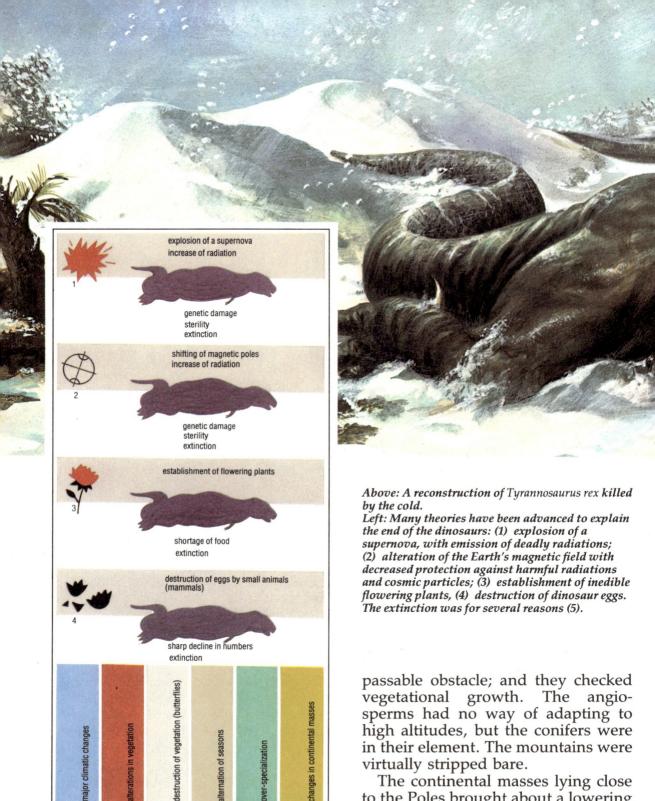

**1**
explosion of a supernova
increase of radiation

genetic damage
sterility
extinction

**2**
shifting of magnetic poles
increase of radiation

genetic damage
sterility
extinction

**3**
establishment of flowering plants

shortage of food
extinction

**4**
destruction of eggs by small animals
(mammals)

sharp decline in numbers
extinction

**5**
major climatic changes | alterations in vegetation | destruction of vegetation (butterflies) | alteration of seasons | over-specialization | changes in continental masses

extinction

*Above: A reconstruction of Tyrannosaurus rex killed by the cold.*
*Left: Many theories have been advanced to explain the end of the dinosaurs: (1) explosion of a supernova, with emission of deadly radiations; (2) alteration of the Earth's magnetic field with decreased protection against harmful radiations and cosmic particles; (3) establishment of inedible flowering plants, (4) destruction of dinosaur eggs. The extinction was for several reasons (5).*

passable obstacle; and they checked vegetational growth. The angiosperms had no way of adapting to high altitudes, but the conifers were in their element. The mountains were virtually stripped bare.

The continental masses lying close to the Poles brought about a lowering of temperature on dry land, which led to snow in the mountains and floods in the lowlands.

Tyrannosaurus rex

Were the dinosaurs killed by cold?

Plants need sunlight to live. Many experts believe the sunlight was cut down for a long time. A falling asteroid might have raised enough dust to be in the Earth's atmosphere for years. Huge plumes of ash and dust could also have been thrown up from erupting volcanoes, obscuring the Sun for a lengthy period. Less light would have led to less plant life. This would result in a crisis both for herbivores and carnivores.

Some scientists point out that a strong dose of radiation could have sterilized all those animals known to have vanished. Radiation might have been caused by the explosion and collapse of a star fairly close to the Solar System. Alternatively, there could have been an alteration in the Earth's magnetic field, so that it no longer provided a shield against radiation from space and the Sun.

These are exceptional events but they could have happened. The theories about mass sterilization, are today considered highly unlikely.

By this time the continents had clearly defined temperate, warm and cold areas; and there were already signs of alternating warm and cold periods coinciding with the seasons. This was an inhospitable environment for the dinosaurs. If they had been cold-blooded, they would have been killed by the cold. If they were homoiothermic they could have generated a certain amount of heat, but they could not have coped with large-scale changes of temperature.

# Fall of the dinosaurs

A determining factor may have been the competition from other animals. Insects are capable of destroying a forest. In the later Cretaceous there was an increase in insects. It is important to realize that the biological control of insect-eating birds was then non-existent or minimal. The idea of herbivorous dinosaurs condemned to die of hunger by the action of butterflies is possible.

Climatic changes could also have altered the life of the plankton in the seas, thus depriving many other animals of their food. This could have been a death sentence for the mosasaurs, pliosaurs and ichthyosaurs, already in decline. The marine pterosaurs, are more likely to have been affected by competition from birds.

The dinosaurs, it is generally agreed, have gone. But if they can still conjure up a feeling of awe and wonder, or compel us to look back with curiosity and interest to those distant ages when they literally ruled the Earth, that surely is a fitting tribute.

*This skeleton of a tyrannosaur in the Royal Ontario Museum, Toronto, is complete with a set of abdominal ribs. These indicate the size of the animal's paunch. A tyrannosaur could weigh up to 10t (11 tons).*

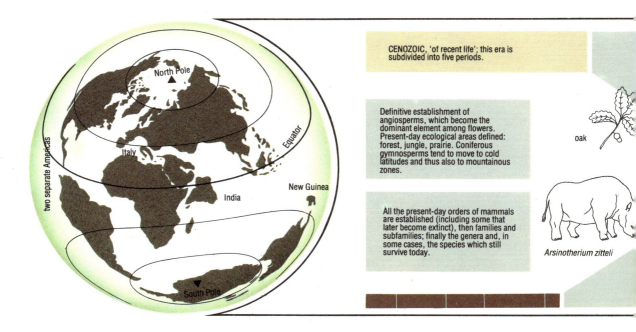

Definitive establishment of angiosperms, which become the dominant element among flowers. Present-day ecological areas defined: forest, jungle, prairie. Coniferous gymnosperms tend to move to cold latitudes and thus also to mountainous zones.

oak

All the present-day orders of mammals are established (including some that later become extinct), then families and subfamilies; finally the genera and, in some cases, the species which still survive today.

*Arsinotherium zitteli*

# CENOZOIC
# Tertiary

The Cenozoic era lasted a little more than 60 million years – a short time compared with preceding eras. Since it is more recent, it is easier for scientists to distinguish the events that are recorded in the Earth's strata. The earlier part of the Cenozoic, known as the Tertiary, is divided into five distinct periods, all of relatively brief duration. The later part, known as the Quaternary, takes us up to the present day.

At the beginning of the Tertiary there were seven continental blocks resulting from the splitting up of the supercontinents: North America, Eurasia, Africa (with Arabia adjoining), India, South America, Antarctica and Australia. These last three were linked at various times by bridges of dry land periodically exposed or submerged.

India lay on either side of the Equator; and Antarctica still contained the South Pole. Throughout the early part of the era, corresponding to the Paleocene and Eocene epochs, there may have been a slight slackening of mountain activity, which had been very marked all through the late Mesozoic, mainly because there were no further major collisions between the continental blocks. On the other hand, the land level in many areas was raised, so that inland seas, lakes and swamps dried up.

Mountain-building received an impetus around the middle of the era when, for example, Italy, Yugoslavia and Greece, advancing from the south, made contact with Europe, thrusting up the Alps. Towards the end of the era the impact of India against southern Asia caused the emergence of the Himalayas, the highest and youngest mountains on the planet.

The climate was fairly cold in the zones around the Poles but quite mild elsewhere.

duration        63 million years

from 65 to approximately 2 (million years ago)

PALEOCENE, means 'old recent'

EOCENE, 'dawn recent'

OLIGOCENE, 'scarcely, slightly recent'

MIOCENE, 'less recent'

PLIOCENE, 'very recent'

duration 11 million years        from 65 to 54 (million years ago)

duration 16 million years        from 54 to 38

duration 12 million years        from 38 to 26

duration 19 million years        from 26 to 7

duration about 5 million years        from 7 to about 2

*Left: A diagram of the Cenozoic era. The entire Cenozoic has lasted for a shorter time than some of the periods making up previous eras. The Cenozoic periods themselves are fairly brief, in geological terms. The appearance of the continents gradually came to take on the shapes with which we are familiar today. There were many volcanic eruptions and earthquakes. The angiosperms dominated the plant kingdom. Mammals established themselves in every environment. Insects were abundant, among them many external parasites which lodged themselves in the fur of mammals and the feathers of birds. Bony fishes, in ever greater variety, were spectacularly represented both in seas and inland waters.*

*Below: The Matterhorn, an enormous mass of uprooted rock which looks as it does today by being thrust up from the Alpine mountain range during its principal formative phases in the Cenozoic.*

# New ways of life

During the Tertiary reptiles were progressively replaced by mammals and birds. The animals of these two classes moved in to occupy new environments, new areas of living space. The environment itself was being transformed by the gradual and irresistible advance of the angiosperms, with visible flowers: huge trees, shrubs and grasses. The last group extended its range over immense areas.

As always, novelties in the plant kingdom preceded those in the animal kingdom. The flowering plants achieved their full glory before the mammals and birds finally established themselves. The plains and prairies stretched to the horizon before the most efficient herbivores (the artiodactyls or mammals with two equal, symmetrical hooves) and the most accomplished grain- and seed-eaters appeared.

The new plants developed interesting methods of pollination, making use of animals and other elements of the environment as carriers.

## The typical mammal

A description of a present-day mammal would also apply to all the fossil species of the Cenozoic. The vertebrates of the class Mammalia are warm-blooded, true homoiotherms, and their bodies are covered by hairs. Sometimes there may be scales in addition to hairs. Numerous glands scattered over the skin produce and secrete various fluids like sweat, odorous liquids, sebum and milk.

The lower jaw or mandible consists of a single dentary bone and articulates with the bone of the upper part

*Opposite: Herbaceous plants on the tundra. The monocotyledons of the family Gramineae, or grasses, gradually became established as the commonest plants of flat lowland zones. With their long, slender stems and tissues permeated with silica, the grasses are sturdy and quickly spread by producing innumerable seeds in spikelets.*

*Below: A comparison between the traditional subdivision of eras based on the presence of animal life and a sub-division taking into account the appearance of plant types. It can be seen that every major change among the animals is preceded by a change among the plants. The drawings show the advantages of being a warm-blooded animal with a covering of fur as insulation, and the principle of homoiothermy, controlled by the brain, typical of mammals and birds.*

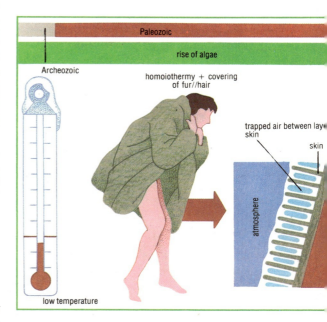

of the skull. The square bone and other bony elements are present in the skull of the amphibians and reptiles. They are much modified in mammals, where they are the basis for the collection of small bones of the inner ear.

The upper part of the skull, which

| Mesozoic | | Cenozoic | | | |

rise of ferns | middle flora | recent flora | | |

Holocene
Quaternary

reddening (blood in surface vessels: dispersion of heat)
sweating (evaporation: cooling)

centrally controlled by the brain

muscular movement (continual shivering)
erection of the hairs (increase trapped air)

when warm

when cool

constant body temperature

contains the brain, is directly attached to the bony skeleton of the palate.

The teeth almost always have roots and are normally of four types: incisors, canines, premolars and molars. There are, as a rule, two sets of teeth: the 'milk' teeth, which are present in the young, and fall out to be replaced by the permanent teeth.

The internal cavity of the thorax or chest is separated from the abdominal cavity by the diaphragm muscle. The heart has four separate cavities, two atria and two ventricles. Metabolism is high and plenty of food is required. There is a balance between the energy that the mammal has to expend on procuring food and the energy it must retain as heat by means of its internal temperature regulating systems.

A vital element for making this regulation system efficient is the insulating cover provided by the fur. A good deal of air is trapped between the hairs; and since air is a poor conductor of heat it prevents heat generated by the animal from being dispersed outside. But the animal also has cooling systems. If, for instance, it is very hot, our skin gets red: blood flows abundantly through the thin surface vessels and the heat which it carries is partially dispersed by the body surface. Certain mammals, including humans, have numerous sudoriparous glands which emit sweat when it is hot. This evaporates on contact with the air, lowering the temperature of the skin and thus of the body. If it is very cold, we shiver. This is caused by a rapid movement of the muscles which ensures the production of a little extra heat that is momentarily needed. The cold may also cause goose pimples, whereby the hairs are erected. This is much more evident among animals hairier than ourselves. In order to cope with the cold, the brain 'orders' the muscles capable of erecting the hairs to place themselves so as to increase the amount of 'trapped' air and thus insulate the body.

Milk is produced by special, transformed sudoriparous glands. These are generally in the female breasts and the milk is exuded from the nipples. The platypus and the echidnas have neither true breasts nor nipples. These mammals called monotremes, lay eggs. The eggs are similar to those of reptiles but have a shell that resembles parchment. The babies are protected inside a deep fold in the mother's abdomen after they have hatched. None of the true mammals lay eggs, so it is possible to accept the argument that the monotremes are not unusual mammals but the last representatives of the therapsids. These are the Permian and Triassic reptiles who walked upright and are regarded as the ancestors of the mammals.

The marsupial mammals give birth to babies that are still virtually embryos and deposit them in the marsupium or pouch. Among the placental mammals development takes place in the mother's womb, where the embryo is nourished and can expel waste substances.

The embryo of placental mammals does not breathe: its lungs are deflated. Blood circulates, through the umbilical cord, through both the body and lungs of the mother. At the moment of birth, the two atria of the baby's heart are subdivided and blood begins to flow to the lungs, which themselves fill with air. This happens when the newborn baby opens its mouth, often uttering its first cry.

In all mammals the red corpuscles of the blood, which help distribute oxygen throughout the body, form as normal cells but later lose their nucleus. These red corpuscles cannot reproduce, but have to be manufactured. No other vertebrate has red corpuscles without a nucleus.

# The typical bird

Birds are warm-blooded vertebrates whose body is covered with feathers that are equivalent to the scales of reptiles, and not to the hairs of mammals. (Scales and feathers are formed in the surface layers of the skin; hairs have a more complex structure and are embedded with their root in the skin itself. In addition the hairs are connected to various glands, for example, the sudoriparous glands which birds and reptiles do not have.) They also have real scales, particularly on the hind legs.

The forelimbs are transformed into organs of flight, or wings. There are many species that are incapable of flying, some of them, like the kiwi, with atrophied wings.

The upper and lower jaws are encased in a horny beak. The upper jaw

*Above: Reafforestation of cypresses. Land plants
with seeds have many ways of ensuring the union
of sexual cells, gametes, and, following that, the
diffusion of the seeds themselves capable of
creating new plants. In the evolutionary history of
plants the seed has the same significance as does
the egg with shell in the history of vertebrates. It
enables the living organism to await the most
favourable moment for development, with less
reliance on water.*

*Right: An exchange of favours between animals,
plants and the environment. The insects pollinate
flowers and extract nectar from them; the wind
carries pollen and seeds; the animals transport
seeds and fruits. They put the seeds back into
circulation by eating the fruits. The seeds are
fertilized by their faeces.*

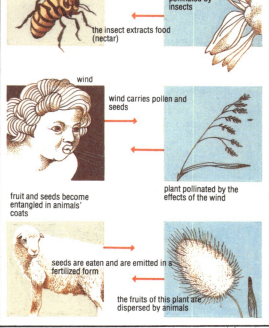

the flower is pollinated

plant pollinated by insects

the insect extracts food (nectar)

wind

wind carries pollen and seeds

plant pollinated by the effects of the wind

fruit and seeds become entangled in animals' coats

seeds are eaten and are emitted in a fertilized form

the fruits of this plant are dispersed by animals

143

is separately mobile. When mammals open their mouth, they lower the mandible; birds open their beak by lowering the mandible *and* raising the upper jaw. As in reptiles, the mandible is formed of several bones.

The clavicles or collar-bones in birds are joined into a single element, commonly known as the wishbone. In the human skeleton the two bones each link the scapula or shoulder-blade to the sternum or breastbone, forming the front part of the shoulder. In birds that fly, the sternum has a broad keel into which are inserted the muscles that move the wings.

Birds do not possess a diaphragm. The movements of the lungs, for breathing in and out, are related to movements of the forelimbs. The lungs of birds have passages, or air sacs, which communicate with all parts of the body, including the skeletal system. The bones, too, have cavities that are filled with air. The pterosaurs had this feature.

The lower portion of the larynx, which is the part of the respiratory system containing the vocal cords in mammals, contains the syrinx or vocal organ, which is only present in birds.

Birds' eggs have a calcareous shell. In the earliest stage of development, the embryos have tiny teeth which later disappear. This is evidence of their common link of descent with reptiles.

# The Paleocene mammals

During the long period when the dinosaurs were dominant, the mammals were mostly insectivores, hunters of small creatures such as worms, caterpillars and tiny vertebrates, and perhaps eaters of eggs, grains and

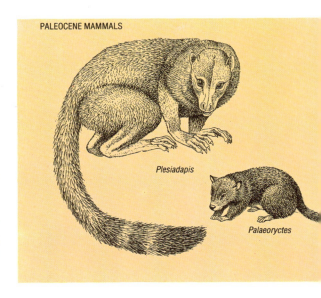

PALEOCENE MAMMALS

*Plesiadapis*

*Palaeoryctes*

seeds. The oldest primates also fed on leaves.

In the Paleocene, the first period of the Cenozoic, a group of quite large herbivorous mammals emerged. These were the Pantodonta, descended from the Condylarthra, hoofed creatures known to have lived in the late Cretaceous. Notable forms of pantodont included *Pantolambda*, the size of a sheep, and *Barylambda*, as long as a horse but much stockier. *Barylambda* may have reared up on its hind legs to reach the high branches of shrubs and trees. Its toes had strange hoof-like nails and it had a large tail. Primates (*Plesiadapis*) and species capable of leaping from a height and gliding, like the modern flying lemur, lived in the trees. Very large numbers of shrews competed with more primitive forms (Multituberculata), now almost extinct.

Carnivorous mammals were fairly slow to appear. The real enemies of the medium- and large-sized herbivorous mammals of the Paleocene were crocodiles on river banks and lake shores, and a number of large birds of prey on dry land, especially in exposed areas.

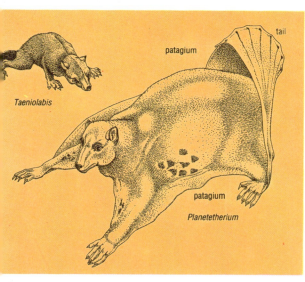

The mammals of the Paleocene were already fairly varied. Most of them were adapted to life in trees or in the thick of the forest.
Left: *Taeniolabis*, a multi-tuberculate, representing a late form already living during the Mesozoic; *Plesiadapis*, a long-tailed primate; *Palaeoryctes*, an insectivore similar to shrews; and *Planetetherium*, an animal with broad strips of skin between the sides of the body and the limbs and between the hind limbs and the tail. This made it possible for the animal to glide short distances, as is the case with the present-day flying lemur, sole modern representative of the order Dermoptera.

Below: *Barylambda*, more than 2m (6½ft) long, and *Pantolambda*, as big as a sheep but looking more like a cat. Both these animals were vegetarians. The claws of *Barylambda* took the form of small, sturdy hooves.

# Warm-blooded giants of the seas

The mammals soon began to explore the possibilities of living in watery environments, especially the sea. A number of types developed which were probably descended from herbivores of the Condylarthra group. These were similar to the present-day Sirenia, the manatee or sea cow and the dugong. The mammals of this order owe their name to the fact that the females have large breasts. It is said that sailors, seeing these creatures emerge from the water, believed them to be the mythical sirens, half-woman and half-fish, so creating the legend of the mermaids. The sirenians of the next epoch, the Eocene, show links with the group from which the elephants were to evolve.

Animals resembling present-day dolphins, derived from primitive forms of predatory land mammals (also classified as Condylarthra), appeared during the late Paleocene. These were the first Cetacea, well documented from the Eocene onwards: genus *Protocetus*. These creatures had strong teeth for seizing and biting fishes and cephalopods. Teeth suitable for cracking shells were no longer needed after the disappearance of the ammonites. So the cetaceans to some extent took over the ecological niche previously occupied by the ichthyosaurs and began interfering with the activities of the sharks.

In the Oligocene, gigantic types appeared which were adapted to the consumption of plankton. These were the baleen whales, the biggest creatures that have ever lived on Earth, feeding exclusively on the tiniest animals of the oceans. The plankton is driven into the whale's mouth

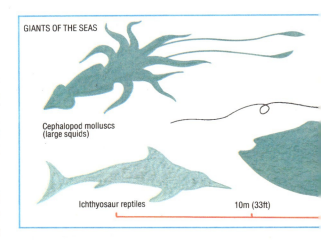

GIANTS OF THE SEAS

Cephalopod molluscs (large squids)

Ichthyosaur reptiles

10m (33ft)

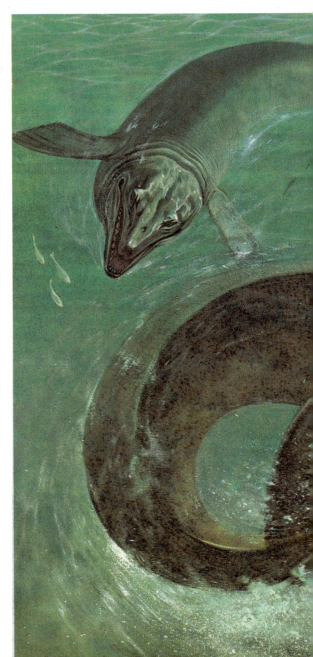

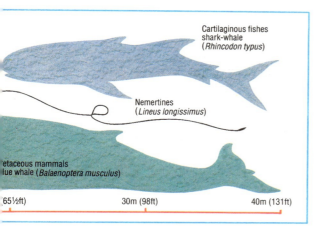

Cartilaginous fishes
shark-whale
(*Rhincodon typus*)

Nemertines
(*Lineus longissimus*)

etaceous mammals
lue whale (*Balaenoptera musculus*)

65½ft          30m (98ft)          40m (131ft)

*Below: A reconstruction of* Basilosaurus cetoides, *an Eocene cetacean which was up to 20m (65½ft) long. The formation of the vertebrae made the body fairly flexible. The forefeet of this mammal were transformed into flippers and the hind feet were reduced to virtually nothing. The body ended in a large, horizontal caudal fin. The dentition was typical of a predator's. The marine environments, with plenty of food, encouraged the development of gigantic animals. Left: Silhouettes of some of these giants. The longest of all these animals was actually a nemertine worm,* Lineus longissimus, *which, although its diameter was only a few centimetres, measured 40m (131ft).*

Basilosaurus cetoides

through a filter of horny baleen plates, set on either side of the palate, which are substitutes for teeth.

During the Eocene there was already one gigantic cetacean, *Basilosaurus*, also known as *Zeuglodon*. The generic name, meaning king lizard, was given after the discovery in 1834, of its long snake-like skeleton, measuring 20m (65½ft). The forelimbs of *Basilosaurus* were already transformed into powerful fins; the hind limbs were reduced to a few small bones inside the body, as is the case with modern cetaceans. The triangular teeth had a serrated edge. This predator must have been a formidable substitute for the mosasaurs.

# Above and below ground

Whatever ecological disaster or combination of disasters occurred at the end of the Cretaceous, only the small or tiny land animals managed to survive. Furthermore, those animals which escaped the catastrophe were, for the most part, homoiothermic. The exceptions included the smaller lizards and the crocodiles who, as amphibians, were not strictly creatures of dry land but creatures of watery environments.

Already during the Paleocene many forms of greatly varying sizes had evolved from these little animals. As a result, the mammals began competing with one another. Many of them developed new specializations or brought old skills up to date. In the following period, the Eocene, we have records of various primates which returned to being active mainly at night, as is indicated by the almost frontal position of the large eyes of the small animal *Tetonius*. Creatures

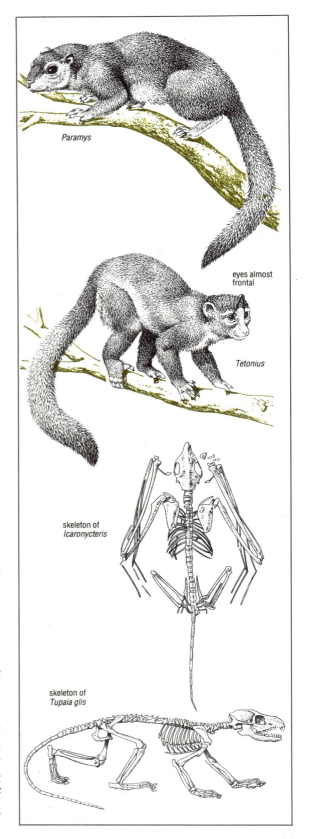

*Paramys*

eyes almost frontal

*Tetonius*

skeleton of *Icaronycteris*

skeleton of *Tupaia glis*

similar to squirrels (Rodentia) also began scampering around in the trees; and many insectivores undoubtedly sought refuge underground, digging burrows, like modern moles and hedgehogs.

Certain mammals developed enormous hands, the fingers of which supported a broad membrane of skin. These were the first bats. From the earliest experiments in gliding, mammals now progressed to true and proper flight.

*Opposite: Eocene mammals.* Paramys, *one of the first rodents, already resembling a squirrel;* Tetonius, *a primate with eyes almost frontally positioned; skeleton of* Icaronycteris index, *the first bat of which we possess reliable remains; and the skeleton of a present-day tree shrew (*Tupaia glis*), quite similar to the Cenozoic forms.*
*Right: Two tree shrews, primates which bear strong resemblances to the insectivores.*
*Below: Two hedgehogs (*Erinaceus europaeus*), insectivores adapted to life at ground level.*

# Eocene land predators

During the Eocene, many predatory mammals emerged which were related in a somewhat complex way to the Condylarthra and Creodonta ('flesh teeth'). These creatures roamed the same habitats that were later to be frequented by the various groups of the order Carnivora. They played the same ecological role as the present-day big cats, the dogs and wolves, the hyenas, the bears, the mongooses and the weasels. But the Eocene animals cannot always be regarded as the direct ancestors of modern species: sometimes the resemblances are due to similar responses to the environment and to specializations in a certain type of hunting or particular kind of prey.

*Dromocyon*, the size of a setter dog, and the colossal *Andrewsachus mongoliensis* were among the forms equivalent to dogs and wolves. Only the skull (84cm [33cm] long) and a few other fragments have been recovered of this latter carnivore, classified as one of the condylarths: so it is difficult to reconstruct its overall appearance. All that is certain is its size, at least 4m (13ft) long and 2m (6½ft) high at the shoulder, judging from the dimensions of the head.

Some of these animals walked on the soles of their feet, as was the case with *Oxyaena lupina*, a creodont which looked like an odd mixture of a marten, a cat, a badger and a hyena. Others were variously adapted to walk on their toes, as do modern carnivores, including domestic cats and dogs.

The nails on the four toes of both hind and front feet were something between a claw and a hoof; and the first toe was already reduced, again as in modern cats and dogs. The strong spinal column of these mammals suggests that they could leap or sprint; yet the large size of *Andrewsarchus* hardly conjures up the impression of the great agility of modern carnivores. Perhaps many of the Eocene predators enjoyed a mixed diet, as do brown bears today, or fed mainly on carrion.

# Early ungulates

Towards the end of the Paleocene and, subsequently, in the Eocene, there was a great increase in the numbers of herbivorous mammals. They roamed both the forests and the newly emerged plains; and with so much food available, they sometimes grew huge.

In order to function perfectly in such different environments, these mammals developed a new type of nail on the foot. All the primitive animals were equipped with tiny claws, as are modern rodents and insectivores. In the herbivores these were replaced by much thicker and sturdier hooves, capable of supporting the weight of the body and distributing it evenly either on soft or hard ground. These hoofed mammals are commonly known as ungulates.

The first hoofed animal, still one of the condylarths, was *Phenacodus primaevus*. It was as big as a wild boar and walked on the soles and toes, like modern bears. This animal resembled the primitive creodont carnivores in various ways, but its diet must have been that of a herbivore.

*Coryphodon*, even more massive, was up to 3m (9ft) in length and known to exist in the late Paleocene. This herbivore may have lived on river banks, like present-day hip-

CLASS MAMMALIA (MAMMALS)
SUBCLASS EUTHERIA (placental mammals)

orders:
   INSECTIVORA (shrews, moles, hedgehogs)
   DERMOPTERA (flying lemur)
   CHIROPTERA (bats)
+ OXYAENIDA (*Patriofelis* and other forms)
   PRIMATES (lemurs, monkeys, apes, man)
   EDENTATA (sloths, anteaters, armadillos, +
     *Megatherium*)
   PHOLIDOTA (pangolin)
   RODENTIA (squirrels, porcupines, rats, mice)
+ HYAENODONTA (*Hyaenodon*)
+ CREODONTA (*Tricentetes*)
   CARNIVORA (weasels, cats, dogs, bears, seals,
     walruses)
   LAGOMORPHA (hares, rabbits)
+ CONDYLARTHRA (*Phenacodus, Hyopsodus*)
+ MESONYCHIDA (*Andrewsarchus*)
+ PANTODONTA (*Coryphodon*)
   CETACEA (dolphins, whales, porpoises, +
     *Basilosaurus*)
   TUBULIDENTATA (aardvark)
+ PYROTHERIA (*Pyrotherium*)
+ ASTRAPOTHERIA (*Astrapotherium*)
+ NOTOUNGULATA (*Toxodon*)
+ LITOPTERNA (*Macrauchenia*)
+ DINOCERATA (*Uintatherium*)
   PERISSODACTYLA (tapirs, rhinoceroses, horses)
   ARTIODACTYLA (pigs, hippopotamuses, camels,
     deer, cattle)
   HYRACOIDEA (hyraxes)
+ EMBRITHOPODA (*Arsinotherium*)
   PROBOSCIDIA (+ mastodonts, + *Deinotherium*,
     elephants)
+ DESMOSTILIA (*Palaeoparadoxia*)
   SIRENIA (dugong, manatee)

*Left: A table showing (with examples) all the modern and extinct orders of the subclass Eutheria (placental mammals). The extinct forms are marked with a +. Various extinct Mesozoic groups (Morganucodonta, Pantotheria, Triconodonta, Simmetrodonta, Multituberculata) and, today, in addition to the Eutheria, the subclass Metatheria, which comprises the marsupials, are included in the class Mammalia. The Monotremata, egg-laying mammals (echidnas and platypus) are nowadays seen by many authors as the last representatives of the Triassic paramammals.*
*Below: Three predatory mammals of the middle and late Eocene, belonging to the orders Oxyaenida and Mesonychida.*

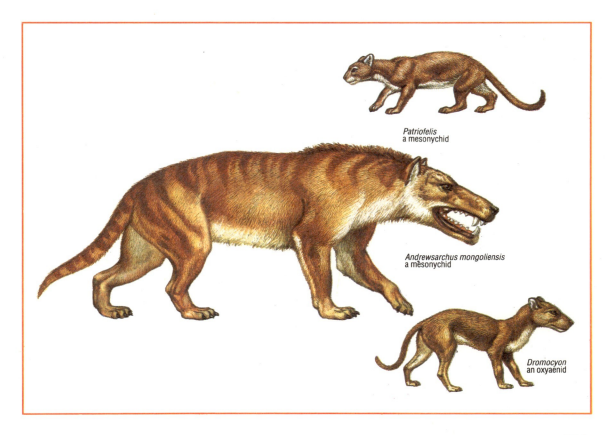

*Patriofelis*
a mesonychid

*Andrewsarchus mongoliensis*
a mesonychid

*Dromocyon*
an oxyaenid

popotamuses. Long upper canines would have enabled it to tear off aquatic plants and may have been used by the males for duels.

In *Uintatherium mirabile*, 3.3m (11ft) long with a skull of 75cm (29½in), the protruding canine teeth are clearly longer in the males than in female specimens. The skull of this herbivore was topped by three bony outgrowths which were covered with skin, like the horns of a giraffe. An interesting feature in *Uintatherium* and in the related form, *Eobasileus*, ('dawn king'), is that the top part of the cranium or brain box is practically concave, which considerably reduces brain capacity. Furthermore, the bones of these skulls are very thick. Perhaps rival males used to butt each other when duelling, as some of the dinosaurs may have done.

These huge ungulate herbivores belonged to the group of Dinócerata ('with terrible horns'); and their feet had massive hooves. In spite of their apparent resemblance to rhinoceroses and hippopotamuses, they are not the ancestors of either kind of animal. As a general rule a huge animal of the past tends not to be the ancestor of a huge animal of the present. In the process of evolution large forms usually develop from smaller ones. This is partly explained by the availability of food and the occupation of new environments in which such food is abundant. Let us see how this might happen.

# A matter of size

A small animal starts exploring an environment which appears to offer plenty of food and does not have too many predators. It eats from necessity. If food continues to be available it is quite probable that its descendants will gradually grow bigger. The biggest individuals are those that can most easily reproduce and thus 'bigness' becomes an established characteristic. This also constitutes a simple defence against predators. In the meantime, predators will be attracted to this new environment and will have tracked the herbivores. So, on the plains, for example, there will be enormous herbivores with ever harder hooves and more efficient feet. The big herbivore must spend much of its time feeding, as elephants do today in the savannah, and so it is increasingly probable that it will be attacked by predators. The only solution is to get even bigger and, at the same time, develop some form of weapon like horns or tusks, capable of wounding and frightening an as-

UNGULATES OF THE PALEOCENE AND EOCENE

*Coryphodon*
(Paleocene-mid-Eocene)

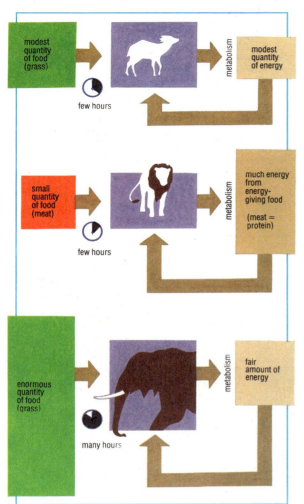

sailant. Then it can charge the enemy, to scare it away.

If we want to find the ancestors of today's giants, we should look at some of the smaller animals of the early Cenozoic, particularly those with features interesting from the evolutionary viewpoint.

## The 'thunder beast'

It sometimes happened that a gigantic animal which at the time proved extraordinarily successful, was not or could not be repeated at a later period. Only other branches of smaller types in its group continued to

*Left: A small herbivore (1), within a comparatively short time, consumes a certain quantity of vegetables and obtains from them a moderate amount of energy to support its life processes. A carnivore (2) eats a small quantity of food very rapidly and derives a great deal of energy from it. A large herbivore (3) spends some time consuming a large quantity of food and obtains from it a fair amount of energy.*
*Below: A reconstruction of three ungulates which followed one another during the late Paleocene and the Eocene.*

Uintatherium
(mid-Eocene)

Eobasileus
(late Eocene)

'thunder horse' of Indian legend

Indians hunting

bison

*Left: The bones of* Brontotherium *were known to the American Indians, particularly the Sioux of Dakota, who attributed them to the legendary 'thunder horse'. This mythical creature literally thundered across the plains, terrifying the bison and so making it easier for the Indians to hunt them. The name of the genus, chosen by Othniel Charles Marsh, means 'thunder beast' and is a direct reference to the Indian legend.*

*Below: A reconstruction of* Brontotherium platyceras, *a huge ungulate belonging to the Titanotheridae. From the evolutionary point of view these animals are related to horses. They stood up to 2·5m (8ft) at the shoulder.*

Brontotherium platyceras

evolve. This was the case with the Titanotheridae, huge ungulates whose most famous representative was *Brontotherium platyceras* ('flat-horned thunder beast') from the North American early Oligocene. The titanotheres, already completely extinct before the Miocene, were part of a huge collection of ungulates from which stemmed two separate lines of descent: on the one side the horses and on the other the tapirs and rhinoceroses. The titanotheres were themselves closer to the horses branch.

*Brontotherium* was 4.3m (14ft) long and stood 2.5m (8¼ft) high at the shoulder. It had a shovel-like snout. The generic name was chosen by the paleontologist, Marsh, in the second half of the 19th century, with reference to the legends of the North American Sioux Dakota Indians. They believed that they were assisted in their hunt for bison by an enormous heavenly horse, whose presence was heralded by the earth-pounding noise of thunder. They collected the gigantic bones of the brontothere, hailing them as the remains of the 'thunder horse'. Trophies made from such fossil bones were found by paleontologists who subsequently discovered entire skeletons of the great herbivores.

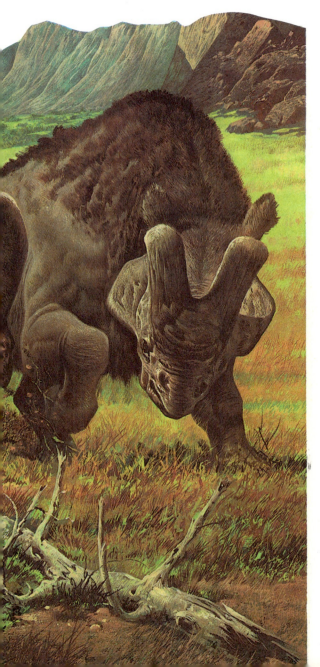

## Odd or even

An animal that needs to run, either for charging or for escaping, is greatly assisted by legs with strong toes. But for a firm grip on the ground it may be equally useful to rely on a limited number of toes. This reduction in numbers, with a consequent strengthening of those that remain, is particularly valuable on hard, fairly unyielding ground, such as the terrain of plains and prairies.

This advantage automatically meant that the animals concerned lost their capacity to climb or to grasp objects. The two major groups of herbivorous ungulates, with fewer but stronger toes, have survived to this day. They adopted one of two patterns. One group tended to retain

155

an uneven or odd number of toes, using the middle or third toe as the principal means of support. The other group tended to have an even number of toes, dividing the weight equally on the third and fourth toes. The first group became the order Perissodactyla ('with uneven toes'), and the second the order Artiodactylia ('with even toes').

The perissodactyls were most successful around the middle of the Tertiary. Nowadays there are only six genera, comprising rhinoceroses, tapirs and horses, including, of course, asses and zebras. The evolutionary history of the artiodactyls,

| number of toes | odd | even |
|---|---|---|
| type of terrain | weight / reaction to terrain | weight / reaction to terrain |
| soft, yielding | *Hyracotherium* | hippopotamus |
| hard | modern horse | giraffe |

*Lophiodon*

*Opposite: The shape and formation of hooves depend on the nature of the terrain. In the vast group of ungulates two quite different types of hoof quickly emerged. In one case the animal's weight tends to fall mainly on one toe (the third), whereas in the other case the weight is borne by two equally big toes.*

*Below: A herd of Paleotherium, a genus very closely related to the group of horses; and of Lophiodon, a genus which originated the tapirs.*

which began in the Eocene, continues. There are some 80 genera, with numerous species, which range from pigs and wild boars to hippopotamuses, from camels to giraffes, from deer to cattle, and from antelopes to goats.

Reduction in the number of toes appears to have been directly related to the transition from relatively soft and yielding terrain to hard terrain. At the same time, both groups developed the tendency to abandon support on toes *and* hoof in favour of support on hoof alone. Both perissodactyls and artiodactyls became unguligrades ('walking on the hooves').

Paleotherium

# Multitudes of birds

There is still comparatively little documentary evidence of primitive flying birds, for only some 80 fossil species have been discovered. In the majority of instances remains of birds simply crumbled away and were scattered beyond hope of recovery. In Tertiary forms there are not even any hard parts such as teeth. Dead birds were often consumed by scavengers, mostly mammals. This was especially true of all woodland forms. The situation was slightly different in the case of aquatic birds; their remains, if they fell into the water and were not devoured, could easily sink to the bottom where, buried by mud, they would become fossilized. So there is rather more evidence relating to birds that lived on sea coasts, along lake shores and in swamps. However, in all probability there were innumerable birds that also lived in trees and on the ground.

In spite of the difficulty in preserving them, the remains of the birds recovered from Tertiary strata show clearly how rapidly they were becoming established. The process dates back to the last phases of the Cretaceous. The only evidence is the odd bone, footprint or feather, yet all these bits and pieces provide clues to the existence of a very large number of species, representing all the principal bird orders that survive today and many others now extinct. It is fair to say that during the Tertiary flying birds came to inhabit all the environments in which they are present today.

The basic structure of all these birds is more or less the same. The front foot generally has only three toes and bears the feathers. The flying birds tend to have a constant number of feathers, the same number as *Archaeopteryx* had. There may be some variation in the numbers and arrangement of toes on the hind feet. The number of neck vertebrae may also vary according to species, up to a maximum of 25 in modern birds. Compare this with mammals, where the number of vertebrae in the neck is *always* fixed at seven, whether the neck is short, as in the mole, of average size, as in ourselves, or enormously long, as in the giraffe.

The class Aves, to which the birds belong, has shown every sign of continuous expansion. The first threats to the existence of particular species probably arose as a result of human hunting activities or, in more general terms, alterations that humans made to the environment.

Some large birds that became extinct because of human interference have survived only in legend. The terrible roc encountered by Sinbad

the sailor on the voyage described in the *Thousand and One Nights*, may have been the flightless elephant bird, *Aepyornis*, which once lived on the island of Madagascar.

In the late Cretaceous there were already birds similar to flamingos (*Gallornis*), to grebes (*Enaliornis*) and to gannets (*Elopteryx*). In the Paleocene and the Eocene we find forms resembling cormorants (*Odontopteryx*), tropic birds (*Prophaëton*) and vultures (*Neocathartes*).

*In the late Cretaceous and early periods of the Cenozoic the number of flying birds greatly increased. There were already many types similar to those existing today and almost all the orders were represented. There are about 800 known fossil species and some 9000 existing species.*
*Right: Some present-day species whose ancestors are known to have lived as far back as the Paleocene and Eocene.*
*Below: A flock of flamingos. The genus Gallornis, similar to a flamingo, dates from the Cretaceous.*

modern tropic bird

modern cormorant

modern gannet

# Flightless birds

At certain times and in certain environments birds became the final element in food chains. In other words, they were the superpredators. On dry land, particularly, they were fierce predators *before* mammals with the same specialized tendency appeared. Even later they were active in areas inaccessible to carnivorous mammals because of natural barriers, like broad stretches of sea, as in South America. Often such adaptations occurred among birds that did not fly. How did these creatures of the air become creatures of dry land? In many sea birds loss of flying capacity has ingeniously led to the wings being used as for swimming, like flippers in penguins. Among the large land birds the wings were reduced because they were not used for flying, so that the animals became absolute bipeds. Even this modification of wings brought some benefit.

Let us take another look at the question of food. The abundance of a certain kind of food may have led to the development of very large birds. These would have experienced considerable difficulty in flying, but were able to give up flying because it was unnecessary for obtaining food. It is likely that adaptation to life on the ground was originally associated with a diet based on leaves, fruit or seeds. Some experts claim, for instance, that even *Diatryma steini*, 2.4m (8ft) high, had a diet of fruit like present-day cassowaries. The large beak may have resembled a parrot's more than an eagle's. What is undisputed is that this gigantic bird was an excellent runner. Its feet had three toes facing forwards and one turned backwards, while the claws were strong and triangular in section. Other related

*Below: Adaptations of small reptiles and birds to diverse habitats.*
*Birds were not always creatures of the air. Some of them adapted successfully to life on the ground.*
*Opposite, below: A table listing all the present-day orders of birds (class Aves) and the principal extinct orders.*

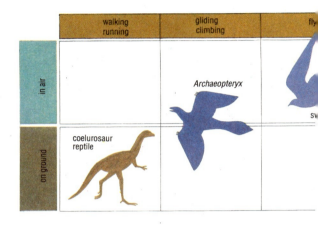

*Opposite, above: A reconstruction of* Diatryma steini, *a large bird dating from the early Eocene. The abundance of grass, leaves, fruit and hard seeds on plains and around the fringes of forests led to the appearance of some very large birds. The size of such birds prevented them from flying and thus their wings were reduced. Later birds resembling* Diatryma steini *certainly used their powerful legs for running and their strong beaks for hunting. The Diatrimidae were therefore the fearsome enemies of herbivorous mammals.*

forms (Diatrymidae) exploited their speed by hunting. So this may have been the evolutionary process: plenty of plant food – no competition – increase of size – loss of flight capacity – development of running capacity – reduction of wings – strengthening of beak – transformation into predators.

| | pecking | running |
|---|---|---|
| running | hunting | |
| | diatrymid | ostrich |

*Diatryma steini*

## CLASS AVES (BIRDS)

orders:
+ ARCHAEOPTERYGIFORMES (*Archaeopteryx*)
+ HESPERORNITHIFORMES (*Hesperornis*)
  TINAMIFORMES (tinamous)
  STRUTHIONIFORMES (ostriches)
  RHEIFORMES (rheas)
  CASUARIIFORMES (cassowaries, emus)
+ AEPYORNITHIFORMES (*Aepyornis*)
+ DINORNITHIFORMES (*Dinornis*, moas)
  APTERYGIFORMES (kiwi)
  PODICIPEDIFORMES (grebes)
  GAVIIFORMES (loons)
  SPHENISCIFORMES (penguins)
  PROCELLARIIFORMES (albatrosses, shearwaters, petrels)
  PELECANIFORMES (tropic birds, pelicans, gannets, frigate birds)
  CICONIIFORMES (herons, storks, ibis)
  PHOENICOPTERIFORMES (flamingos)
  ANSERIFORMES (ducks, geese, swans)
  FALCONIFORMES (vultures, falcons, eagles, hawks)
  GALLIFORMES (pheasants, partridges, peacocks, grouse, guinea fowl, turkeys, hoatzins)

GRUIFORMES (cranes, rails, bustards, seriemas, + *Phororhacos*)
CHARADRIIFORMES (plovers, sandpipers, coursers, gulls, terns)
COLUMBIFORMES (sand grouse, pigeons, doves)
PSITTACIFORMES (parrots, macaws)
CUCULIFORMES (cuckoos and related forms)
STRIGIFORMES (owls)
CAPRIMULGIFORMES (goatsuckers)
APODIFORMES (swifts)
TROCHILIFORMES (hummingbirds)
TROGONIFORMES (trogons)
COLIIFORMES (colies)
CORACIIFORMES (kingfishers, hoopoes, rollers, hornbills)
PICIFORMES (woodpeckers, toucans)
PASSERIFORMES (the largest order, with 5000 described species: sparrows, swallows, thrushes, shrikes, tits, starlings, finches, warblers, wrens, dippers, larks, crows, magpies, birds of paradise, nuthatches, bowerbirds, etc)

161

# Snouts and humps

Pigs are related to camels – which may sound rather strange if we look at these animals today. However, inspection of their feet shows that they are both artiodactyls. They both have an even number of toes. Pigs have four, the first has disappeared, the third and fourth are large, the second and fifth small and slightly divergent. Camels have two, the first, second and fifth have disappeared.

The basic pattern for mammals is for the feet to have five toes (pentadactylous). This is the number found in all the primitive mammals and forms related to them.

If we look at the evidence for the evolutionary history of the artiodactyls, we cannot doubt the link between the familiar farmyard pig, with its characteristic snout, and the humped ship of the desert.

Descendants of the primitive condylarths had an even number of toes, and they gave rise to the swine and the hippopotamuses. Others were the ancestors of llamas and all the remaining artiodactyls.

During the Eocene, one prominent group was the Anthracotheres or 'coal beasts'. They were so named because the principal finds have been in deposits of lignite, a relatively recent coal formation. These animals were bigger than present-day pigs. The skull alone of *Anthracotherium magnum* measured 70cm (27½in). The front feet had five toes, the first very small, and the hind feet *already* had only four. There were tusk-like canines and spoon-like incisors for tearing relatively soft grasses. The anthracotheres lived close to river banks.

The earliest animals leading to the evolutionary line of the camels were of modest size. In the late Eocene and early Oligocene there were animals with the dimensions of a big hare (*Cainotherium*); and the ungulates known as oreodonts were widely distributed. The oreodonts were larger and some were well adapted to an aquatic life, whereas others lived on dry land and hard terrain. *Poëbrotherium*, of the Oligocene, was already similar to a llama.

Another anthracothere of the Oligocene was *Bothriodon*, probable ancestor of the hippopotamuses. A little later came animals similar to peccaries, from which came true pigs, both wild and domestic.

However, the trump card held by the artiodactyls was the evolution of a digestive mechanism adapted for obtaining the maximum nutritional value from the plants on which they habitually fed.

*Subhyracodon*

# Ancestors of tapirs and rhinos

The perissodactyls prospered during the Eocene. They were established as an independent group before the artiodactyls appeared, but were also descended from the condylarths. These mammals were soon to abandon their aquatic or semi-aquatic environments, and their sturdy odd-numbered, hooved toes were ideally suited to the terrain of plains and forest glades. The large forms indicate that plenty of food was available and that they did not need to compete seriously with the artiodactyls. If the need arose, they were, in some cases,

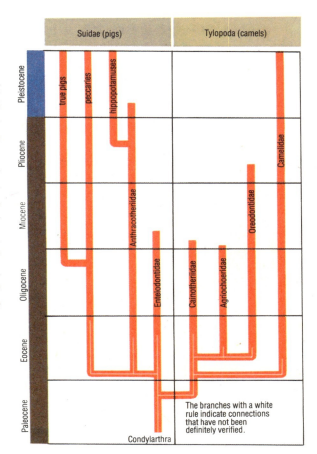

*Right: The evolutionary (phylogenetic) tree of the two groups of Artiodactyla: the pig–peccary–hippopotamus group and the camel group.*
*Below: Mammals of the North American Oligocene. They are all artiodactyls,* Protoceras, *somewhat similar to a deer, is a ruminant artiodactyl; except for* Subhyracodon, *which is a perissodactyl resembling a hornless rhinoceros.*

The branches with a white rule indicate connections that have not been definitely verified.

well adapted to live peacefully side by side with the artiodoctyls.

The perissodactyls are distinguished by two lines of evolution, one of types resembling horses, the other of tapirs and rhinoceroses. We have described the gigantic ancestors of the horse: *Brontotherium* and the other titanotheres. Now we come to the biggest of the rhinoceroses and, so far as we know, the largest land mammal that has ever lived. This was *Indricotherium parvum*, from the early Oligocene of Mongolia and China. Although *parvum* is Latin for small, this ungulate was 8m (26¼ft) long and stood 5.5m (18ft) high at the shoulder. Its long neck evidently meant it could browse on the leaves of tall trees. It had two downward pointing incisors in the upper jaw and two that were pointing upwards in the lower jaw. The structure of the skeleton and the muzzle itself shows clearly that *Indricotherium* and other related forms, known as Baluchitheridae, belonged to the evolutionary line of rhinoceroses. However, they had not yet developed the characteristic horn implanted in the nasal bone. The name rhinoceros means horn on nose. This horn, in some rhinos there are two, one in front of the other, is made up of horny pieces similar to hairs. These are joined together to form a rigid structure. It is quite likely that the large size of the animal, sustained by a great deal of food, was enough to discourage even the most daring of predators. In due course the horn on the nose was also a means of recognition within the species.

There is evidence of perissodactyls resembling tapirs back in the late Eocene. They do not differ conspicuously in build and size from their modern descendants.

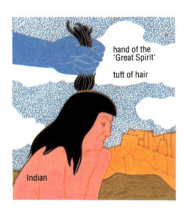

hand of the 'Great Spirit'

tuft of hair

Indian

Rhinoceros horn is really a tuft of dense hairs

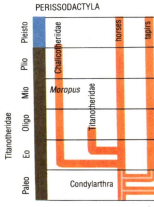

*Above: The horn of the rhinoceros consists of horny formations similar to hairs, welded together so as to form a rigid structure. Some species, such as the white rhino, have two horns. It is really a kind of plait or tuft, like that worn by the American Indians of the Chumash tribe from south-western California. This tuft was designed to be grasped by the Great Spirit to prevent fallen warriors who had been summoned to the Heavenly Pastures from tumbling back to Earth.*

*Above right: The phylogenetic tree of the Perissodactyla. The tapir–rhinoceros group is quite distinct from the horse group.*
*The brontothere and other Titanotheridae were close to the evolutionary line of horses.*
*Opposite: A reconstruction of Indricotherium parvum, the largest land mammal that has ever lived. The indricothere was a huge rhinoceros, hornless and with a long neck. It stood 5·5m (18ft) at the shoulder and fed on grass and leaves.*

running
rhinoceroses
(*Hyracodon*)

Amynodontidae

*Indricotherium parvum*

# Carnivores: perfect hunting machines

Most books dealing with zoology subdivide the order Carnivora into two suborders: Fissipeda (land forms) and Pinnipedia (forms adapted to marine life). Seals, sea lions and walruses are all pinnipeds. We have few clues as to how the pinnipeds evolved. During the lower Miocene there were mammals already adapted to life in a watery environment. The closest descendants of such aquatic mammals are probably the bears. The real distinction is that in the majority of cases the pinnipeds are not carnivores, but ichthyovores (eaters of fish).

All the carnivores are descended from the predatory condylarths and from the creodonts. Probably the different evolutionary lines, including the aquatic forms, were already defined in the Eocene. Some scholars believe that all the predatory animals which became the true carnivores should be united in a single group called Hyaenodontidae. This family is well represented by a form such as *Hyaenodon horridus*, dating from the early Oligocene. This animal was 1.4m (4½ft) long and had a skull of 27cm (10½in) long. The large size of the carnassial teeth, the premolars which rip up meat, indicates that in general the hyaenodonts did *not* behave like present-day hyenas, which feed on carrion and have teeth mainly adapted for grinding bones. They were active predators who tore the skin of their victims and ripped the muscles from the bones. The feet of *Hyaenodon* still have five toes even though the first is already reduced.

The groups today represented by bears, martens, weasels, hyenas, cats and dogs took shape between the late Eocene and the Oligocene. The oldest

forms, like the hyaenodonts, soon gave way to newer ones. Modern dogs and cats have a common ancestor in the Miacidae.

The evolutionary history of the cat is especially well documented. The Felidae, as the family is known today, are perfectly adapted for their role as predators. It is possible to detect many signs of the changes as they developed from small mammals similar to insectivores (condylarths and primitive creodonts) to big cats such as the lion and the tiger. The cat family shows a wide range of sizes and specialized skills which are not to be found in the dog family (Canidae) or the bear family (Ursidae). There are no dogs as big as a tiger and no bears as small as the domestic cat.

Although the gestation period is comparatively short, it seems to be adapted to the need of the mother cat to remain as agile and active as possible. Consequently, the newborn kittens are unable to look after themselves; they are usually incapable of walking and their eyes do not yet see. To make up for this, the mother or, in

CATS THAT SLASH

*Hoplophoneus*

MACHAIRODONTIDAE
'Sabre-toothed' forms

*Homotherium*

*Smilodon*

CATS THAT BITE

FELIDAE

*Panthera leo spelaea*
(cave lion)

*Lynx lynx*
(common lynx)

*Felis silvestris*
(wild cat)

*The cat-like carnivores evolved along two main paths. One was the Machairodontidae (sabre-toothed forms, all extinct), the other the Felidae. The Felidae contained various forms and is today represented by the three subfamilies Felinae (cat, lynx, ocelot and puma), Pantherinae (lion, leopard and tiger) and Acinonychinae (the cheetah, Acinonyx jubatus).*

167

some cases, the family group are ready to fend off any enemies threatening the helpless litter. Such parental care helps the kittens to develop a strong social sense which is useful later in group hunting activities.

Reduction in the number of toes, so marked among the ungulates, is not an equally distinctive feature of the carnivores, who never have less than four on each foot. Many of them still possess the first toe of the forefoot, even though it is small. For example, the forepaws of the domestic cat has the first toe which is mainly a claw. This first toe helps the carnivore to take a firmer grip on the ground or on a tree trunk after making a leap. The carnivores have never lost their ability to climb trees. This was a characteristic of all the primitive mammals, and is still true of modern insectivores, rodents and primates. The claws have developed to be used primarily for killing prey or at least grasping it firmly. Thus the toes have become remarkably flexible. When a cat pounces on a mouse, it expands its toes just as a pianist spreads the fingers to span an octave on the keyboard. Furthermore, in order to prevent sharp claws wearing down, most of the Felidae have a remarkable mechanism which allows them to retract the claws when not in use by pulling back the end bone of the toe that bears the claw. The only exception is the cheetah. Dogs and their relatives, bears, martens or hyenas, do not have this ability.

The earliest cats were quite small, roughly the size of our common tabby, and the origins go back to the Oligocene, taking two distinct lines of evolution. The genus *Dinictis* is considered to be the ancestor of both the true Felidae, cats that have teeth for biting, and of the sabre-toothed cats,

specialists in stabbing and slashing. The body of *Dinictis felina* was 1.1m (3½ft) long, and the height at the shoulder was 60cm (23½in). The feet still had five toes, without retractile claws. The upper canines were very large but not yet sabre-like: there was a kind of lobe in the lower jaw which fitted the tip of the canines of the upper jaw.

In the opinion of many paleontologists, the sabre-toothed cats should be classified in a separate family, the Machairodontidae, so named after one of the most typical genera, *Machairodus*, from the early Pliocene.

In *Hoplophoneus*, from the Oligocene, the upper sabre-like canines were already very long; and the connecting lobes of the lower jaw were also present.

During the late Pliocene and early Pleistocene, one of the most fearsome and widespread predators, ranging from Europe to southern Asia, was *Homotherium*. This animal had fairly short sabre-teeth, forelegs that were longer than the hind pair, and a short tail.

Perhaps the best-known animals were those of the genus *Smilodon*, 'chisel teeth', which were about the size of a tiger, with a short tail. In some Machairodontidae the angle between upper and lower jaw was around 95°; in a yawning lion it is about 65°. These animals had very powerful neck muscles, but the masticatory muscles, which close the mouth, were, in proportion, weaker than in a modern lion or tiger. Apparently the sabre-toothed species killed their victim with a single blow, inflicted with crushing force. It is likely that they fed mainly on the entrails and blood of their prey without needing to chew the muscular meat with their enormous teeth.

The main evolutionary line of Felidae also boasted forms with huge canines, such as *Nimravus*, from the late Oligocene, but their dentition was chiefly notable for their grinding teeth.

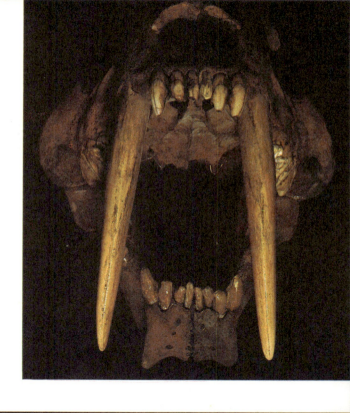

*Right and below: A skeleton and detail of the dentition of a machairodont of the genus Smilodon. The legs are strong and rather stocky. There was ample room for the neck muscles which brought the sabre teeth scything down with a swift movement to lodge in the body of the prey.*

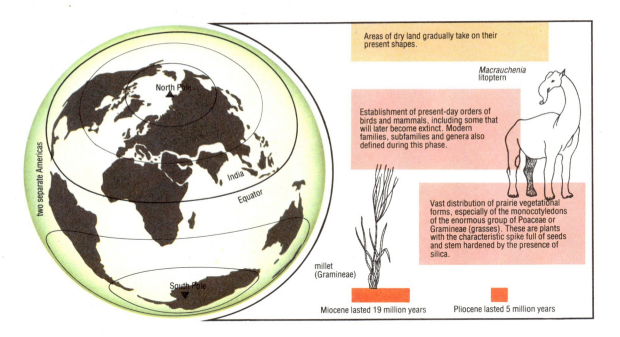

Areas of dry land gradually take on their present shapes.

*Macrauchenia* litoptern

Establishment of present-day orders of birds and mammals, including some that will later become extinct. Modern families, subfamilies and genera also defined during this phase.

Vast distribution of prairie vegetational forms, especially of the monocotyledons of the enormous group of Poaceae or Gramineae (grasses). These are plants with the characteristic spike full of seeds and stem hardened by the presence of silica.

millet (Gramineae)

two separate Americas

North Pole

India

Equator

South Pole

Miocene lasted 19 million years     Pliocene lasted 5 million years

# Late Tertiary

*Above: A diagram of the late Cenozoic era. Opposite: The excavation of Miocene strata near Orchard, Nebraska, USA, revealed numerous remains of hippopotamuses and equids buried by a volcanic eruption. During the geological phase from which these layers date, the nearest active volcanic cones were in New Mexico, a thousand or so kilometres from Orchard. The cloud of ashes and dust must have been enormous.*

## Miocene and Pliocene

In the late Tertiary the continents got closer to the positions they occupy today. The final periods were characterized by marked orogenetic activity when many mountains came into being or grew bigger and by numerous volcanic eruptions.

North America and South America continued to get nearer to each other, and there were frequent phases when the isthmus that is nowadays Central America was alternately submerged and exposed. Thus the two continental masses were occasionally isolated and occasionally joined. This had marked effects on the distribution of animals. Central America is still very 'active' from the geological viewpoint, with frequent volcanic eruptions and earthquakes.

India's long sea voyage now came to an end. In geological terms it had been an astonishingly rapid journey, the speed being estimated at about 16cm (6¼in) per year. At the end of the Tertiary the continental plate finally linked up with Asia. Italy and the Balkans joined with the rest of Europe. The Mediterranean basin, a relic of the ancient Tethys Sea, was enclosed to the east. This resulted in new mountain-building activity in the Pyrenees, the Caucasus and the Atlantic. The Andes were formed on the west coast of South America as a result of the continuous drifting of that continental plate; and during the late Tertiary the same happened with the Rocky Mountains of North America.

170

# Evidence from catastrophes

The reason that we have such detailed information about certain geological events is that, in terms of the Earth's age, they are comparatively recent. For example, we know precisely the areas of major volcanic activity. This gives us insight into aspects of life in the Tertiary that would otherwise have been hidden, for example, some biological association or a phase in the development of a particular species.

Recently, near Orchard, Nebraska, USA, the remains of a varied group of animals killed by the ashes of an exceptionally powerful volcanic eruption were discovered. The cone that must have disgorged these ashes was found some 1000km (620 miles) away, in New Mexico. This catastrophe evidently took place approximately ten million years ago, in the late Miocene. The remains of a one-toed horse, *Pliohippus*, and of a three-toed horse belonging to the genus *Hipparion* were found in addition to many animals of considerable interest.

# The triumph of the horse

When we compare animals that are part of the present-day fauna with fairly similar forms found among the faunas of the last phases of the Tertiary, it is easy to make an error of judgment by seeing today's species as the final destination, the peak of the evolutionary process. It is true that modern animals represent one stage reached by various groups in the course of their evolution, a stage that was not reached by extinct animals; but it cannot be said that we and the species that exist alongside us necessarily represent the final goal or an end to something that is still happening. For instance, the order Proboscidea (the elephants) is today in decline; there are only two genera, with one species in each, compared to ten or so genera that existed in the Pliocene.

The evolution of the Equidae, the family that is now the horse, the zebra and the ass, all species of the single genus *Equus*, reached its peak during the Pliocene and the Pleistocene.

The perissodactyl of the family Equidae which had the widest distribution and which remained longest on the scene was *Hipparion*. This was a horse with three toes, which carried all its weight on the central or third toe. The side toes did not even touch the ground but were perhaps of some use on soft terrain. *Hipparion* appears to have been perfectly adapted to running on the plains. Its molars were well developed and could be used efficiently both for tearing leaves off trees and for chewing grass.

The story of the Equidae begins in the Eocene with *Hyracotherium*, which lived in Europe and in North America, and is also known by the old generic name of *Eohippus*, 'dawn horse'. In this animal, about the size of a large hare, there is hardly any sign of a reduction in the number of toes; there are five on the forefeet, and four on the hind feet. Each toe has a small hoof and the feet are adapted to soft, swampy ground, where *Hyracotherium* habitually fed. The molars have four cusps and there are premolars with three cusps, canines and incisors.

The horse evolved mainly in North America, and the various genera that emerged spread to Eurasia by what is

*Pliohippus*
one-toed foot

*Hipparion*
(three-toed foot)

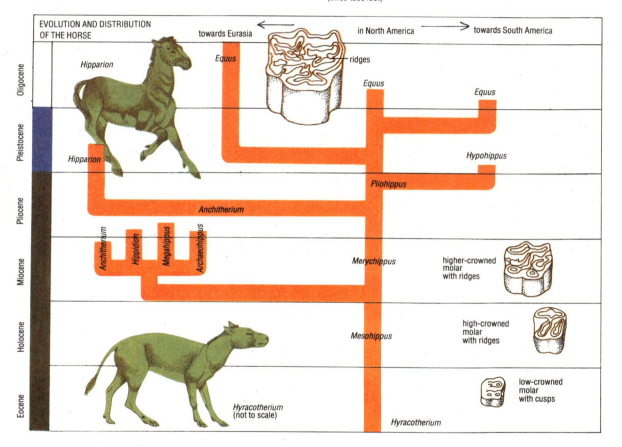

EVOLUTION AND DISTRIBUTION
OF THE HORSE

← towards Eurasia     in North America   → towards South America

*Hipparion*

*Equus* — ridges

*Equus*

*Equus*

*Hipparion*

*Hypohippus*

*Pliohippus*

*Anchitherium*

*Anchitherium*   *Hippidion*   *Megahippus*   *Archaeohippus*

*Merychippus*

higher-crowned
molar
with ridges

*Mesohippus*

high-crowned
molar
with ridges

low-crowned
molar
with cusps

*Hyracotherium*
(not to scale)

*Hyracotherium*

Oligocene · Pleistocene · Pliocene · Miocene · Holocene · Eocene

now the Bering Strait, which at that time was dry land. Some forms later reached South America as well, when there was a land bridge between the two subcontinents. These were animals already veering towards the smaller branch of single-toed horses.

There are about 350 known species of fossil Equidae. In the various evolutionary steps that led to *Hipparion* the muzzle gradually became longer, as did the bones corresponding, in

*Top: Details, based on photographs, of the forelimbs of two equids found in the Miocene graveyard at Orchard, Nebraska. On the left is the single hoof of a form belonging to the genus* Pliohippus, *on the right the hoof with a small central notch of the third toe and the shorter second and fourth toes of a form belonging to the genus* Hipparion.
*Above: The phylogenetic tree of the Equidae. The central branch represents the evolution of North American forms; the branches on the left relate to forms that subsequently migrated to Eurasia as well; and the branches on the right relate to the few forms known to have existed in South America.*

Machairodus

the human skeleton, to the palms of the hand and the soles of the feet.

The dentition of these animals became a battery of molars, with the premolars tending to assume molar form. The cusps were joined and the crown, which became steadily higher, exhibited characteristic ridges. The canines were reduced to mere stumps. *Hipparion* survived for a considerable time possibly because its foot was rather less specialized. This three-toed horse became extinct in Eurasia less than two million years ago. Meanwhile, and alongside it, one-toed forms such as *Pliohippus* and *Equus* evolved. They subsequently became extinct in the two Americas and survived only in Eurasia. The horse was reintroduced to America only in the early 16th century when the Spanish *conquistadores* invaded. The animals panicked the native Indian warriors and terrified the population.

## The elephants and their relatives

The elephants and their ancestors belong to the order Proboscidea. The animals of this order are related to mammals of other orders and to the group of hoofed mammals known as ungulates. In the elephants and related mammals, however, the hoof is not as fully developed as in the ungulates proper; thus the various orders concerned are known as penungulates, 'almost ungulates'. The group is

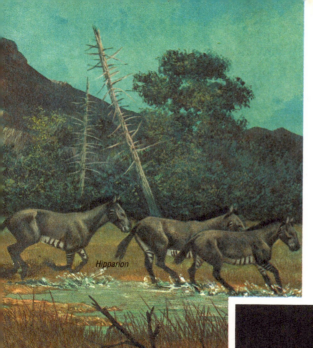

Hipparion

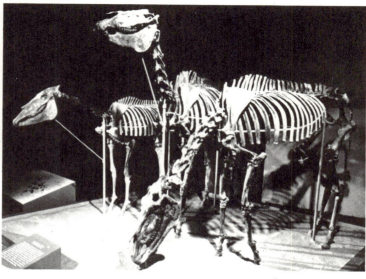

made up of the present-day orders of Proboscidea, Sirenia and Hyracoidea and certain extinct orders. It is likely that all the penungulates were derived from the condylarths, the group which preceded the majority of predatory mammals and the ungulates.

The present-day order, Hyracoidea, has only the hyraxes, but in the past it contained many more species. The present-day hyraxes resemble marmots, but numerous features of their body show that they are not in any way related to these rodents. The paw of the hyrax displays a thick pad under the skin, formed of highly elastic tissue. This is a characteristic of an elephant's foot. The nails are flat and thick, except for the second toe of the hind paw, which is a small claw. The upper incisors grow continuously, as in rodents, and correspond to the tusks of elephants; because they sometimes protrude sideways these teeth look like the canines of carnivores.

Another characteristic that links the hyraxes with elephants and walruses is that the male testicles do not project outside the body but are contained in the abdominal cavity throughout life. Hyraxes live in trees or on the ground in steppe zones and are exclusively vegetarian.

Modern hyraxes measure at most 0.5m (1½ft) and are divided into three genera: *Dendrohyrax*, tree hyraxes, *Procavia*, rock hyraxes, and *Heterohyrax*, steppe hyraxes. In the past there were huge forms, such as *Megalohyrax* from the African Oligocene, as big as a sheep but resembling a stocky pony.

# The elephant's ancestors

We do not know anything about the very earliest proboscideans. It has often been claimed that the sole ancestral form of all the elephants was *Moeritherium*, from the late Eocene in Egypt. This genus is represented by several species in a single place, the fossil site of al-Fayyūm, south-west of Cairo. It lies close to Lake Moeris, known to the ancients, so that the generic name means beast of Moeris. Since it has not been discovered anywhere else, it is more logical to assume that this was a form close to that of the true ancestor but *not* the sole founder of all later lines of evolution. The species *Moeritherium lyonsi* stood 70cm (27½in) high at the shoulder. The second incisors of both the upper and lower jaws resembled short tusks. The upper lip protruded but did not yet form a true proboscis or trunk. The trunk is not actually an outsize nose, but an enormous very muscular, extension of the upper lip, with the openings of the nostrils at the tip.

The plant-eating *Moeritherium* species lived like hippopotamuses at the water's edge and perhaps in the water itself.

Two distinct evolutionary lines can already be identified in the Oligocene, represented by the genera *Phiomia* and *Palaeomastodon*.

*Phiomia* had four tusks, two on top and two below; the trunk was still rudimentary, little more than a very flexible snout. Animals that came later in this line of evolution had blade-like lower incisors; *Platybelodon*, for instance, had a flat, muscular upper lip, like a huge spade, which covered the long lower jaw. Later still, in the Pleistocene, animals such as *Anancus arvernensis* looked much like elephants, with tusks in the upper jaw only. These tusks were very long and straight, the name means 'without curves', but with molars very different from those of modern elephants.

Elephants' molars have developed into grass-grinding machines. Those that did not have molars must have fed on leaves but not grass, as was the case with *Anancus*.

*Opposite, above: The phylogenetic tree of the Proboscidea. Only the more important genera are shown. The order was once very prosperous, with numerous species. Today it is clear that the elephants are on the decline: there are only two genera, each with a single species (there is disagreement about the status of subspecies). Opposite, below: The African elephant belongs to the genus Loxodonta. It may stand 4m (13ft) tall at the shoulder and weigh up to 7·5t (8¼ tons). The Indian elephant belongs to the genus Elephas. It is up to 3m (10ft) tall and may weigh as much as 5t (5½ tons).*

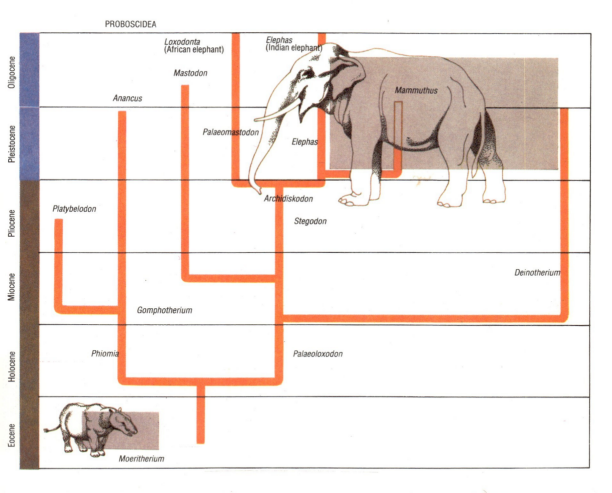

PROBOSCIDEA

Oligocene | Pleistocene | Pliocene | Miocene | Holocene | Eocene

*Loxodonta* (African elephant)

*Elephas* (Indian elephant)

*Mastodon*

*Mammuthus*

*Anancus*

*Palaeomastodon*

*Elephas*

*Platybelodon*

*Archidiskodon*

*Stegodon*

*Deinotherium*

*Gomphotherium*

*Phiomia*

*Palaeoloxodon*

*Moeritherium*

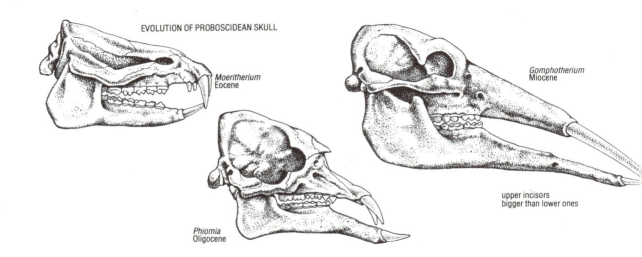

EVOLUTION OF PROBOSCIDEAN SKULL

*Moeritherium*
Eocene

*Phiomia*
Oligocene

*Gomphotherium*
Miocene

upper incisors
bigger than lower ones

*Archidiskodon imperator*

*Smilodon*

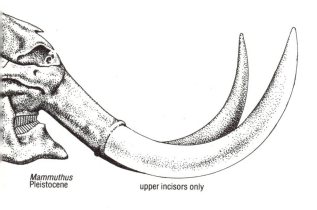

Mammuthus
Pleistocene

upper incisors only

*Left: Skulls of proboscidians from various periods of the Cenozoic.*
*Below left: A reconstruction of an attack by two smilodonts on* Archidiskodon imperator, *which is sinking into a pool of asphalt. The predators also trapped in this substance are unlikely to escape. There have been numerous finds of such situations in deposits from Rancho la Brea, now Hancock Park, Los Angeles. In the region where the great Californian city was later to be built, during the late Cenozoic and the Pleistocene, there were broad areas of natural asphalt, which were often covered by marshes or shallow pools. The animals which ventured near these waterholes to drink would sink in the underlying asphalt layer and be unable to get out.*

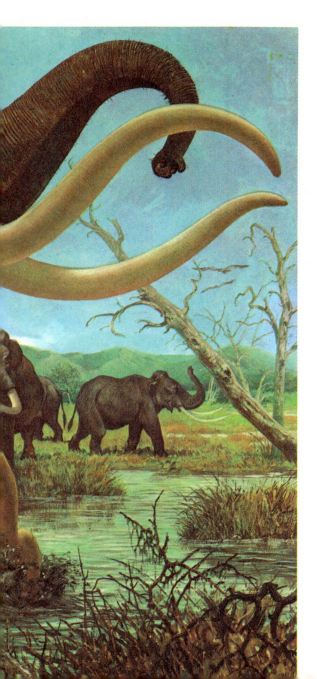

The proboscideans became enormous animals because they always had plenty of food. This grass had to be consumed in large quantities; and the time needed for stocking up with food was limited, since even an animal such as the elephant, which is always eating, has to take a rest. Also, it is obvious that long hours spent on grazing are also hours exposed continually to predators. Size and tusks are two possible deterrents. An elephant's molar teeth must operate with high efficiency so as to ensure that not too much time is spent in feeding; and it is also important that these teeth should never wear out or, if need be, that they should immediately be replaced.

The animals belonging to the *Palaeomastodon* line developed huge molars with cusps, which were suitable for eating grass. The cusps were somewhat rounded, resembling nipples.

*Top: Two paleontologists working to recover the skeleton of a mammoth. The huge proboscidian with its woolly coat became extinct in fairly recent times (about 10,000 years ago). It was built like an Indian elephant but was bigger. Its molars were blade-like, as in modern elephants.*
*Above: A mammoth skeleton (Mammuthus primigenius) now in the Smithsonian Institute at Washington, DC, USA.*

# Teeth for grinding

The generic name *Mastodon* and the common name mastodont for various Pliocene proboscidean species means 'with nipple-type teeth'. In the course of evolution these characteristic cusps of projections of the molar teeth tended to be linked so as to form long tubercles or rounded ridges, all in the same direction, both in the upper and lower jaw. This is known as 'bunodont' structure.

Fairly primitive nipple-type cusps are found on the molars of *Deinotherium*, represented by several species, some of average size, others

over 3m (10ft) tall. This type, belonging to the *Palaeomastodon* stock, possibly went on to follow an independent evolutionary path. The legs are long, the trunk short. There are no upper incisors, but the lower incisors are well developed. The lower jaw has been twisted more than 90° so that the tusks are directed downwards, probably enabling the animal to dig up tubers and roots. The deinotherians survived in Europe and in Africa up to about two million years ago.

Another evolutionary line led from *Palaeomastodon* to *Stegodon* and *Archidiskodon*. In these animals the structure of the molar teeth is perfected,

the cusps joining crosswise to form folds; between these folds there is hard tissue known as cement.

In the mammoths (genus *Mammuthus*) and in the modern Indian and African elephants (genera *Elephas* and *Loxodonta* respectively) the molars are crowned by more numerous and higher ridges, welded together by plates of cement. The molars, used as a set, are gradually replaced as they wear down, from the back towards the front of the mouth. As a rule the animal uses only two molars in each half of either jaw, making a total of eight. This type of dentition fulfils the same purpose as did the massed teeth of the duck-billed dinosaurs.

The mammoths of the species *Mammuthus primigenius* became extinct about 10,000 years ago. They were eagerly hunted by primitive man, and their remains have given rise to numerous legends. In Siberia it was claimed that earthquakes might be caused by mammoths living below ground; when they awoke they caused the earth to shake. It is easy to understand how such stories could spread, for the visible evidence of the creatures was there to hand. In these intensely cold regions the remains of many mammoths have been found frozen, their flesh still intact and complete with their thick, woolly coat.

It is interesting to note that most of the ivory still in commercial circulation is mammoth ivory, which for centuries has been a source of immense profit, shipped from Siberia and Russia to dealers all over the world. In America ivory has come from remains of mastodonts as well.

The genus *Mastodon* represented the last of the evolutionary line stemming from *Palaeomastodon*. It emerged during the Pliocene and survived up to about 10,000 years ago. *Mastodon americanus* was certainly hunted in America by humans. Such animals stood over 3m (10ft) high at the shoulder and had a coat of thick fur. The cusps of the molars were still of the nipple type, with hardly a sign of true ridges.

*Below right: A reconstruction of a mastodont and a pair of musk oxen* (Ovibos moschatus).
*Below: The skeleton of the American mastodont* (Mastodon americanus). *This proboscidian, which became extinct some 10,000 years ago, had molars with characteristic nipple-type ridges.*

# The all-purpose trunk

Why do elephants have a trunk? For an animal that is so big and therefore very tall, the problem of feeding is of vital importance. A herbivore must look for leaves high up, or the more plentiful grass at ground level. A long neck was not the answer for a creature that already had a large skull and huge teeth. The 'nasal hand', as it was once called, was therefore an extraordinary innovation. The proboscis enabled the animal to collect food from the ground, at head height or even higher. We can see that modern elephants also use the trunk to shower themselves with water or to blow dust all over the body to clean it. Other extinct animals also adopted

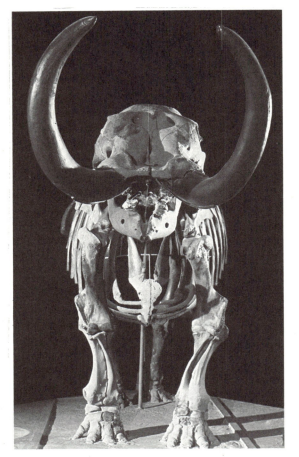

*Ovibos* (musk-ox)

this all-purpose device, and present-day tapirs have a much reduced trunk. The tip of the trunk is extremely sensitive to touch, and can thus be used as a finger. The Indian elephant has a single trunk, placed high up. The mammoth also had a single trunk as can be seen in the discoveries of frozen specimens. This shows the close relationship between the genera *Elephas* and *Mammuthus*. The African elephant has a long trunk above and a much shorter one below.

The feet of the proboscideans have evolved to support a body that became progressively bigger and heavier. The toes are linked by muscles and skin. As a rule the first and fifth toes are small and without hooves. The weight of the body thus rests on the three middle toes and on a thick, elastic pad situated behind them. The skin of the bottom of the feet is covered by horny plates. The joint of the foreleg that resembles a knee is really the elephant's wrist. Elephants are digitigrades, walking on the toes, and have thus readopted the walk of the gigantic sauropods.

Mastodon americanus

# The primates: two hundred living species

The history of the order Primates does not differ much from that of any other order of mammals. The oldest forms, very closely related to the Mesozoic mammals and the insectivores, set a pattern that led to animals being well adapted to living in forests and particularly in trees. One of the evolutionary lines of the order led to man, an animal with an exceptional adaptation to the environment. This is the only living being which has managed to modify this environment considerably and adapt it to his own needs. The story of our species is comparatively complex because of the continuous change in relation to the environment and the relationship between one individual and another. The process cannot be analyzed properly without taking into account cultural and social factors which have operated at different periods. So we shall divide the story into two chapters, the first dealing principally with monkeys, apes and related forms, the second with man.

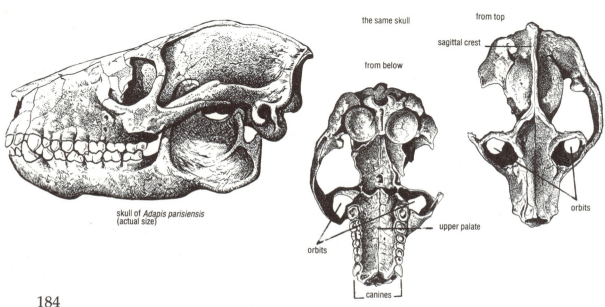

skull of *Adapis parisiensis*
(actual size)

the same skull

from below

from top

sagittal crest

orbits

upper palate

orbits

canines

The name of the order, derived from the Latin *primus* (first), was chosen because of the presence in the group of man, regarded as the first of all living beings. Considering what harm man has since done to nature, the description now has a somewhat ironic implication, but the name remains.

The order comprises two suborders: Prosimii and Anthropoidea, man belonging to the latter. Among the general characteristics are the following. The primates are placental mammals of small and medium size ranging from that of a mouse to that of a gorilla, averaging 180cm (70in) in height. Hands and feet generally have an opposable thumb and big toe, adapted to life in the trees, where an immediate and solid grip is essential; both fingers and toes have flat nails, rarely claws. The brain is quite well developed, particularly that part pertaining to the sense of sight. The skull is always distinguished by the eye orbit bordered by a bony arch in the region of the temple. As a rule there are two nipples on the breast. The penis always hangs outside and

*The order Primates comprises two suborders, Prosimii and Anthropoidea, the latter being the monkeys, in which group man is included. The prosimians are probably closer, both in physical make-up and habit, to the primates of the early Cenozoic. Well adapted to life in the heart of the forest, they have eyes placed almost frontally and therefore have stereoscopic vision.*
*Opposite, above: A living prosimian, the black lemur (*Lemur macaco*).*
*Opposite, below: During the Eocene there were prosimians fairly similar to those of today; one was* Adapis parisiensis.

*This page: Two examples of monkeys; on the left, the vervet or green monkey (*Cercopithecus aethiops*), of the superfamily Cercopithecoidea, family Cercopithecidae; on the right, a chimpanzee (*Pan troglodytes*), of the superfamily Hominoidea, family Pongidae.*

185

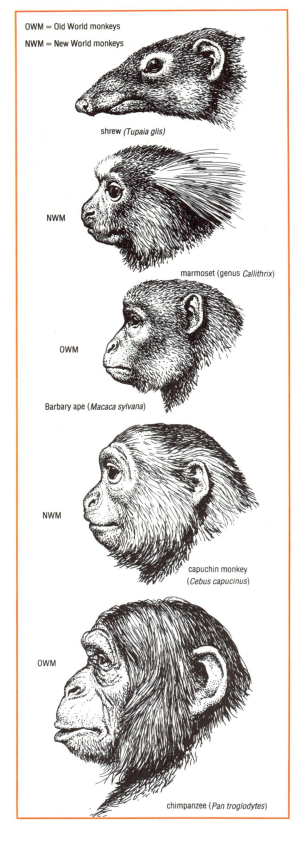

OWM = Old World monkeys

NWM = New World monkeys

shrew (*Tupaia glis*)

NWM

marmoset (genus *Callithrix*)

OWM

Barbary ape (*Macaca sylvana*)

NWM

capuchin monkey
(*Cebus capucinus*)

OWM

chimpanzee (*Pan troglodytes*)

the external testicles are contained in a sac of skin, scrotum.

The present-day animals that probably most resemble the very earliest representatives of the order in appearance are the tree shrews. These prosimians are agile little creatures somewhat larger than ordinary shrews. They have a broad, conspicuous tail. In one species which leaps from branch to branch, the tail looks like a huge feather and serves as a parachute. The toes carry short claws. The placenta of tree shrews is similar to that of insectivores, an indication that the two orders are related.

Other prosimians include the lemurs, the indris, the lorises, the bush babies, the aye-ayes and the tarsiers. During the Eocene one lemur-like animal was *Adapis parisiensis*. Today's prosimians are of modest size and their eyes are always frontally placed, giving them stereoscopic vision, extremely valuable for leaping from branch to branch in the tangled forest environment. The bony structure of the ear is quite simple; only in the tarsiers and in the monkeys is there a true duct leading to the inner ear (auditory meatus). This is very

*Left: In the course of primate evolution there has been a progressive shortening of the face, and the faculty of smell has become less efficient. The most primitive forms, still close to the insectivores, have a very long head and snout.*

*Opposite: The phylogenetic tree of the Primates. The drawings show some important remains: teeth of the earliest forms identifiable as primates; a lower jaw fragment of a form belonging to a group that was probably ancestral to all monkeys; fragments of the skull of* Ramapithecus.

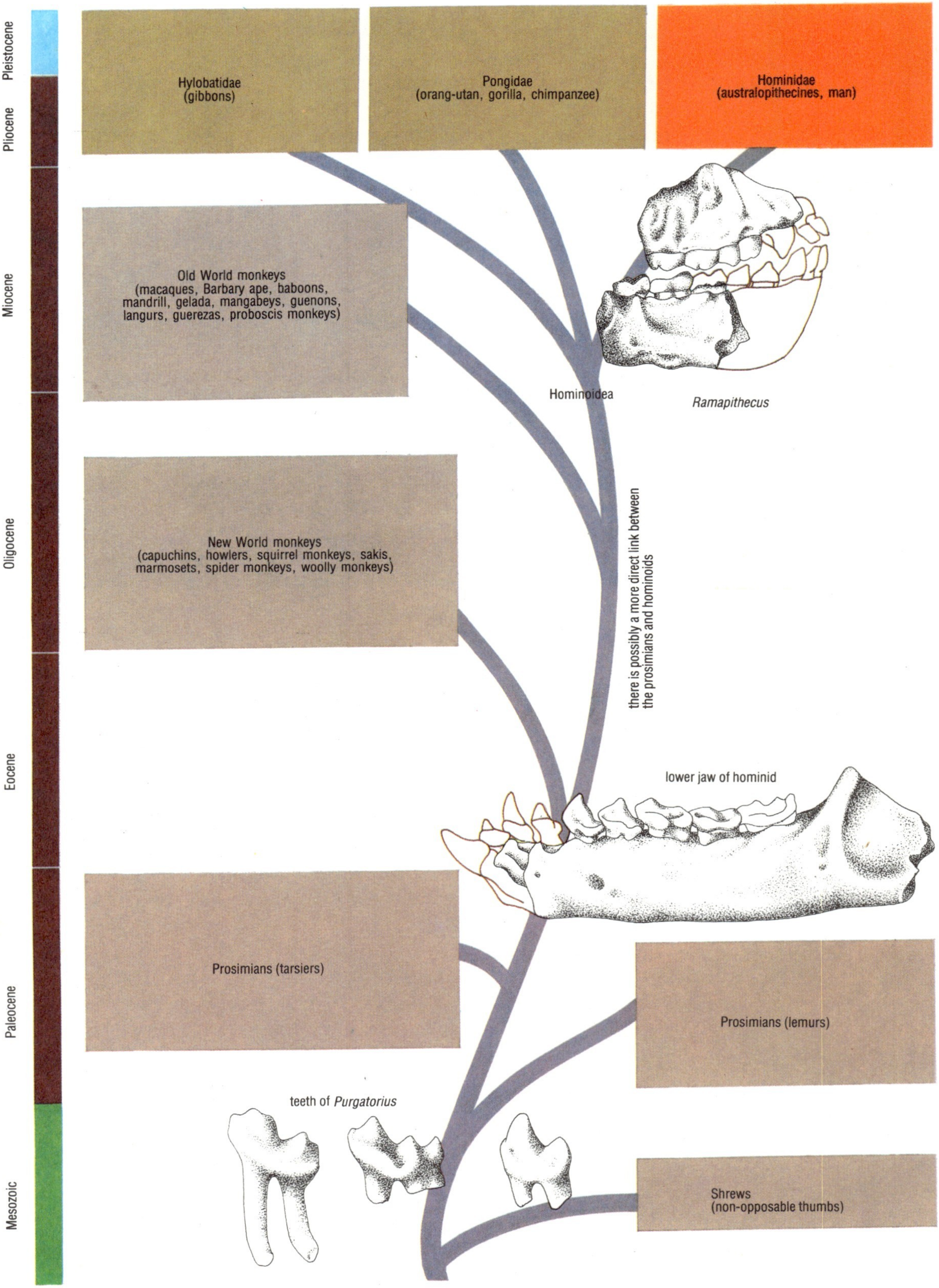

Hylobatidae
(gibbons)

Pongidae
(orang-utan, gorilla, chimpanzee)

Hominidae
(australopithecines, man)

Old World monkeys
(macaques, Barbary ape, baboons,
mandrill, gelada, mangabeys, guenons,
langurs, guerezas, proboscis monkeys)

New World monkeys
(capuchins, howlers, squirrel monkeys, sakis,
marmosets, spider monkeys, woolly monkeys)

Hominoidea

*Ramapithecus*

there is possibly a more direct link between
the prosimians and hominoids

lower jaw of hominid

Prosimians (tarsiers)

Prosimians (lemurs)

teeth of *Purgatorius*

Shrews
(non-opposable thumbs)

Pleistocene

Pliocene

Miocene

Oligocene

Eocene

Paleocene

Mesozoic

187

important for distinguishing the two primate suborders. Among the especially interesting extinct forms of prosimians are the Homomidae, distributed during the Eocene in Europe, eastern Asia and North America. From these animals were descended all the monkeys, by way of two evolutionary paths, one in America, the other in the Old World.

The monkeys, in fact, are divided into two major groups: the New World monkeys (platyrrhines) and the Old World monkeys (catarrhines). Our own species forms part of the latter group.

The New World monkeys characteristically have a flat nose with two nostrils set widely apart (platyrrhine means 'flat nose'). As a rule they have a tail, which is usually prehensile. They live in trees, never descending to the ground, and are widespread through South America. Mainly vegetarian, they sometimes feed on insects, worms and small vertebrates. All the platyrrhines are members of the superfamily Ceboidea. Among the best-known representatives of the group, sometimes kept as pets and common in zoos, are the capuchins, the marmosets, the howlers and the squirrel monkeys. There are many fossils dating back to the Miocene.

The Old World monkeys have nostrils set close together and a rather pronounced nose, which as a whole gives the impression of hanging down, 'catarrhine' means 'nose downwards'. There are two superfamilies: Cercopithecoidea, forms that usually have a tail, and Hominoidea, generally tailless forms. Among the best-known Cercopithecoidea are the macaques, the Barbary ape, the rhesus monkey, the baboons, the gelada and the vervet or green monkey.

# The Hominoidea

Several sites in Africa have provided a series of clues which, examined as a whole, reveal a fairly logical sequence of events.

There are three evolutionary lines in the superfamily Hominoidea. An animal such as *Propliopithecus* (with a lower jaw 6cm (2¼in) long and a complete dentition of 32 teeth, including quite large canines) may reasonably be regarded as a predecessor of the gibbons *or* of the apes (gorilla, chimpanzee and orang-utan, all belonging to the family Pongidae) *or* of the family (Hominidae) in which man developed. Pehaps such a creature was genuinely a common ancestor or at least quite similar to what a common ancestor must have been. It is interesting that these Oligocene types show relationships to the prosimians. Possibly there was a linked descent of prosimians and very ancient hominoids, without the latter coming from the other Old World branch, that of the cercopithecoids. *Parapithecus* (with a 35mm [1¼in] lower jaw) may have been a very primitive hominoid, perhaps already pointing the way towards the evolutionary line of gibbons. The direct ancestor of these last monkeys was *Prohylobates* from the mid-Miocene. Representatives of the branch Pongiade along the way include *Aegyptopithecus*, *Proconsul*, *Dryopithecus*, with various species, and *Sivapithecus*.

*Opposite: One of the sites which has provided remains of hominids, on the shores of Lake Turkana, in the Ethiopian Afar. Inset: Fragments and reconstructions of the lower jaw, upper jaw and complete skull of Ramapithecus, nowadays considered the first known hominid. Remains of Ramapithecus have been found at various places in the Old World. It was only quite recently, however, that these fragments were correctly interpreted.*

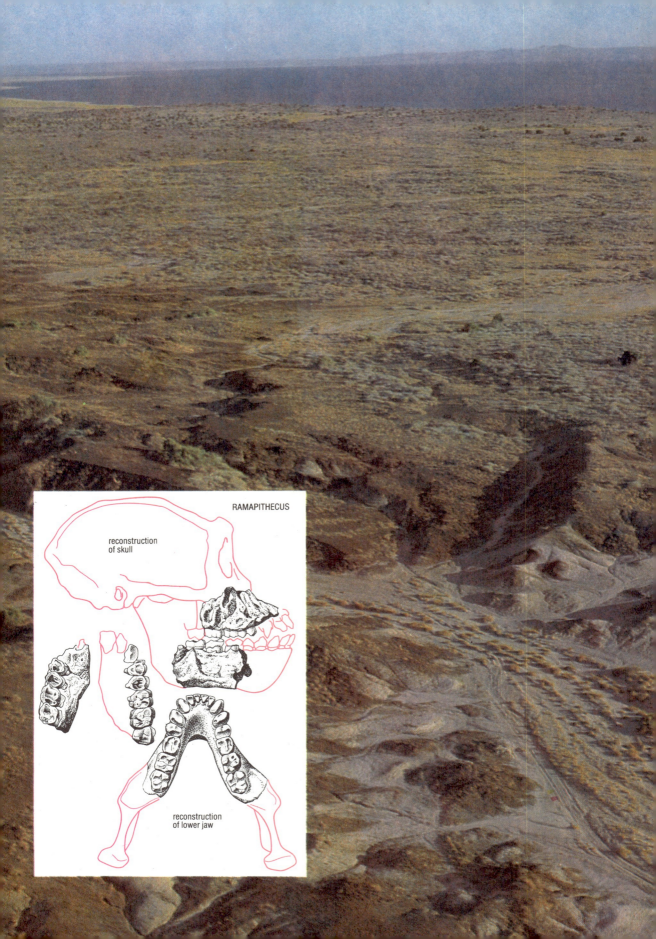

RAMAPITHECUS

reconstruction
of skull

reconstruction
of lower jaw

# The Rama monkey

In 1936 the remains of an extremely interesting primate were found on the Siwalik hills in India. A correct interpretation of this discovery only came later after other remains of the same or a similar form were found at various Old World sites, Kenya, Greece, Turkey and Hungary. This primate was given the generic name of *Ramapithecus* (Rama monkey) in honour of the hero of the great Indian epic poem, the *Ramayana*. Why were the remains of *Ramapithecus* of such importance? The answer is that midway between the Miocene and the Pliocene (dating from approximately 12–9 million years ago), this primate showed, in its dentition and in certain features recognizable from a few fragments of skull, various elements that were fairly similar to comparable elements existing in man. They were not to be found in monkeys either of past or present.

For example, the dental arch, along which the teeth are arranged, had a curved shape, very like that of human dentition. The rounded, not flat, palate was closer to that of a man than a monkey. As for the teeth themselves, the arrangement of the cusps of the molars was similar to that found in certain primitive monkeys, but also in *Dryopithecus*. Evidently this was a primitive characteristic which had been retained because it was useful.

What did *Ramapithecus* eat? Probably, in the course of its evolution, which may have lasted as much as five million years, there was a gradual alteration in the way of life. From a life in the forest, *Ramapithecus* progressed to a life spent mainly in clearings and later in open regions. An original diet of leaves, fruit and small insects or other invertebrates was transformed into one that included grass, shoots, roots, hard fruits and seeds. This may be deduced from its dentition. It is likely that *Ramapithecus* held its body upright when seated on the ground; and it may have walked on the soles of its hind feet, so leaving the hands free.

In some cases, especially on the Kenya site, pieces of volcanic rock resembling splinters or chips, were found. Perhaps *Ramapithecus* made these objects or perhaps he merely collected and used them.

Today it is suggested that *Ramapithecus*, which lived from 20 to a little over 12 million years ago, should be included in the family Hominidae, our own family.

The first chapter of our evolutionary story, which leads from the tree shrew to man, ends here with this description of *Ramapithecus*, our ancestor.

# Ruminants: chewing the cud

The land mammals that rely in varying measures on plants for their food are of many different shapes and sizes and belong to various orders. They range from small or tiny rodents, which escape predators by hiding in holes and burrows, to enormous elephants, which are rarely attacked because of their size. The perissodactyls include the rhinoceroses, whose tough hide is virtually a protective armour and who can scare off enemies by charging at them; and also the swift-running Equidae, horses, asses and zebras, who have exceptional stamina and can leave any pursuer far behind.

The vast group of artiodactyls

known as Ruminantia, also represented by animals of all forms and sizes, survive in the same ways. The little chevrotains, deer-like creatures about the size of a hare, and the muntjacs, for example, can easily slip away into the surrounding vegetation. Buffalo, bison and gnu, huge animals with aggressive instincts, charge their attackers; and the agile gazelles, antelopes and roebucks can usually outrun their enemies. These animals are adapted to any environment capable of providing them with sufficient plant food. The ruminants, however, have an additional advantage. The special form of their stomach enables them to absorb and digest their food efficiently and safely by 'chewing the cud'.

We have seen how a grazing animal is particularly vulnerable to attack when it is busy feeding. The longer the meal takes, the more dangerous is the herbivore's situation. Ruminants solve the problem simply by cutting short the time spent every day in feeding. They do eat in a great hurry but while they are actually grazing they do not trouble to break the food down into the substances which can be absorbed into the body system. They merely swallow as much food as they can, as quickly as possible. The whole process is completed in a relatively short time. In an emergency, such as the unexpected appearance of an enemy, the ruminant can always rely on its long legs or, in many cases, sharp horns, effective for both offence and defence.

What happens to all this vegetable material that is swallowed almost whole? Land plants have cells with rigid walls, made up of a substance called cellulose, which is similar to a complex type of sugar. The molecules of cellulose contain a great deal of

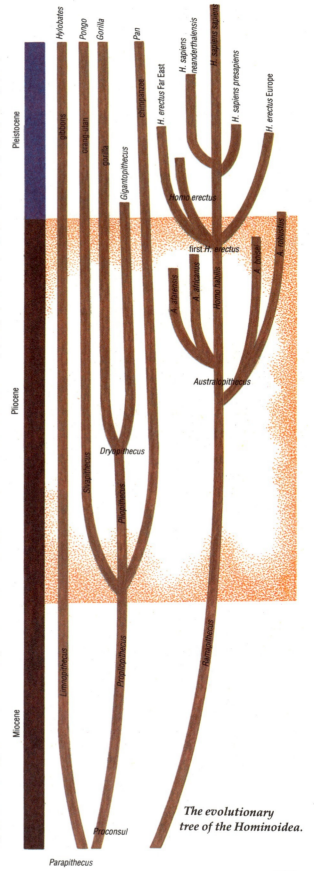

*The evolutionary tree of the Hominoidea.*

chemical energy, as do sugars as a whole. Cellulose is difficult to digest, and not easily transformed into energy and other useful, simpler substances.

# A stomach for the job

Many animals do not digest cellulose because it is so hard to assimilate, but largely eliminate it in their excrement. There is a considerable difference, for example, between the appearance of the excrement of a horse or an ass which are not ruminants, and that of a cow. Examination of a horse's faeces show scraps of vegetable matter still virtually intact; and birds often peck at these when searching for seeds. The faeces of a cow seem soft, like a blackish pulp; nothing that has been eaten is recognizable.

Ruminants have vast numbers of bacteria in their stomach that are capable of breaking down cellulose. This allows the digestive juices of the stomach to act on every part of the substance and to extract every useful compound, especially proteins and vitamins, from it. The plant material is wholly digested and completely transformed, partly by the bacteria, partly by the ruminant itself. Like the sauropods, which could be described as stomachs on four legs, the ruminants might be compared to living fermentation vats or chemical treatment chambers. In the case of ruminants efficient digestion is increased by the constant high body temperature (in spite of their size, it is probable that the body temperature of the dinosaurs fluctuated somewhat) and, above all, by a truly extraordinary mechanism for preparing the plant matter. Ruminants are therefore able to cope with far tougher types of grass than those eaten during the Mesozoic by the sauropods.

The ruminant stomach is composed of four separate chambers. The vegetable matter is hastily chewed and travels from the mouth, down the oesophagus, into the rumen. This is where the bacteria break down all the molecules. The pulp then passes into the reticulum, and by a muscular contraction is sent back into the mouth, were the cud is all chewed again. This second chewing operation does not need to be carried out in the open, but can be done quietly and safely in a clearing, a wood or a shed. The material then returns by a different route to the omasum and the abomasum, where proper digestion takes place. The abomasum has the outlets of the glands secreting digestive liquids. Every substance is transformed and assimilated. This is why the excrement contains no recognizable traces of the original plant matter.

It is interesting to note that a similar but far simpler apparatus, capable of achieving quite an efficient form of rumination, also exists in camels and llamas. It is likely that in these artiodactyls, belonging to the suborder Tylopoda, and not officially designated as Ruminantia, adaptations of the stomach happened independently of such adaptations among the true ruminants.

*Opposite, above: The important subdivision of the order Artiodactylia into its two main branches, with the suborder Non-Ruminantia or Suiformes (pigs, peccaries and hippopotamuses) and the suborder Tylopoda (camels and llamas) and the equally vast suborder Ruminantia (more than 70 living genera). Camels and llamas can ruminate but the stomach is made differently from that of true ruminants. It is certain that they acquired this capacity independently. The diagram shows the stomach structure of a typical ruminant. The arrows indicate the direction followed by the food. Proper digestion only takes place in the abomasum.*

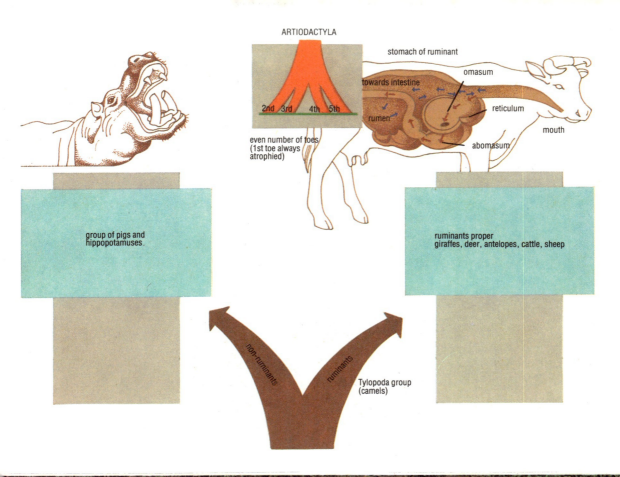

ARTIODACTYLA

2nd 3rd 4th 5th

even number of toes
(1st toe always
atrophied)

stomach of ruminant

towards intestine

omasum

rumen

reticulum

mouth

abomasum

group of pigs and
hippopotamuses

ruminants proper
giraffes, deer, antelopes, cattle, sheep

non-ruminants

ruminants

Tylopoda group
(camels)

bony horn with covering of skin

*Prolybitherium* ancestor of giraffe

giraffe

In deer the horns (antlers) sprout covered with skin; the skin then dries and falls; these antlers are changed every year.

rosette (base of antler)

# Horns and teeth

The ruminants appeared during the Eocene, before the subdivision of artiodactyls into non-ruminants, swine, peccaries and hippopotamuses, and tylopods, camels. It may be that there was a direct descent from the condylarths.

The most primitive forms are those belonging to the Tragulidae, nowadays represented by the little chevrotains, inhabitants of Indonesia. *Archaeomeryx* had no horns but, like the chevrotains, had projecting upper canines. This is a feature which, since it is found in a herbivore, can be compared with that of the ornithischian *Heterodontosaurus* (as noted by Halstead). Protruding teeth serve here both as a defensive weapon and as a threat to would-be predators.

Other ruminants closely related to the tragulid group appeared during the Oligocene and throughout the Pliocene. These were medium-sized or large animals, equipped with short horns but also with curious, long bony appendages above the nasal bones. In the live animal these would probably have been covered with skin. Typical genera were *Syndyoceras* and Synthetoceras.

The first true deer date from the Miocene (genus *Dicrocerus*), descended from animals like *Cranioceras*,

*Syndyoceras*

*Procam[e...]*

*Merycodus*

*Above: A reconstruction of some artiodactyls of the North American Miocene. Among them are non-ruminants, Entelodontidae, such as* Dinohyus, *similar to a gigantic wild boar; tylopods, such as* Alticamelus, *a form close to the group of Camelidae; and ruminants, forms close to the pronghorn, like* Syndyoceras *and* Cranioceras.
*Top: Only ruminants have horns, which may be of two types: bony projections covered by skin, as in giraffes and related extinct groups, or bony formations which are renewed every year, becoming steadily larger and more branched. These are the type deer have. The horns of the Bovidae are horny sheaths stiffly set over bony projections.*

Alticamelus

Dinohyus

Cranioceras

which have affinities with the tragulids.

These ruminants were quick to establish themselves, and produced gigantic animals until the Pleistocene. Their horns, or, to be more precise, antlers, were renewed each year, with increasing numbers of branches. These were bony elements covered by skin, with nerves and blood vessels (the velvet), only when they are growing. The skin then dries and flakes off.

Whereas the tragulids and extinct forms related to them had a complete set of teeth, the deer had a reduced dentition. There are no upper incisors and the lower canines resemble incisors. There is no real sole on the foot and the third and fourth toes have hooves.

Antlers are usually present in both

sexes, but in a few species are only seen in the males. The formation of the antlers is quite varied and helps to distinguish the different species.

The giraffes were animals of the Miocene. Their horns are protuberances of bone covered by skin. In some of the extinct types these horns were extremely big. The long neck has only reached its greatest length in modern giraffes. But giraffes were not the only animals to possess such a feature. A North American tylopod of the Miocene (*Alticamelus latus*) had a very long neck for feeding on the leaves of trees, a characteristic that earned it the name of giraffe–camel. The giraffe is very interesting for having particular parts in its network of blood vessels which regulate the blood pressure in the head region, keeping it steady even when the animal bends its long neck from a height of 6m (20ft) down to ground level.

The female giraffe gives birth while standing, and the newborn calf drops on to its side so that it is unharmed from a height of over 2m (6½ft). It seems reasonable to suppose that both the physical peculiarities and the special behaviour patterns of the modern giraffe evolved in a complex manner over a long period.

There are many living and fossil species of antelope. All but one of the present-day antelopes belong to the family Bovidae, the exception being the pronghorn (*Antilocapra*) which makes up the family Antilocapridae. The Bovidae are divided into four subfamilies. Probably all these animals came from types similar to the tragulids, by a long evolutionary path far removed from that of the deer and giraffes.

The Bovidae are extremely specialized. In the upper jaw there is a sort of horny pad against which the lower incisors rub. The teeth are highly efficient for cropping grass; and the same is true of the digestive apparatus.

Behaviour patterns are elaborate. The Bovidae use a vast range of signals among members of the same species. The horns, made of a horny sheath implanted over a bony projection, are permanent. In many cases they signal to other species, especially predators, that the owners can look after themselves in a tight corner.

The Bovidae emit sounds of various tones, including loud bellows. These also serve for communication. Scent signals are equally important. All the Bovidae possess special glands which secrete odorous substances, used both for sexual activities and for marking territory.

Domesticated species include the cow (genus *Bos*, subfamily Bovinae), the goat (genus *Capra*) and the sheep (genus *Ovis*, both these in the subfamily Caprinae). Semi-domesticated forms of ruminants are the reindeer (genus *Rangifer*) and some buffaloes.

*Opposite, above: The branch of antlers of the Irish elk, Megaloceros giganteus, a deer which became extinct in western and central Europe about 12,000 years ago. The huge antlers were in proportion to the animal's size, which was over 2.5m (8¼ft) at the shoulder. The Irish elk inhabited open grasslands. Perhaps it was incapable of eating leaves, bark and tough vegetable matter.*
*Opposite, below: A group of fallow deer (Dama dama) in an English park.*

# Centuries of isolation

During the Tertiary there were some interesting evolutionary developments either because of absence of competition or as a result of seclusion. In Africa, for example, the hyraxes spread far and wide because in the early and middle phases of the era there were no horse-like ungulates on the continent. The cetaceans, too, began their development in Africa with carnivorous forms finding ample food in the extensive watery areas then covering the continent.

One large herbivore with very unusual feet, resembling those of the penungulates, is known only from Africa. This was *Arsinotherium zitteli*, dating from the Oligocene in the al-Fayyūm region. This creature, given an order of its own (Embrithopoda), had two curious appendages like huge half-moons on the nasal bones. As big as a rhinoceros, the animal appeared suddenly and vanished just as quickly, leaving no descendants. This truly mysterious process can partly be explained by the animal's solitary, isolation. No other remains remotely resembling those of this embrithopod have so far been found in other regions.

Highly interesting examples of evolution due to geographical isolation have also occurred in South America, Australia and Madagascar. In the first two regions the marsupial mammals played an important role in the local fauna.

# South America

During the Paleocene the southern American subcontinent was the home of very few mammals. Some armadillos and several ungulates descended from the condylarths were among the placentals. There were also a few primitive marsupials.

Theosodon

The area once occupied by carnivores, the more evolved condylarths and the creodonts, was now taken over by marsupials. These were animals derived from the fairly ancient type of opossum. The family Borhyaenidae was particularly successful; the largest species of the genus *Borhyaena* were the size of a wolf. These creatures became very big because there was so much prey. The last of the Borhyaenidae (*Arminiheringia*) were the size of a brown bear. Later, in the Pliocene, the group of South American marsupial carnivores developed its own type of sabre-toothed tiger, with the characteristic lobes in the lower jaw to accommodate the large canines; the genus was appropriately called *Thylacosmilus* (chisel-pouch). This predator lasted until the beginning of the Pleistocene, about two million years ago. Several large birds were also formidable predators.

Many marsupials fed on insects and other invertebrates. There were also several herbivores, of small or medium size, some adapted to living in trees.

*Mammals of the South American Miocene. On the left are a pair of* Theosodon, *with a baby. These ungulates, 2m (6½ft) long, were part of the now-extinct order of Litopterna. The feet of these animals always had an odd number of toes – a clear example of convergent evolution with the perissodactyls.* Theosodon *still had three toes but other litopterns only retained the third toe, showing a more pronounced reduction than is evident in horses. Horses have rudiments (stylets) of the second and fourth toes, which are entirely absent in the litopterns.*
*At the right of the picture is a group of Borhyaenidae (genus* Borhyaena*), predatory marsupials as big as bears.*

Borhyaena

## Placental mammals

During the Tertiary several order of ungulates appeared in South America, with no representatives elsewhere.

The Litopterna were animals adapted to live like camels and horses: in some cases they even imitated elephants. Reconstructions of these ungulates look distinctly odd to us because although we are accustomed to seeing such features in present-day animals, they are not nowadays found all together in the same species. The litopterns of the genus *Macrauchenia*, from the Paleocene, looked something like a three-toed camel but had the neck of a giraffe and a form of trunk into the bargain. The nasal opening projected far back towards the forehead, so that the upper lip undoubtedly formed a proboscis, which the animal used, like an elephant, for tearing leaves and grass; but because of the length of the neck, this trunk must have been on the shortish side.

199

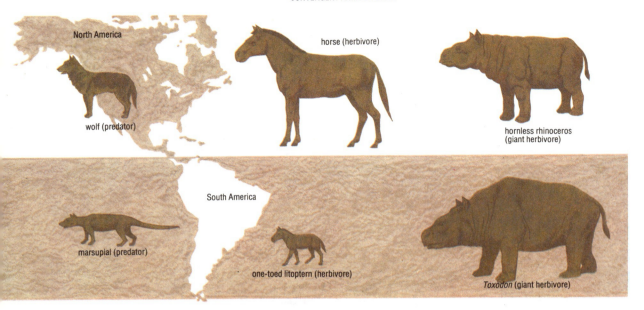

North America

wolf (predator)

horse (herbivore)

hornless rhinoceros (giant herbivore)

South America

marsupial (predator)

one-toed litoptern (herbivore)

*Toxodon* (giant herbivore)

In the order Notoungulata (southern ungulates) there were sturdy, massive animals like rhinoceroses (genus *Toxodon*), from the Pliocene. Some remains of such animals were found by Darwin on his voyage in the *Beagle*. During the Eocene the notoungulates included some huge herbivores (*Homalodotherium*), which had their counterparts, in North America, in the enormous perissodactyls known as Chalicotheria, a divergent branch of the Equidae. Like the chalicotheres (*Moropus*), the homalodotheres lacked true hooves but were equipped with strong claws suitable for digging up roots and tubers and perhaps also for tearing leaves and fronds off trees. In both North and South America, many carnivores of various sizes emerged because of the large numbers of herbivores. In the northern subcontinent some of these animals hunted, in packs, like wolves; in the south the equivalent habitats were occupied by predatory marsupials and running birds.

*Relatively similar types of animal (both in build and appearance) tend to evolve in similar environments even if the groups concerned have no close relationship. This is known as convergent evolution.*
*Above: In the late Cenozoic the animals of the two Americas displayed many examples of convergence. Here mammals of various orders are compared. In South America there were no placental predators, but marsupials that resembled wolves did emerge.*

*Opposite: A reconstruction of* Macrauchenia, *a litoptern of the South American Pliocene with a long neck and a short trunk. In the background is* Toxodon, *a notoungulate the size of a rhinoceros.*

# The edentates

A group of very curious South American mammals, misleadingly called Edentata, flourished in the Tertiary. From fossil remains it is clear that there were at least ten times as many species in the order at that time as there are today. Edentate means without teeth, and the name rightly applies only to the anteaters, in which an atrophying or wasting process causes the rudimentary teeth of the

*Macrauchenia*

*Toxodon*

discovered which were apparently used by primitive humans as elementary prefabricated huts.

Other well-known edentates are the sloths. Modern forms live in trees. The three-toed sloth, an inhabitant of South American forests, attaches itself by its strong claws to branches and hangs upside-down. Its silky, wet fur harbours various algae, which the animal eats by combing out.

From the Eocene to the late Pleistocene, in the Quaternary, animals similar to sloths, but living on the

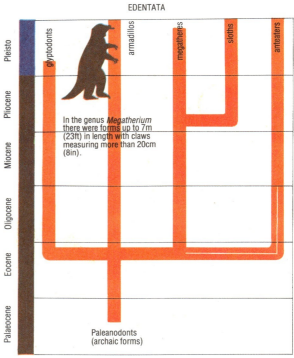

EDENTATA

In the genus *Megatherium* there were forms up to 7m (23ft) in length with claws measuring more than 20cm (8in).

Paleanodonts (archaic forms)

embryos and young to disappear entirely in the adult animals. Other forms of edentates, such as armadillos, have up to 100 teeth, although all uniform and very small.

Some edentates specialize in eating very small insects that are available in vast numbers – the social insects, like termites and ants, nesting in their millions. The armadillos are the only modern mammals equipped with a genuine suit of armour, consisting of jointed elements of bony tissue. The animals can roll themselves into a ball and are safe from any predator. During the Eocene, such armour-plated mammals also included the Glyptodonta, which looked even more impressive, up to 4.5m (15ft) long. Shells of glyptodonts have been

*Above: The phylogenetic tree of the Edentata. The oldest armadillo known to us, which may perhaps be seen as the prototype of the common ancestor of all the edentates, was Utaetus, from the later North American Paleocene. Evidently these animals crossed by land bridge from the region of Central America into the southern subcontinent and completed their development there.*
*Top left: The skeleton of Megatherium.*
*Opposite: A three-toed sloth, above, and a nine-banded armadillo, below.*

ground, emerged. These were the Megatheria. The biggest (*Megartherium*) was almost 7m (23ft) long. The enormous tail and positioning of the hind legs show that the creature often stood upright to reach the high branches of trees. The powerful hands and feet were used for digging and shaking trunks. The remains of a megathere were found in a cave in Patagonia, together with relics of human settlement, conjuring up an image of a captive animal. It is more likely that the huge creature, perhaps only wounded, was dragged into the cave by hunters, and that its carcase provided a plentiful stock of fresh meat. Megatheres and glyptodonts survived for a long time and escaped the isolation of South America, for during the Pleistocene, when the isthmus was land, they crossed to the northern subcontinent and were widely distributed there.

A later branch of the Edentata gave rise to the anteaters, whose great speciality is devouring social insects. They have no teeth but a complex muscular system enables the animal to dart out a very long tongue covered with mucus, to which the ants and termites literally stick fast. The earliest fossil finds of anteaters date from the Miocene. If 'terrible-handed' dinosaurs such as *Deinocheirus* already used their claws to break open the nests of social insects, the specialized anteaters were merely copying them. Other mammals with claws are also expert in feeding on insects. The pangolin and aardvark, for instance, are not edentates but belong respectively to the orders Pholidota and Tubulidentata.

There are certain features of present-day armadillos which do not obviously appear an advantage and thus a useful element of natural selec-tion. The limbs contain dense networks of blood vessels which allow plenty of oxygen to be distributed when an effort has to be made. On the other hand, the armadillo is not completely warm-blooded and, rather like a modern reptile, is quite sensitive to temperature fluctuations. A really cold season can kill armadillos.

The embryos of armadillos develop in a most remarkable way. After fertilization, the egg begins to develop normally and then stops. Fourteen weeks later the egg attaches itself to the wall of the uterus, so that the embryo can continue growing. Four embryos, furnished with a single placenta, always develop from each egg, and four identical babies of the same sex are born.

# A flightless bird of prey

The flightless running birds of South America were well established in the late Tertiary being isolated and, particularly in open regions, having no competitors. *Phororhacos inflatus*, from the mid-Miocene, stood up to 3m (10ft) high and was a formidable predator.

Although there may be doubts as to whether some of the more ancient flightless birds such as *Diatryma steini*, were exclusively predators, there can be none where *Phororacos* is concerned. The feet of this animal had claws for slashing, comparable to those of the allosaurs. The skull, with its strongly curved beak, is 35cm (14in) long; the wings are reduced to stumps. Yet although the bird must have been as big as an ostrich and its beak similar to an eagle's it was actually the forerunner of the modern seriemas. These birds from Patagonia

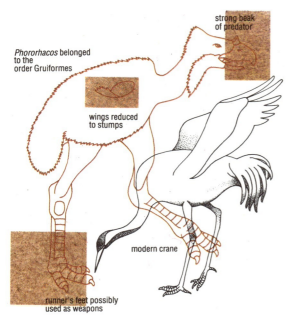

Phororhacos belonged
to the
order Gruiformes

strong beak
of predator

wings reduced
to stumps

modern crane

runner's feet possibly
used as weapons

**Left:** *Phororhacos inflatus,* **a huge predatory bird of the South American Miocene, had feet with three strong toes and a rudimentary fourth toe facing backwards. The head was up to 60cm (24in) long (the beak alone, with the upper part curving sharply downwards, measured 35cm (13¾in). The wings were reduced to mere stumps with feathers. The bird stood up to 3m (10ft) tall.**
*Phororacos* **is classified among the Gruiformes, the order of birds that comprises cranes, coots and bustards, despite the fact that many external features remind us of present-day ostriches or cassowaries.**

**Below:** **A reconstruction of** *Phororhacos inflatus.* **Feet and beak indicate that this bird had carnivorous tastes. It stood at the summit of the various food chains on the high grasslands and plains of Patagonia.**

*Phororhacos inflatus*

are less than 1m (3ft) high and are related to cranes.

To complete our survey of South America, it is worth mentioning that perhaps during the Oligocene there was a land bridge which permitted the rodents and the primate to travel southwards. The primates quite soon gave rise to various forms of platyrrhine monkeys.

*Below: A koala with its baby.*
*Opposite, above: A table listing the families of marsupials and the phylogenetic tree nowadays generally accepted, partially on the basis of recent fossil finds.*
*Opposite, below: Two red kangaroos (Macropus rufus).*

# Australia

The oldest marsupials known to us (*Eodelphis* from the North American upper Cretaceous) paved the way for a variety of species that were distributed almost everywhere, including Eurasia. During the lower Tertiary fairly small marsupials migrated from Asia to Australia, which led to an extraordinary development of these animals there, not equalled even in South America.

Geographical isolation enabled the marsupials of Australia to establish unchallenged mastery in every land environment. The different forms that emerged played a comparable role and were astonishingly similar in appearance to placental mammals of other continents. The oldest Australian fossil marsupial thus far known is *Wynyardia*, from the Tasmanian Oligocene. It was a vegetarian, similar to a wombat.

We still know very little about the actual relationships of the various groups of marsupials. Some recent discoveries of remains dating back to the late Oligocene and early Miocene make it possible to construct a family tree which is reasonably convincing. It shows similar sequences to those of the placental mammals.

The main trunk of this tree may have consisted of animals similar to the present-day bandicoots. They are quite small animals, sometimes with longish hind legs, so as to resemble jumping mice, which feed on insects and worms and sometimes roots and cereals. The bandicoots, like many other creatures living in burrows, have a marsupial pouch opening towards the rear. This prevents it from filling with soil while the animal is digging, which would obviously harm the babies.

**CLASS MAMMALIA (MAMMALS)**

**SUBCLASS METATHERIA**

All the animals of this subclass belong to the order MARSUPIALIA (MARSUPIALS) which comprise the following nine familes:

DIDELPHIDAE (American opossums)

DASYURIDAE (marsupial mice, dasyures, including Tasmanian devil, *Sarcophilus harrisi*, and the thylacine or marsupial wolf, *Thylacinus cynocephalus*)

MYRMECOBIIDAE (numbat or banded anteater)

NOTORYCTIDAE (marsupial moles)

PERAMELIDAE (bandicoots)

CAENOLESTIDAE (South American mouse-opossums)

PHALANGERIDAE (phalangers, cuscuses, gliders and koala, *Phascolarctos cinereus*)

VOMBATIDAE (wombats)

MACROPODIDAE (kangaroos, wallabies)

Altogether the marsupials living today belong to 71 genera with 241 species.

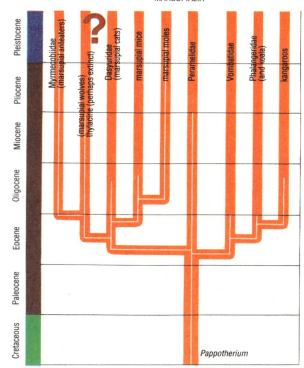

MARSUPIALIA

Pleistocene · Pliocene · Miocene · Oligocene · Eocene · Paleocene · Cretaceous

Myrmecobiidae (marsupial anteaters)

? (marsupial wolves) thylacine (perhaps extinct)

Dasyuridae (marsupial cats)

marsupial mice

marsupial moles

Peramelidae

Vombatidae

Phalangeridae (and koala)

kangaroos

*Pappotherium*

The Dasyuridae, today represented by animals similar to cats, probably emerged after the bandicoots. Likely relatives of this group include the marsupial anteaters or numbats, the marsupial wolf or thylacine, thought now to be extinct, and the marsupial mice and moles. Other evolutionary branches account for the modern wombats, similar to badgers, the koalas and the kangaroos.

Ground-dwelling and insect-eating marsupial mammals were followed by tree-dwelling forms, exactly as happened among the placental mammals.

One of the most striking features that underlines the resemblance of certain groups of marsupials to placental counterparts is the structure of the muzzle, the projecting part of the head containing the jaws, mouth and nose, primarily concerned with eating. The kangaroos have a muzzle similar to that of antelopes and deer in order to browse twigs and leaves. The marsupial moles have a snout that is in all respects like that of placental moles. The thylacine looked very much like a coyote; and the koala, in spite of an obvious difference in size, clearly resembles a small bear.

Why have the marsupials developed such a complicated and apparently strange system of reproduction? There is no easy answer that is valid for every single case, but we can gain a better understanding of the marsupials, as a group, by examining the female kangaroo and the astonishing relationship she has with her young. At one time, she may maintain links with *three* children at different stages of development. She has in her womb one or more already fertilized eggs and can virtually control their rate of development; secondly,

there may be a baby, little more than an embryo at this stage, in the pouch; and thirdly, that same pouch may accommodate a bigger youngster from time to time, more or less capable of fending for itself. This older 'joey' still sucks its mother's milk and has a nipple all to itself, while the newborn baby remains firmly attached to another nipple. The milk flowing from the two nipples has a different chemical composition, suited to the growth needs of the two offspring. The mother can thus protect her young over a lengthy period, although the risks are high and it is very likely that only one of these two children will survive.

Recent fossil evidence proves that the marsupials prospered in their new land, for some gigantic forms have been found. From Pleistocene strata comes the wombat *Diprotodon*, as big as a rhinoceros, the kangaroo *Procoptodon*, 3m (10ft) high with a short tail, a giant koala called *Phascolarctos ingens*, and an animal similar to a large leopard, *Thylacoleo carnifex*, perhaps not a predator, as its specific name would suggest, but a fruit-eater. Some diprotodonts have been preserved in perfect condition because they were buried in saline lakes during the Pleistocene. These lakes were usually covered by a thick layer of salt. The crust may have held up smaller animals but possibly the diprotodonts were too heavy, some of them sinking and drowning.

There were clearly many habitats with plenty of food for herbivores. In addition to the marsupials of Australia and neighbouring islands, such as New Zealand, huge flightless birds emerged. Some of these birds were destroyed by man quite recently. The giant moa (*Dinornis maximus*) survived until the 17th century.

Dinornis maximus

*A reconstruction and skeleton of the giant moa (Dinornis maximus), a huge flightless bird from New Zealand which is known to have existed since the Pleistocene up to, possibly, a couple of centuries ago. This bird was certainly hunted by the first immigrants (Maoris) to the islands, but its extinction is probably due not to direct extermination but to the destruction of its habitats as a result of the introduction of farming. The wings of the moa were completely reduced, as is evident from the skeleton.*

This bird was over 3m (10ft) tall. Smaller species became extinct at the beginning of the 19th century. In none of these birds, Dinornithiformes, is there any trace in the skeleton of wings. Their plumage was threadbare, the legs very strong. The egg of *Dinornis* weighed up to 7kg (15½lb).

# Madagascar: a miniature continent

This large island in the Indian Ocean has been isolated from Africa since the beginning of the Cenozoic. The first animals to reach there were probably insectivores and fairly primitive primates, carried there on drifting tree trunks. These creatures evolved in a spectacular manner. Most of the island's animals were and are prosimians. Among the insectivores, there was considerable development of forms similar to the modern tenrec, an astonishingly prolific animal. A female common tenrec can bear 31 embryos, a record for a mammal. Present-day tenrecs, up to 40cm (16in) long, are similar to shrews but usually have a stump of a tail.

There were some gigantic prosimians. *Megaladapis*, a later form from the Pleistocene, was as big as a calf. This huge lemur probably became extinct only in modern times. In the upper Tertiary Madagascar was reached by carnivores of the group of genets (Viverridae) and by rodents of the hamster type. These animals also developed locally in interesting ways but were not as numerous as the prosimians.

Birds typical of this island fauna included the gigantic elephant birds of the genera *Aepyornis* and *Mullerornis*, standing 3m (10ft) high, and the dodo (*Raphus cucullatus*), a kind of pigeon but bigger than a turkey. These flightless birds were destroyed by man or by introduced animals both on the main island and others close by; the dodo became extinct on Mauritius chiefly because its eggs and chicks were preyed on by pigs that had been allowed to run wild. Eggs of elephant birds, measuring 35cm (14in) long and 262cm (8½ft) across,

*Tenrec ecaudatus* (living)

with a shell 3mm (⅛in) thick, have been found. These remains were discovered in areas which were and still are sandy. The huge birds probably dug nests in the dunes and used the heat of the sun to hatch the eggs. The elephant birds were certainly vegetarians but perhaps supplemented their diet with insect larvae.

Megaladapis edwardsi

Varecia variegata (living)

Aepyornis maximus

Lemur catta (living)

Alectroenas nitidissima

hippopotamus

Geochelon sumierei

SKULL OF MEGALADAPIS

length 35cm (13¾in)

*Above: The animals which make up the fauna of Madagascar, most of them now extinct. The tenrec (several species), the ringtailed or cat lemur (Lemur catta) and the ruffed lemur (Varecia variegata) are the sole survivors of those reconstructed here.*

*Left: The skull of Megaladapis, 35cm (13¾ft) long. This large Pleistocene prosimian (shown at top of picture) probably became extinct after man's arrival.*

211

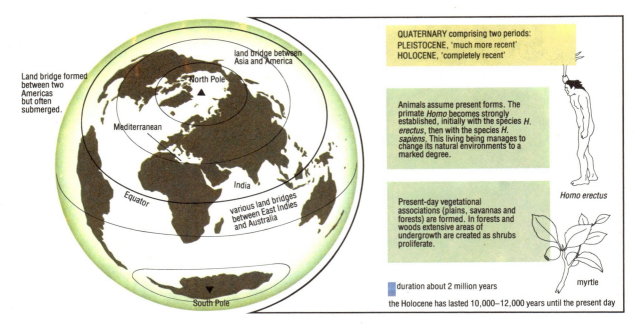

QUATERNARY comprising two periods:
PLEISTOCENE, 'much more recent'
HOLOCENE, 'completely recent'

Animals assume present forms. The primate *Homo* becomes strongly established, initially with the species *H. erectus*, then with the species *H. sapiens*. This living being manages to change its natural environments to a marked degree.

Present-day vegetational associations (plains, savannas and forests) are formed. In forests and woods extensive areas of undergrowth are created as shrubs proliferate.

*Homo erectus*

myrtle

■ duration about 2 million years

the Holocene has lasted 10,000–12,000 years until the present day

# Quaternary

The final phases of the Tertiary were characterized by drastic climatic changes. The transition from the Miocene to the Pliocene was marked by a progressive lowering of temperature. The luxuriant vegetation, which still formed tropical-type forests in many areas, was wholly transformed. Vast areas were taken over by grasslands. At the same time, the herbivores became more strongly established, particularly the proboscidians and artiodactyls.

At the end of the Pliocene, movements of the continental land blocks resulted in the Earth's appearing as it does in any modern world atlas. The last mountains finished growing. Continental platforms were significant features bordering the continents.

Rivers coursed freely in all direc-

tions and as mountain ranges took
shape the river beds cut more deeply
into the valleys. Many altered their
previous course and, with their
tributaries, formed new basins and
lakes.

Lower temperatures in mountain
regions stimulated the growth and
spread of conifers. This also happened at more moderate altitudes
over vast areas of the northern continents where the climate gradually
grew colder.

The beginning of the Quaternary
already displayed signs of what was
to be the most dramatic and spectacular phenomenon of the past two million years: glaciation.

Scholars have long debated the
reasons for this glaciation or Ice Age,
seeking clues in the Earth's strata. It
was generally assumed that the Pleistocene glaciation was unique. We
now know that this was only the
latest of several Ice Ages in the
Earth's history, and that glaciation
has been a recurrent theme.

Authors of the past therefore advanced many theories to account for
what seemed an exceptional occur-
rence. Some claimed that the glaciation could be due to profound
changes in the way the planet rotated, an alteration perhaps in the
angle of the rotating axis. Others
attributed the sudden lowering of
temperature to a series of fluctuations
in the flow of energy from the Sun.

Nowadays it is admitted that astronomical phenomena may have played
some part in influencing the general
course of events. Perhaps there were
showers of meteorites or a fall of
asteroids; the same occurrences as
were claimed as possible reasons for
the extinction of the dinosaurs. Scientists now give greater weight to the
fact that there have been numerous

glaciations and try to find a common, linking factor. Most glaciations have been recorded when immense continental masses were· concentrated around the polar regions. This does not appear to be coincidental or accidental. Vast accumulations of snow and ice form on these land masses and create extensive icefields. It is significant that today some 99% of the Earth's glaciers are to be found in Antarctica and Greenland, the two biggest areas of dry land closest to the polar regions.

Where there are extensive stretches of open sea around the Poles, the ice layers are thinner and less massive. The blocks of ice tend to break up and the water becomes liquid again, as happens today with the pack-ice around the North Pole.

It may be that astronomical phenomena or other events not so far understood can explain events associated with glaciation, that is the recurrent periods of thaw which bring about distinctive phases in the course of an Ice Age, the cold phases (glacials) and the milder phases (interglacials). There is plenty of evidence to show that ice retreated from time to time during glaciations, but the reasons are still unclear. Although these phases have been confirmed for the latest Ice Age, it is likely that the same alternating periods also occurred in earlier glaciations.

It is pointless to discuss here the innumerable theories advanced, so we shall confine ourselves to the simplest account, based on geological evidence, of what may have happened, and the impact these phases had on plants and animals.

# Pleistocene glacials and interglacials

During the glacial phases the thickness of the icecaps must have been more than 3km (1¾ miles) in some places. The mass of frozen water was enormous. The sea level therefore dropped and numerous dry patches of land appeared. Among these were the link between Asia and North America, the isthmus of Panama and many land bridges between the islands of Indonesia. Once more it was possible for large numbers of animals to migrate as their environments changed.

The conifers moved southwards, literally pushed in front of the advancing icecaps, depriving other trees of living space and thus altering the ecology of immense areas. In temperate latitudes the climate was probably cold and fairly dry. Humidity was concentrated in the equatorial belt and in parts of the adjacent tropical zones where there was abundant rainfall. About one million years ago the first cold waves struck. The oldest glacial age, although it is not now universally agreed, is the Donau.

Donau is the German word for Danube, and the names given to the succeeding glacials, applicable to the Alpine region and Europe in general, are derived from this river and its tributaries. The Donau was followed by an interglacial and then the Gunz glacial. Subsequent glacials are the Mindel, the Riss and the Würm (this lasting from about 80,000–70,000 years ago to about 12,000–10,000 years ago). Each glacial was followed by an interglacial (Gunz–Mindel, etc).

A different nomenclature is used for the North American glacials and interglacials, based on the valley states of the upper Mississippi. The sequence, from the oldest, is Nebraskan glacial, Aftonian interglacial, Kansan glacial, Yarmouth interglacial, Illinois glacial, Sangamon interglacial and Wisconsin glacial. The last coincides with the European Würm glacial.

The entire period from the beginning of the Quaternary to the end of the Würm is known as the Pleistocene epoch. The last interglacial begins the Holocene or Recent epoch, in which we live today.

*Right: A scene from the Amazon jungle.*
*Below: Migrating reindeer on the taiga, the forest of conifers and other rare angiosperm plants nowadays restricted to the northern part of Siberia and some territories of Canada. The present climate is of an interglacial, probably similar to that of the other Quaternary interglacial phases.*

# Adapting to cold

These frequent changes of climate and temperature imposed a series of stresses and strains on both plants and animals. The plants evolved rhythmical life cycles to coincide with the different seasons and climates. The animals also adapted in various ways, mainly by developing new species. It was not that simple, if only because the alternation of cold and warm phases occurred more rapidly than the normal rhythms of the evolutionary processes. Decreasing quantities of food and shrinking of the Earth's habitable zones did a great deal of harm to some plants and animals. In tropical and equatorial zones there were phases of congestion, with species becoming impossibly overcrowded. Many species became extinct because of the fierce competition from other species. By contrast the temperate and cold regions saw continuous movement, as animals followed the periodic advance and retreat of grasslands and woodlands. Those who could not adapt to the continual movement became extinct.

Some adaptations, however, were notably successful. Reduction in size assured rodents and related animals safety since they did not need a great deal of food. Others grew bigger and

*Herbivores and carnivores during one of the Pleistocene glacial phases. In this reconstruction a pack of wolves are attempting to bring down a bison (Bison latifrons) but are driven off. Bison were widely distributed in the Pleistocene throughout the temperate regions, with a fair number of species. Nowadays the genus Bison is represented in North America by the American bison (B. bison) and in Eurasia by the European bison (B. bonasus, with two subspecies). The best known of the very few habitats where these artiodactyls still roam wild is the Bialowieska forest, south-east of Bialystok, in Poland.*

Bison latifrons

Canis lupus

survived because they were better able to withstand adverse climatic conditions. They could eat a lot and by doing so accumulate fat or other reserve substances in expectation of difficult times. Gigantic animals appeared in many orders: mastodonts and mammoths among the proboscidians, huge deer and cattle among the artiodactyls, giant beavers in the rodent group and, among the perissodactyls, the rhinoceros *Elasmo-*

*therium*, with a horn 2m (6½ft) long, and a 1m (3ft) skull and a total body length of over 6m (19½ft). There was also a giant primate, the ape *Gigantopithecus*, 3m (10ft) tall. All the mammals also acquired added protection by growing thick fur.

During the glacials some large animals developed or at least perfected hibernation. This is a period of winter sleep when the metabolism slows down and the animal lives on the fat

Mammuthus primigenius
(3.5m (11½ft) tall at shoulder)

Megaloceras giganteus
(as big as a modern elk (moose) )

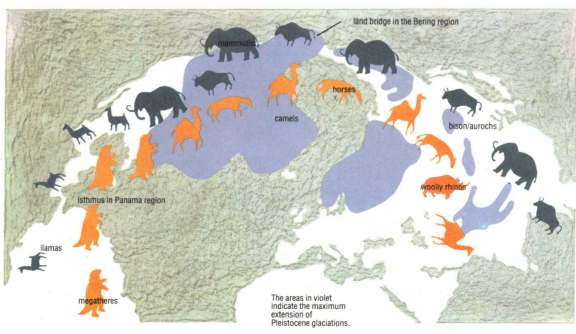

land bridge in the Bering region

mammoths

horses

camels

bison/aurochs

woolly rhinos

isthmus in Panama region

llamas

megatheres

The areas in violet indicate the maximum extension of Pleistocene glaciations.

stored up in the previous season or period of plentiful food.

Did the dinosaurs also attempt to apply the principles of hibernation? The enormous reptiles may have been prevented from this because of their immense size and because they probably had no way of storing food efficiently in their body. Only small reptiles, lizards and some snakes, are known to hibernate.

We must remember that during the Pleistocene, no matter how cold the climate, there was always an alternation of seasons. In certain areas there were summers with plenty of vegetational growth.

During the glacial phases migrations were frequent. Animals from temperate zones moved from north to south and vice-versa repeatedly, crossing the equatorial regions. In this way the megatheres and glyptodonts reached North America.

In some isolated areas medium-sized or small animals appeared which were derived from larger or gigantic animals living elsewhere. These dwarf animals behaved in much the same way as their bigger counterparts. In Sicily, for instance, during the interglacials, new species included miniature deer, a megathere only the size of a cat, and dwarf elephants (*Palaeoloxodon falconeri*), a mere 90cm (35in) high at the shoulder. Other dwarf elephants appeared in islands off the coast of Indonesia and in the Celebes group, while small woolly mammoths lived at Santa Barbara, California.

Yet as some large animals became smaller, others of medium size grew into giants, because of their isolation. Huge dormice and rats, for example, inhabited various Mediterranean islands.

*Ursus spelaeus*
(cave bear, bigger than a modern grizzly)

*Ovibos moschatus*
(musk-ox, living)

*Rhinoceros etruscus*
(woolly rhinoceros, bigger than modern white rhinoceros)

tigers

hippopotamuses

deer

St Martin-in-the-Fields  Houses of Parliament  Big Ben  London Bridge

# Melting ice

During the interglacials there was obviously a lot of animal movement in a south–north direction. Suitably adapted animals returned to occupy temperate and cold areas which were once more going through a milder phase. Flooding caused difficulties in communications; lakes and swamps spread out, restricting areas of grassland. Animals from the equatorial belt, accustomed to a semi-aquatic life, were able to colonize zones previously barred to them. Competition was undoubtedly intense.

The retreat of glaciers meant that the continents were carrying far less weight, so they tended to rise, like rafts floating freely after shedding part of their load. Many coastal areas

Palaeoloxodon antiquus

buffalo

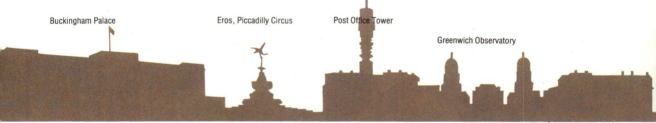

Buckingham Palace — Eros, Piccadilly Circus — Post Office Tower — Greenwich Observatory

OLBER

*The reconstruction shows some of the mammals which, in the Riss-Würm interglacial, roamed the lower reaches of the Thames, later the site of London. About 100,000 years ago, the area now occupied by the English capital (some of whose principal landmarks are shown in silhouette below) was the home of lions, tigers, hippopotamuses, elephants (Palaeoloxodon antiquus), deer and aurochs (Bos primigenius). The environment was similar to that of the present-day African savannah but the climate may have been wetter and there were many swampy zones.*

were similarly raised, exposing vast beaches and lowlands. There were new opportunities for animals associated with water, including many birds, and certain kinds of marine mammal. Giant Sirenidae, like Steller's sea-cow, a type of dugong, about 8m (26ft) long, was destroyed by human activity in the 18th century. During the Pleistocene, however, the marine faunas did not undergo major

221

changes, except for the continuing development of the bony fishes. They had been on the ascendant throughout the Tertiary and triumphed conclusively in the upper Pleistocene.

As for the land animals, it is relatively easy to carry out a roll-call of survivors from the glacials; we can see which species were present during the various interglacials and deduce how many vanished, how many escaped the worst conditions, how many altered and how many were replaced by new forms.

The last machairodonts, sabretoothed tigers, gave way to cave lions and the giant deer yielded their place to more modest-sized forms, the modern deer. The mastodonts probably vanished just before the mammoths. The ratio of predators to prey more closely approached that which exists today in protected areas where a natural balance is preserved.

One important new element, however, soon began to affect the stability of these animal communities, and steadily assumed greater significance. This was the appearance of man.

*This table shows the varied fauna of the different interglacial periods. On the left are the names applied to the alpine region and to Europe in general, and on the right those adopted for North America. The European interglacials take the double name of the preceding and following glacial phases whereas the North American interglacials use different names (present-day US states or counties). The figures are not to scale, and those of predators are in red. The human figures, with various weapons and tools, are deliberately placed beside those of other animals.*

222

Wisconsin

Sangamon

Illinois

Yarmouth

Kansas

Afton

Nebraska

AMERICAN NAMES

# Man

## Myth versus science

We have traced the story of life on planet Earth over a period of more than four thousand million years up to the Pleistocene, the sixth epoch of the Cenozoic era, which began about two million years ago. It was during the Pleistocene that primitive man began to make an impact, although his origins may be even earlier.

We shall trace the evolution of man over a span of some twelve million years, treating him as an animal like all the others, with lines of descent and relationships which are still not entirely clear. Man developed from prehistoric forms, adapted to the changing environment, acquired special skills and emerged a survivor, with creative and destructive powers unrivalled by any other species on Earth.

The evidence of fossils allows science to demonstrate that species have changed; that one species, gradually and almost imperceptibly, has led to another; and that sudden changes in the environment have perhaps caused equally sudden changes in living forms. Yet even where physical facts are presented as evidence, there must be areas of doubt. Terms like 'probably' and 'perhaps' cannot be avoided. This is part of scientific procedure. Science can never explain everything.

Science seeks to discover how an organ, such as a limb, came to be transformed, how a foot became a wing, or a scale or a feather. It will propose a theory, a partial explanation, though never one that can be valid in every case.

Now that we have clear evidence of man's remote past, we naturally want to know in what way we are related or descended from these animals of the past. Things were far simpler up to a few centuries ago, before any human fossils had been found. Early human artefacts, such as stone chips and flakes, were dismissed as 'whims of nature' or 'petrified thunderbolts'. The antiquity of the human species was roundly denied.

Darwin's interpretation of human events in an evolutionary context in *The Descent of Man* (1871) came up against immediate prejudices. To accept the antiquity of man implied accepting his 'animal' nature, admitting that he was not a superior being, contradicting all traditional beliefs.

So the whole argument was simplified. Once again, to explain things in a few words meant to distort it. If the living forms most resembling man were the anthropoid (man-like) apes, Darwin's theory could be summed up by saying that 'man is descended from monkeys'. Such a statement – never made by Darwin – led to endless debates and arguments. They were all conducted in the most misleadingly simple terms, such as the public could readily understand, and all with the intention of discrediting the theory of evolution.

Even if we accept the idea of continuous evolution, how can we pinpoint the moment of transition from animal to man, from the creature which is not aware of anything but its immediate needs to the creature which perceives everything and can use reason as well? We are undoubtedly beings of this kind: we use our intellect as well as our senses. Science can only offer *some* explanations, clarify certain obscure points. It can help us understand that man evolved 'bit by bit', that learning to think and make decisions was part of that process. However improbable it may at first seem, it is not impossible that in several million years man could have progressed from using flint tools to thinking up the *Mona Lisa*, *King Lear* and the *Jupiter Symphony*. And we can come to only one conclusion – that Leonardo, Shakespeare, Mozart and every one of us is directly descended from the individual who first picked up a stone and cut off a flake.

# Apes and hominids

There have been and still are many theories about 'the origin of man'. These theories are liable to change even from one year to another as a result of research and fresh discoveries. Yet if the process of human evolution does not necessarily differ greatly from that of other groups of animals, the consequences of that process have been significant for more than our species alone. There has been an unusually close relationship between species and environment in human evolution. This virtually upsets the fundamental notion of every animal species having its 'ecological niche'. We shall return to this point later. Despite the numerous theories which subsequently appeared, Darwin's basic proposition is still valid: it is highly probable that in the distant past there was an ancestral form (it used formerly to be known as the 'missing link') from which both man and the apes were descended.

Confining ourselves to the evolution of the primates, we have already seen that animals going back to the middle Oligocene of Egypt could be considered forerunners both of the Pongidae, the present-day anthropoid apes such as the orang-utan, gorilla and chimpanzee; the Hylobatidae, the modern gibbons; and also of the group that includes *Ramapithecus*.

The common ancestor might have been a monkey, still unknown, from the Egyptian Oligocene. We have also described the most interesting features of *Ramapithecus*. It is one ancestral form already so strongly orientated towards the branch of mankind that it should be included among the family Hominidae.

The 'bone history' of the hominid family can be quite thoroughly reconstructed because there are so many fossil remains of bones, especially skull bones that come from animals in the hominid family. Only the later forms tend to be given the generic name *Homo*. The multiplication of scientific names has led to much confusion and argument, though fortunately the trend nowadays is to simplify this classification. Attributing a skull or a limb-bone to a particular hominid form is difficult and bound to cause controversy. The important thing to note is that with the passage of time the various skulls give proof of the gradual increase in the size of the brain. From a certain point onwards, fossil bones have often been found with stone flakes and then with objects – tools, weapons and implements – of increasing complexity. These signs have sometimes been wrongly interpreted by authors, but they clearly point to developing intelligence and skills.

Discussing other animals of the past we have asked ourselves how they developed or became extinct, why some triumphed and others failed. The answer has often been associated with the fundamental operation of eating. The search for food, the availability of food, the abundance or scarcity of food – these are essential elements in the relationship between species and the environment.

Investigations into man's past have been complicated by the fact that too much emphasis has usually been placed on those qualities that distinguish humans from other animals (marked intelligence, capacity to make objects, ability to use articulate language, capability of abstract thought, etc). Too little emphasis has been placed on the basic problems of living, in particular the activity of eating. Obviously, proper account must be taken of man's developing intelligence, but it is significant that many human patterns of behaviour have been and still are determined by the urgent need to resolve the fundamental problem of obtaining food.

# Diet and behaviour

According to Clifford J. Jolly, a valid comparison can be made between the way in which primitive hominids must have behaved and the way in which their contemporaries the apes behaved. We can observe the different life styles of various modern monkey communities. Jolly compares the behaviour of the gelada (*Theropithecus gelada*, a form similar to the baboons) and other monkeys related to them, such as the hamadryad (*Papio hamadryas*), the mandrill (*Mandrillus sphinx*) and the drill (*Mandrillus leucophaeus*).

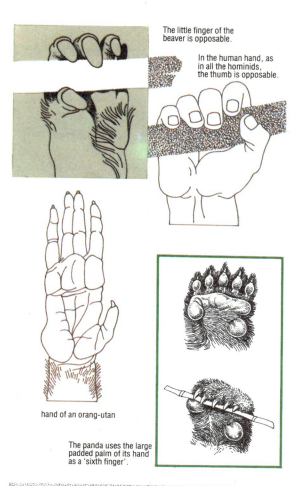

The little finger of the beaver is opposable.

In the human hand, as in all the hominids, the thumb is opposable.

hand of an orang-utan

The panda uses the large padded palm of its hand as a 'sixth finger'.

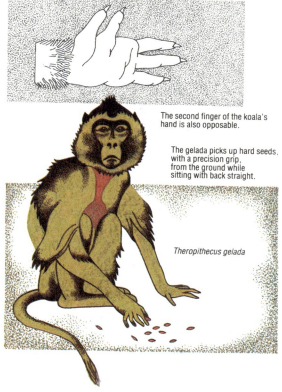

The second finger of the koala's hand is also opposable.

The gelada picks up hard seeds, with a precision grip, from the ground while sitting with back straight.

*Theropithecus gelada*

The gelada lives on the plains, in the savannah, close to the fringes of the forest. Its environment is therefore similar to the environment inhabited by primitive hominids. The forest proper is the typical habitat of modern apes, and probably of primitive apes as well. The mandrills feed on relatively soft leaves, fruit, twigs and sometimes on invertebrates or small vertebrates. Their diet does not differ much from that of the apes. The gelada, however, lives mainly at ground level and feeds principally on roots, grass and hard seeds. To collect these fairly small items, the gelada usually *sits* on the ground, back straight, and without letting the head droop, explores all around itself with its hands. It then picks up the small edible items with thumb and index finger with a precision grip rather like that of a human, and transfers them into the palm of the hand. When it has assembled a tidy pile it carries hand to mouth and begins to gobble the food. To do this, the gelada moves the lower jaw sideways as well, using the teeth for grinding. This may explain why the canines are reduced, since they would be an encumbrance for such an activity. In fact, both the canines and the incisors are smaller than they are in mandrills; but the lower jaw is very strong in the molar region. These characteristics are present, and accentuated in the primitive hominids (e.g. *Ramapithecus*). The gelada's forehead is perhaps less receding in relation to the upright bearing of the head than that of the mandrills. Furthermore, because it lives on the ground, the gelada does not use its foot much for grasping, the big toe being hardly opposable. In other forms that live in trees, thumb and big toe are fully opposable.

Jolly has examined other characteristics. By and large, it appears that from a fairly uniform group of forest-dwelling monkeys, one, the gelada, went exploring, and evolved in a special manner, its food consisting of small, hard objects, much like the diet of the most ancient hominids. In contrast, those primates, mandrill, drill, etc., which remained in the forest, evolved less. This was the case, broadly speaking, with the apes.

*Many animals are able to grip an object with the hand or foot; it is typical of mammals as well as birds. As a rule, however, there is a difference between grasping it and holding it firmly in order to carry out a particular function, as, for example, sewing.*
*Opposite: Different forms of grip employed by certain mammals. At the bottom is a gelada, a type of baboon which, while sitting upright, picks up seeds from the ground with a precision grip possibly similar to that of the early hominids.*

Jolly's methods seem reasonable. He does not try to find affinities or, even less, lines of descent between the hominids and these monkeys. He explains how, starting from the same point, two groups of animals went their distinct ways and how similar environmental conditions led to similar adaptations and patterns of behaviour. It appears logical that the hominids eventually acquired an upright stance, a precision grip, a mandible strongest in the molar region, and a less recessive forehead simply because they lived in environments such as clearings and savannahs where there was plenty of food on the ground. The food was mainly tough vegetation and hard seeds.

# New prospects

Until quite recently it was widely claimed that our ancestors emerged from the forest and took the 'giant step' towards the savannah with the deliberate intention of becoming hunters. Unfortunately such a theory comes up against the difficulty of having to explain why. Long, powerful canine teeth would have been an obvious advantage to would-be hunters, but fossil evidence shows a clear reduction in size both of canines and incisors. It seems more logical to suppose that the earliest hominids were, in fact, granivores, that is, eaters of grain and seeds. Only at a later stage did they begin, occasionally, to feed on flesh, first perhaps by sampling carrion and then by hunting other animals. In the seed-eating phase canines would have been of lesser importance, even a hindrance; but when the hominid began to tear and devour flesh, there was no turning back on the evolutionary path. He could not suddenly find bigger and

stronger front teeth; so he retained his reliable molars and contrived to use his hands to pick up pieces of wood, bones and pebbles. His bipedal gait was not an absolute novelty, as there had been two-legged dinosaurs and running birds. It did make it possible for him to run as well as walk; furthermore he could assume this upright stance as and when he wished, and could squat in the grass, if he wanted to remain hidden.

The hominid could thus cover considerable areas of grassland and could look down on it from a height of several feet, which gave him the chance to scan the surroundings for some distance in all directions. As a collector of roots and seeds he probably had few competitors, certainly none of any size. But in a time of drought or when grass was only growing sparsely, he might have been compelled to supplement his diet with the odd scrap of meat. He may have become a hunter almost against his will; and in doing so he found himself confronted by formidable rivals, notably big cats and hyenas. He would have eaten the remains of their feasts and, if need be, defended himself with sticks. Then the skilful hands began to change the shapes of objects that happened to be lying around. Bit by bit they made weapons both for defence and attack, or tools which were more than substitutes for teeth.

*After discovering how to grip objects firmly, humans soon learned how to manipulate them. At first they made use of stones picked up from the ground by cutting flakes from them; later they realized that such stones could be chipped into various shapes and began to produce different kinds of tools.*
*Opposite: Groups of Neanderthals may well have used assembly-line methods, as shown here, to make stone tools.*

*Homo sapiens neanderthalensis*

# Team work

Certain animal communities live in habitats similar to those occupied by the first hominids. Observing these provides us with information as to how our ancestors may have behaved.

It has been said that the hominids attempted to conquer their new grassland environment by challenging the existing animal predators with stone weapons. This is not really correct, for they probably managed to prosper here for thousands of years, fearing no rivals, and coming to territorial agreements with herbivores.

Today we see many examples of peaceful coexistence among various animals in such a situation, either because they specialize in different kinds of food or feed at different times of day. Wildebeeste and zebras, which eat the same food, may live quietly alongside each other provided there is plenty of grass; groups may remain separate but territories of the two species may partly overlap.

Where considerable areas are involved, an animal obviously will not operate alone; nor do members of a species necessarily lead a solitary life. As a rule they form groups consisting of a few individuals. Living alongside one another is often an advantage to all species concerned. In instances where baboons live in conjunction with antelopes, particularly impala, the impala, who have a keen sense of smell, will run off and thus warn the monkeys of the arrival of a predator. It may be that the hominids cooperated in the same way with their animal companions.

In some cases small groups can operate more efficiently. This happens, for example, with the gelada. The attentive search for roots and seeds is usually done by groups of 3–5 individuals. In the evening the small gelada groups combine into bigger troops and generally retire to sleep on hills overlooking the savannah or at the edges of clearings. It is logical to regard such behaviour as an indication of the kinds of group that were formed by the earliest hominids.

*Below: Grades of rank in a herd of African elephants. Highest in the social scale are the adult females.*
*Opposite: Among some animals that live in groups the leader demands submission from his inferiors. In the case of wolves, the act of submission is a symbolic gesture. The young male bares his throat to the pack-leader who, instead of attacking, admits him to the group.*

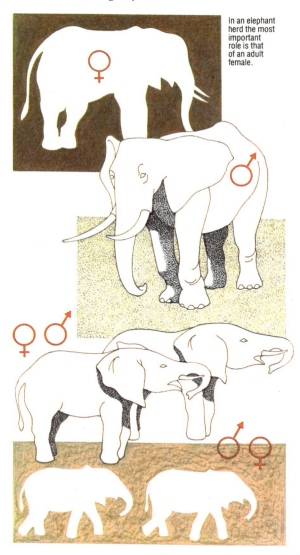

In an elephant herd the most important role is that of an adult female.

The hominids would have done their food gathering in groups containing more than single families because they covered a much larger area. There would hardly have been any effective division of labour in individual groups while they remained food gatherers. This would have happened later, probably when the hominids began competing with the predators, first by taking carrion, then by turning into hunters. Longer scavenging or hunting trips were carried out by the males, while the females gathered seeds and roots and looked after the children.

The males of small, distinct family groups of hominids would therefore have met and challenged other males when out looking for food; or the various men might have made an agreement to join forces. A hominid who chipped off a sliver of stone would have taught a friend how to do it. This was something entirely new. Man is a cultural animal, capable of transmitting knowledge to others. By doing so, the early hominids developed the ability to engage in an activity denied all other living creatures: to conquer the world, to change it and to ruin it.

# Ruin and destruction

We have mentioned that paleontologists have found flakes of stone alongside or near the fossilized bones of hominids. Such objects do not appear everywhere in strata from the same period. Furthermore, they are initially scarce and later become more numerous. Evidently, after the hominids discovered how to make these articles, they made them in large quantities; but not all hominids learned how to use such skills at one and the same time. These two facts show clearly the manner in which the technical skill in craftmanship was transmitted or, in certain cases, *not* trans-

*Left: Forests are being destroyed in the search for oil. This is an aerial view of a drilling plant in the Nigerian rain forest.*
*Opposite: The geology of entire regions may be ruined by crops. An aerial photograph of a farming zone in Nebraska, USA.*

*Below: Fish are killed outright in rivers polluted by industrial waste. They may die, too, as a result of lack of oxygen in waters where such wastes, rich in phosphates or nitrates, favour the explosive growth of aquatic plants which literally suffocate them.*

INDIRECT MASSACRE OF LIVING SPECIES

Industrial wastes poison waters; furthermore, phosphorus- and nitrogen-based substances 'fertilize' them to the extent of encouraging the growth of vegetation which stifles animal life.

dead fish

mitted. If a particular group was not informed of a new technique, a considerable time might elapse before the group rediscovered it. Voluntary communication or non-communication, cultural transmission or non-transmission, became extremely important factors in natural selective processes. Soon in the sense that these kinds of difference emerged more rapidly than purely physical differences in form there were educated groups and ignorant groups.

So the distinction between groups that had knowledge and those that did not was much more quickly evident than that between groups with a slightly bigger or smaller brain.

As time passed, the manufacture of stone flake objects became increasingly refined. By working in a group, (thus imitating many predators), the hominids achieved remarkable results. Then they learned to do something systematically that other animals only do occasionally. They learned how to maim and kill at a distance. For practical purposes, this was as good as growing longer limbs. The time needed to learn how to accomplish this and communicate it to the whole group was much shorter than the time it would have taken to bring about a physical change, like increase in body size, that would have been equally efficient. So the hominids began making weapons, firstly spears, then slings and, later still, bows and arrows. In the meantime they added another weapon to their stockpile: fire. This enabled them to be active at night, to surprise their victims while asleep. For the first time, here was an animal capable of operating both by day and by night. He could work in two shifts, which gave him an enormous advantage over single-shift creatures.

How has man been able to use his

weapons for large-scale destructive purposes? He has the option either of attacking enemies directly or indirectly. The early hominids could do exactly this, either by killing their prey directly or by terrifying it so that it would run away and perhaps tumble from a cliff, after which the injured animal could be killed.

In the course of his existence on Earth, man has probably helped a number of animal and plant species to become extinct. Today these actions receive wide publicity and are there for all to see. The laws of supply and demand place no restrictions on his aggressive activities against other species and their environments. Massacres, whether carried out di-

233

rectly or indirectly, are everyday events; nor are they confined to other species, for the majority are perpetrated against our fellow humans.

Were things always like this? Was prehistoric man just as aggressive as modern man? The chances are that he was. Considering the means at his disposal and judging by the efficient manner in which prey was disposed of, according to remains found at sites frequented by hunters, there can be little doubt that these predators were enormously capable. Another proof comes from evidence of the distribution of these hominids. At one stage they seem to have lived virtually all over the world; so they must have multiplied and spread very rapidly. Large populations mean many mouths to feed, so they were undoubtedly highly efficient in finding enough to eat.

As we have already hinted, man quickly became just as efficient in devising ways to harm his own kind. Groups of hominids must surely have learned very soon how to inflict injury and death on members of other groups.

Conquest and massacre, however, were not the only reasons for the decline or disappearance of a group. The leak of transmission of knowledge could be just as fatal. A group that had not yet discovered fire would be easy victims for another group which already knew the secret of fire with its many uses. A group which did not know the bow and arrow would be at the mercy of another which possessed the weapon. The group which had less education and less technology, ate less food, was thus less efficient and less cunning. It experienced hunger and starvation as it was incapable either of attacking others or defending itself.

# Too many people?

The situation was then not all that different from the present state of affairs. Two groups, which subsequently came to make up entities such as tribes, races and nations, fighting for everything: material pos-

*Opposite: The world's human population is continually growing and severe overcrowding is very common in some countries. Elsewhere critical situations arise because resources are not distributed evenly. Some people have too much food, others not enough.*
*Below: The enormous increase in the numbers of our species is a phenomenon which, according to some experts, can be explained by taking into consideration the basic components of the human diet (diagrams derived from theories advanced by Marvin Harris). The determining factor, in this context, was the transformation of man the hunter–gatherer into man the farmer–livestock raiser about 10,000 years ago.*

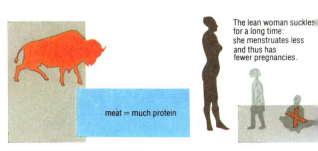

meat = much protein

The lean woman suckles for a long time: she menstruates less and thus has fewer pregnancies.

DIET AND DENSITY OF POPULATIONS

sessions, power, culture. None of these was of the slightest interest to a third group which we now call the Third World, with its starving millions. So is there a connection between and food and culture?

A group that acquires a measure of technical ability and the opportunity to communicate this information to all members of the group or groups which are looked upon as friends or

abies die

cereals and bread = much carbohydrate

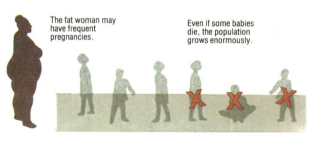

The fat woman may have frequent pregnancies.

Even if some babies die, the population grows enormously.

allies, is more efficient in providing food. So culture, that is knowledge and education, produces food. And could the reverse be true as well, that food produces culture?

An abundance of food is likely to lead to an increase in the size of the population. This makes it possible for people to travel, to meet and to have exchanges with people of other groups. In this way their culture develops, and in this sense food creates culture. Of course, things are not always that simple. In particular, if populations become too big, the beneficial effects may be slowed down. Too many individuals are in danger of forming a shapeless and somewhat inert mass. What has caused modern over-population? Some say because conditions of life have improved. That was certainly true at one time, but not borne out by later events. There have been too many periods of human history in which the masses have faced death by starvation, and our own age is, unhappily, one of these periods.

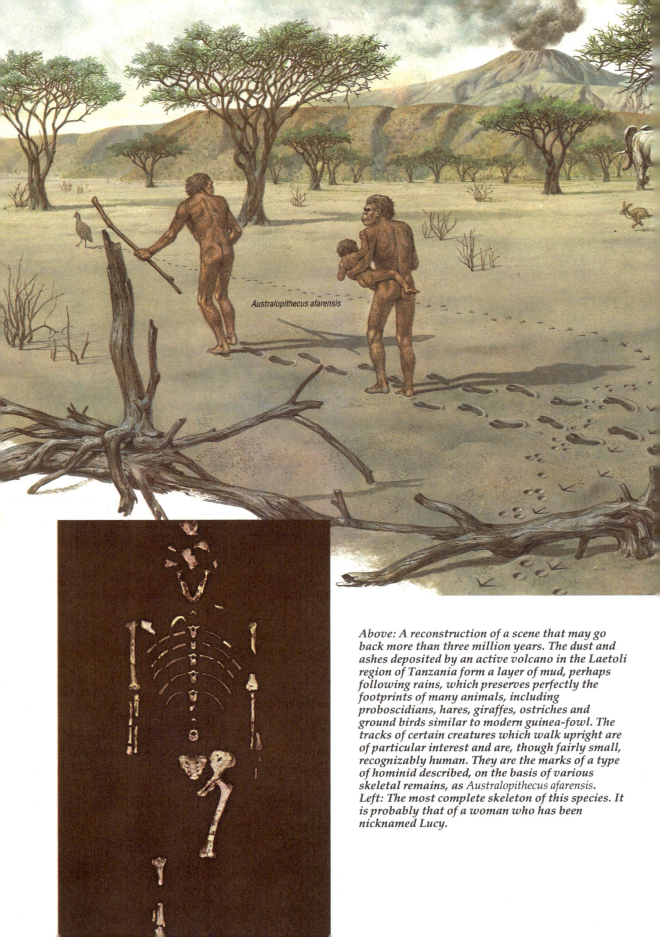

*Australopithecus afarensis*

Above: A reconstruction of a scene that may go back more than three million years. The dust and ashes deposited by an active volcano in the Laetoli region of Tanzania form a layer of mud, perhaps following rains, which preserves perfectly the footprints of many animals, including proboscidians, hares, giraffes, ostriches and ground birds similar to modern guinea-fowl. The tracks of certain creatures which walk upright are of particular interest and are, though fairly small, recognizably human. They are the marks of a type of hominid described, on the basis of various skeletal remains, as *Australopithecus afarensis*.

Left: The most complete skeleton of this species. It is probably that of a woman who has been nicknamed Lucy.

# Food and reproduction

According to Marvin Harris, it is not enough to talk only of food in general; we have to look at the characteristics of that food. Harris compares the period when man lived exclusively as a gatherer and a hunter (about 10,000–12,000 years ago) with the period when man began systematically to cultivate the plants which furnished edible seeds (barley, wheat, rice, etc) and to rear livestock. We shall be dealing further with this transition in due course. For now we should note, with Harris, that the diet of the hunter–gatherers was richer in proteins than was the subsequent diet of the farmer–livestock raisers. The diet of the farmer consisted mainly of carbohydrates, that is, compounds of carbon, hydrogen and oxygen contained in the cereals. Equally valid comparisons can be made today between people who still live as hunter–gatherers and those who live by farming. A diet rich in protein, naturally combined with the carbohydrates of wild plants, encourages good health: the tendency is not to put on too much fat, ageing does not appear too early and life expectancy is longer. Reproduction or multiplication of individuals follows a normal pattern. The women, in order to limit the number of children, sometimes, though rarely, resort to abortion, but more often an unwanted newborn baby is abandoned and left to die. The women of certain hunter–gatherer populations also use another method to delay a new pregnancy. They suckle their children for as much as three or four years. In this way their bodies, well nourished with a rich protein diet, are starved of carbohydrates and fats. Scarcity of fat in the bloodstream prevents the cycle of ovulation being restored, so that another pregnancy can temporarily be avoided. In farming communities the diet contains a high percentage of carbohydrates, a shortage of protein and hence an increased amount of fats. Plenty of fat in the bloodstream leads to frequent ovulation among women and consequently more pregnancies. Primitive birth-control methods such as abortion and infanticide are no longer sufficient to prevent the population growing.

These, briefly, are Harris's conclusions. In his view, the transition to the systematic consumption of cultivated cereals has placed man in a situation where the outlook was and still is one of continuous overpopulation. The discovery of the means to produce food, and thus to be free from the risk of starvation, has inexorably resulted in there *always* being too many of us.

# The southern apes

Now that we have discussed these basic matters, we can examine, the 'bone story' of our ancestors in some detail. It is a *true* story. We can see what happened before our own eyes, even though only in the form of fragments of bone. Of course such evidence can be interpreted in different ways; as with statistics, bones can virtually be made to mean whatever one wants. But what we have discussed previously enables us to make a choice from the various theories and fasten on the one that seems to tell a reasonably likely story. We must always ask ourselves how certain changes came about; and, almost always, we shall be able to attribute what happened to 'a question of food'.

We have already met *Ramapithecus*. Now we shall be concerned with the more recent representatives of the family Hominidae. They belong to two genera only: *Australopithecus* and *Homo*. Some authors have suggested adding other genera but these usually create complications arising from the multiplication of names, and we shall only mention them as and when really necessary.

Nowadays four species of the genus *Australopithecus* are recognized and described: *A. afarensis, A. africanus, A. robustus* and *A. boisei*.

There is a gap between the latest *Ramapithecus* known to us and the oldest *Australopithecus*, of over four million years for the *afarensis* species, and of under three million years for the *robustus* species. It is hard to say what happened in that interval and what species may have existed during that period. Furthermore, it is significant that the few fossils of *Ramapithecus* have been documented in several Old World sites, whereas the much more abundant remains of *Australopithecus* have been discovered only in Africa, in two zones: southern Africa and the eastern belt between Tanzania and Ethiopia. Is it possible that future finds of *Australopithecus* will be made elsewhere, outside Africa? Very probably. Maybe this fact will help us to understand better how *Ramapithecus* developed into later, more recent, forms of genus *Homo*. Already we are in a position to identify some essential factors of the process.

Broadly speaking, the genus *Homo* follows the genus *Australopithecus* in time; but at certain sites the two genera have been found alongside each other. The australopithecines were certainly later than *Ramapithecus* but here too there may have been a phase when both lived at the same time. This might of course indicate the possibility of an intermediate and so far unidentified genus. What did an australopithecine look like? Our description comes from a skeleton that was found in excellent condition and almost complete. This individual was almost certainly a female. Today she has become universally famous as 'Lucy'. She was so named by the discoverers because while the search was going on a tape-recorder in the camp happened to be playing the Beatles' song *Lucy in the Sky with*

*Australopithecus africanus*

Top: A reconstruction of a group of Australopithecus africanus. This hominid may have fed on carrion in competition with other animals such as hyenas. He may also have used rocks and bones as weapons.
Above: A cast of the skull of the famous Taung baby, a young specimen of A. africanus.
Right: The lower jaw of A. africanus.

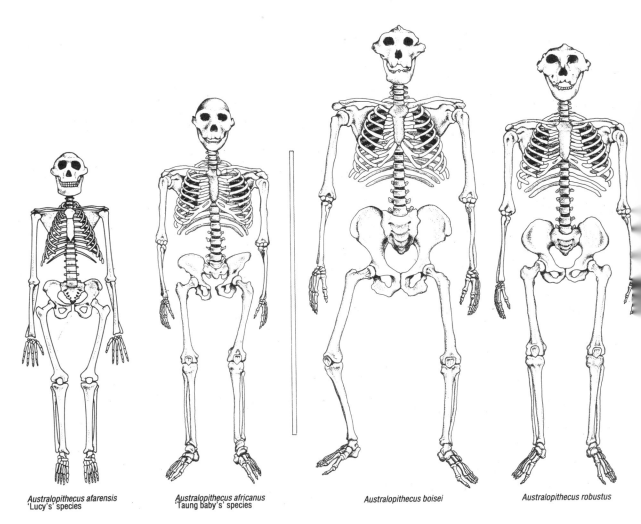

Australopithecus afarensis
'Lucy's' species

Australopithecus africanus
'Taung baby's' species

Australopithecus boisei

Australopithecus robustus

*Diamonds*. The find was made at Hadar, a site in the immense triangular Afar depression north-east of Addis Ababa, capital of Ethiopia. The expedition was led in 1974 by Donald C. Johanson, and the description of Lucy's species (*Australopithecus afarensis*) was provided by him and by Timothy White. It took into account various other remains of hominids fairly similar to hers, particularly those of a group of seven or perhaps more individuals again found at Hadar, and those discovered at Laetoli, a site in northern Tanzania to the west of Kilimanjaro.

The individuals in the Hadar group were designated 'the first family': indeed, all these hominids, including some children, appeared to have

lived, and certainly died, together, perhaps as the result of an epidemic.

At Laetoli, on the other hand, a large number of footprints of various animals were revealed as well as those of hominids who, more than three million years ago, had walked in the volcanic dust dampened by the rain. The prints were as perfectly preserved as if they had been in wet cement.

Lucy was a little over 105cm (41in) tall and must have weighed about 27kg (60lb). She was an adult, with all her teeth, characteristically worn down from use. The strong bones showed clear signs of where the muscles had fitted and, in fact, Lucy must have been a fairly muscular type. She was undoubtedly bipedal, as was

Opposite: *A reconstruction of the skeletons of four hominids nowadays attributed to the genus* Australopithecus. *From left to right,* A. afarensis (*based essentially on the remains of Lucy*)*,* A. africanus*,* A. robustus *and* A. boisei.

Right: *The skull of* A. boisei.
Below: *A fragment of a mandible (compared with that of a modern man) which, according to Richard Leakey, may have been that of* A. robustus*. This fossil is of enormous interest because it can be dated back about five and a half million years.* A. robustus *may thus be extremely old and his evolution quite independent of the other two forms of* Australopithecus.
Bottom: *A reconstruction of the* robustus *and* boisei *forms, often described jointly as* A. robustus*. They are markedly specialized for a vegetable-based diet.*

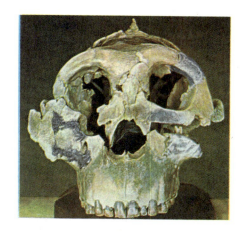

lower jaw of modern man

fragment of Lothagam jaw

*Australopithecus robustus*

shown, too, by invaluable footprints from Laetoli. The lower jaw was fairly massive in relation to the rest of the skull. The dentary arch was similar in shape to that of *Ramapithecus*, and there was a pronounced ridge above the orbits. But the cranium was 'vaulted', with a brain capacity of 450cm³ (27in³) (modern man's is about 1400cm³ [85in³], this being the average calculated on the basis of various *afarensis* specimens).

The species *Australopithecus africanus* has been known for some 60 years. In 1926 Raymond Dart discovered a small skull in a cave near Kimberley, South Africa. The dimensions were those of a monkey, but various other characteristics, volume of cranium, lower jaw, teeth and ridges above orbits, were those of a humanoid. The site was called Taung, Bantu for 'place of the lion'. Professor Dart realized that this was the skull of a young individual, which explained the small dimensions, belonging to some unknown species fairly close to human forms. At that time the find created enormous excitement, partly because it could be dated to about two million years ago, and thus an ancient ancestor. The Taung child became world-famous. Dart invented the name *Australopithecus* (literally 'southern ape') and added the specific name *africanus*. In due course there were further discoveries which greatly enlarged scientific knowledge of this form.

Bipedal, with an upright bearing, *A. africanus* was 115–125cm (45–49in) tall and weighed 28–35kg (62–77lb). The cranial capacity was 450–460cm³ (27–28in³). Incisors and canines were well developed, and the dentary arch, the curve formed by the position of the teeth, was U-shaped with enlarged sides.

What food did *A. africanus* eat? Everything that could be found in their environment of savannah, stony ground along rivers and clearings, but chiefly meat. Did they use tools? It is difficult to answer this precisely. In sites which they occupied, the cracked long bones of other animals were found, evidently to prise out the marrow, but whether these fragments were taken up and used as weapons is an arguable point.

Specimens of *A. africanus* have been found which range from under three million to about two million years ago.

# The robust hominids

Several sites in southern and eastern Africa which were explored during the 1930s and 1950s have yielded the remains of two other australopithecines, *A. robustus* and the closely related *A. boisei*. These hominids have also been given the generic names respectively of *Paranthropus* (almost man) and *Zinjanthropus* (Zinj man). Zinj is a legendary region of eastern Africa. Nowadays these names are generally considered to be out of date, and *Australopithecus* is used to describe both forms.

The robust australopithecines were big: 135–155cm (53–61in) tall and weighing 40–55kg (88–121lb). The lower jaw was huge and the muscles for chewing must have been very powerful, judging by the large cheekbones and the sagittal crest of the head. The latter is a bony ridge, resembling the ornament of an ancient helmet, which extends from the forehead to the back of the neck and is present, for example, in the male gorilla. It provides plenty of room for the insertion of the cheek muscles. The dentary arch was in a fairly

*Bottom: A reconstruction of a group of hominids of the species* Homo habilis *feasting on a zebra. This was the first representative of the genus to which we ourselves belong.*

*Below: In many cases remains of* H. habilis *have been found in association with rough stone choppers. The finds of bones alongside fragments belonging to animals which they may have eaten suggest that these hominids lived in groups in which food was divided.*

CHOPPERS
(roughly chipped stones)

narrow U-shape; the incisors and canines were small and the molars very big. The 'robust' hominids were principally herbivores, living in forests or in the zones between these and the savannahs. The brain capacity was on average, 550cm$^3$ (33in$^3$), so in proportion to the size of the body, it was smaller than that of *A. africanus*. At Lothagam, on Lake Turkana, in Kenya, Richard Leakey found a fragment of lower jaw with a large molar in 1976. The tooth evidently belonged to an *A. robustus* and was dated to five and a half million years ago. The last representatives of *A. robustus* have been found in strata dating back one and a half million years, and the last *A. boisei* individuals just over one million years.

Homo habilis

# Skilled workmen

There is evidence that a new type of hominid was living about two million years ago. The bones of these individuals were usually found with manufactured objects, notably stone flakes and stones with clear hollows. These were used for repeated striking movements, like hammers for hitting other objects. Also found were the marks of rows of rocks, taken to represent simple artificial shelters, or perhaps reinforcements for actual huts of wood or leaves. This type therefore represents the transition to the 'cultural' phase of hominid evolution. It was the first example of the genus *Homo*.

In 1960 Louis S.B. Leakey (father of Richard) discovered at Olduvai Gorge, to the east of Lake Victoria, in Tanzania, the remains of the hominid which in 1964, after considerable debate and rethinking, was given the name *Homo habilis* (handy man). Many other remains attributable to this species were subsequently found (at Olduvai again, on the Omo river, on the shores of Lake Turkana and in the Afar of Ethiopia). A skull found on the Turkana site (now known as Skull 1470) probably dates back some two and a quarter million years.

*Homo habilis* stood 125–135cm (49–53in) tall, the males were taller than the females; the capacity of the brain was around 650–700cm$^3$ (40–43in$^3$), with a maximum, as in Skull 1470, of 775cm$^3$ (47in$^3$). The ridges over the orbits formed a kind of thick visor, and the face was less prominent than that of *A. africanus*. The teeth were those of an ominivore but incisors and canines were both well developed. This hominid was omnivorous but he was, above all, a meateater. Scavenging for carrion and hunting game were group activities; and after a successful expedition the food would be shared out. Meals were important events in the life of the entire group and therefore the chosen diet had considerable social implications. When the hominids had simply gathered vegetable matter like roots, seeds, fruit, leaves and grass it was not easy to collect big amounts of food. Since they had no containers each individual was virtually on his or her own. It was basically a question of gathering, uprooting or tearing off, and then immediately eating. But when the hominids began feeding on meat, things had to be handled differently. The hunting group had to provide the food and carry it between them, in large quantities, back to the communal shelter, there to be divided up. Certainly there must have been quarrels but the operation would have been an important factor in maintaining firmly the unity of the group. The family would have become larger, developing into a clan.

It is likely that *H. habilis* lived alongside other hominids, such as *A. robustus*; but as *A. robustus* tended to be solitary or only to form small, non-social groups, they probably preferred to stay in the nearby forests where they could find plenty of their favourite food of mainly leaves, fruit, insects and small vertebrates. It may be that the two species sometimes clashed; but most of the time they would have lived peacefully together, since there was no real competition between them for food.

During one period dating from a little over one and a half to about one and a quarter million years ago, a more highly evolved type of *Homo* appeared in the Turkana region. In this type of *Homo* the proportional sizes of premolars and molars were

Homo habilis

lower jaw of *Homo habilis*

*Above: The earliest forms of the genus* Homo *have been found at various sites in East Africa. They belong to the species* H. habilis *and, as recently described by some authors,* H. ergaster.
*Right: A mandible of* H. habilis *found in the Ethiopian Afar and a complete palate of the same species. In some areas* H. habilis *lived alongside groups of* Australopithecus robustus. *There was no direct competition for food between the two types of hominid. The* habilis-ergaster *forms survived until about one and a quarter million years ago.*

similar to those of modern man, the second molar was bigger than the third, and the ridge over the brows was more pronounced. The estimated height was 130–145cm (51–57in) and the weight 35–48kg (77–106lb). Could this still be an example of *H. habilis* or had it followed a parallel and independent course of evolution? On the basis of these finds some authors have described a distinct species, *Homo ergaster* (the adjective being Greek for workman). The articles found with the bones do appear to be better made than those associated with the remains of *H. habilis*.

Considered together, these very first representatives of the genus *Homo* must have established themselves very solidly, for they were already quite capable of withstanding likely rivals. Perhaps a climatic change compelled the *A. robustus* hominids to abandon their forests, where the quantity of plant food might have declined drastically. If so, they would have adapted to other diets and tried to trespass upon the territory of the earliest members of the genus *Homo*. But their attempts to compete with the handy men and the workmen was doomed to failure. They eventually died out.

## The leap forward

Another important find in the Turkana region, dating back just under one and a quarter million years was a skull known as Skull 3733 with a cranial capacity of 850cm³ (52in³). The discovery was made by Richard Leakey who considered this 'man' to be the oldest representative of the species *Homo erectus* (upright man) yet to emerge. The species had been known for some time through more recent specimens.

This human form evidently lived almost everywhere in the Old World for a period of about half a million years, surviving until less than 250,000 years ago. Fossil remains, especially of skulls, are well preserved and it has therefore been possible to describe different features of

*According to Richard Leakey, around one and a quarter million years ago, the first individuals of the species* Homo erectus *appeared. The species was subsequently identified at many sites in the Old World, surviving until quite recently, even less than 250,000 years ago. The various specimens have a number of differences which make it possible to identify six or seven subspecies. Above: A frontal view of the Mauer jaw, from a site near Heidelberg, West Germany.*

*Opposite, left: The Mauer jaw compared with the jaw of a modern man.*
*Opposite, right: The skull found in the Arago cave, in the eastern Pyrenees, France. This belonged to a* H. erectus *from about 200,000 years ago.*
*Opposite, below: A reconstruction of the subspecies* Homo erectus heidelbergensis **(Mauer).**

the species. These are interpreted as subspecies. Is this just another example of name invention? Not really. The *H. erectus* subspecies serve to make us aware, for the first time, of the huge potential variability of what might be called the human 'model'. Just as a good model of a motor car can be marketed for many years, appear in various series and be offered with new accessories, so *H. erectus* showed itself adapted to live and become widely distributed in many environments for about one million years.

skull of Arago
*H. erectus*, Pyrenees

European *Homo erectus*

In what ways did *H. erectus* change over such a long period? Above all, in brain capacity. This ranged from 850cm³ (52in³) (3733, Turkana) to above 900cm³ (55in³) (Trinil, Java), 1067cm³ (65in³) (Olduvai), around 1200cm³ (73in³) (Petralonia, Greece), 915–1225cm³ (58–75in³) (for a series of individuals from Chukti'ien, near Peking), about 1300cm³ (79in³) (Ternifine, Algeria) and 1055–1300cm³ (64–79in³) (various individuals from Ngandong, Java). As for stature, this varied form 155–160cm (61–63in), estimated for the Trinil specimens, to 160–168cm (63–66in) in the case of the Ngandong examples. These variants are quite considerable, though less so than in modern individuals.

The picture is very different when we come to the tools. In this area there are some truly amazing developments. Firstly, stone utensils become increasingly refined, with successive stages of reworking in order to produce the finished article. Then, just over half a million years ago, fire came into general use as man's friend and ally. The traces are unmistakable. On many sites, often occupied by huts, as is proved by the discovery of stone foundations, there are the marks of hearths which must have operated uninterruptedly for years. The use of fire, once the initial instinctive fear of it had been overcome, served to strengthen still further the bonds of each individual group. And it also made new foods available, such as fish (virtually inedible raw but now quite tasty).

Traces of human activity also tell us much about his other discoveries. The fact that he could accurately fashion a stone utensil implies that he had some idea of time and also of abstract thought. Performing an action in order to obtain food needs no such

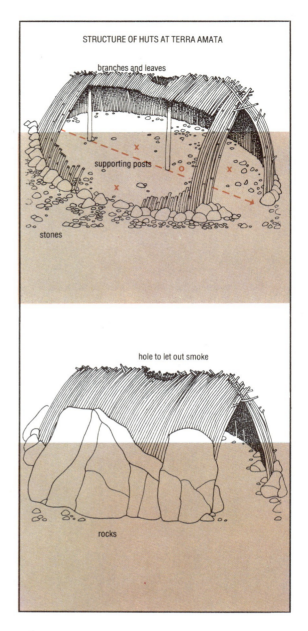

STRUCTURE OF HUTS AT TERRA AMATA

branches and leaves

supporting posts

stones

hole to let out smoke

rocks

abstract thinking. A man kills and then he eats; this is a logical sequence, typical of the majority of animals. But to make something which cannot be eaten is not so simple and logical: a man must work for a day, and then he will have an object with which he can procure food tomorrow. Furthermore, this object which he is now making can be used tomorrow and for many more

European *Homo erectus*

*Dicerorhinus* (Merck's rhinoceros)

*Opposite and above: At Terra Amata, near Nice, France, Henri de Lumley found evidence of a settlement occupied by groups of* H. erectus *during a phase of the Mindel glaciation, about 350,000 years ago. These people had built a huge hut with numerous supports and stone blocks to reinforce the walls. Many stone implements were found close to the choppers used for making them; so there was something resembling a small factory at Terra Amata where utensils were manufactured. Among the animal bones were many belonging to the woolly rhinoceros.*

days in order to procure food. The idea of tomorrow implies the idea of time. It is probable, too, that in order to transmit knowledge, in this case 'instructions how to make a stone utensil', a rich and versatile system of communication would have been required. This is how language was born. Bony remains indicate that the palate of the hominids became progressively bigger, developing a roof,

249

thus enabling them to chew the cereals more efficiently and perhaps the meat which now formed the staple diet. Food was directed towards the molars by complex tongue movements. So the mouth, an instrument for eating, also developed into an instrument for speaking. It may have started by man learning to imitate the sounds of nature, and perhaps the calls of other animals, as an aid to hunting. These sounds may then have formed the basis for words that represented actions and objects.

Another innovation of a less creative nature was the practice of cannibalism, as testified by finds at Ngandong. This is not really so strange. It is highly probable that our ancestors ate their dead companions or their defeated, dead enemies, for there was no room for waste. At Ngandong, however, things seem to have been different. The remains consist only of skulls, often without the lower jaws. No other parts of the skeletons remain. What is the explanation? It seems quite likely that the individuals concerned were beheaded, that their brain was perhaps eaten and that the empty skulls were finally collected as trophies; they may have belonged to chiefs of the community or to defeated enemies, and thus been conserved as sacred relics. Man was already able to consider actions that had no immediate effects but which could be imagined as capable of producing an effect later. *H. erectus* had therefore already discovered the particular application of abstract thought which is the province of magic and religion. Eating a part of some other individual, similar to oneself, had great significance in terms of ritual magic. It was to be used later in various forms of both animal and human sacrifice.

The evolution in hominid-man of the body itself enabled him to recognize ways and means of moulding his environment, of influencing his world. But from now on his evolution was not so much physical as cultural. Man had learnt skills from other individuals, not only through the genes, but also through methods of communication such as imitation and language. By using these, he could rise above his apparent limitations. Every evolutionary process has certain risks. There are spectacular examples of this in the past history of living things. In the words of the great evolutionist, Ernst Mayr, man could now 'specialize in despecialization'. His accessories (abstract thought, the capacity to communicate and the tendency to socialize) helped him gradually to overcome the threats and dangers of his environment. He was able to adapt to all kinds of situations, to live virtually everywhere, to eat all types of food, to be active by day and by night, in heat or in cold, to find shelter in huts or in caves.

## The rise of *Homo sapiens*

We come now to a new human species, the last, so far, and the one to which we all belong: *Homo sapiens*. The name was first applied in 1758 by Linnaeus, who correctly listed our species among the primates, alongside the monkeys. Usually, in his classifications, Linnaeus would follow his Latin names (indicating genus and species) with a short description consisting of a few Latin words. In this instance, however, Linnaeus added no description to his name *Homo* but merely quoted the advice given by the oracle of Apollo at Delphi: *Nosce te ipsum*, 'know thyself'. The word *sapiens* means wise or con-

Below: A reconstruction of Homo erectus pekinensis, commonly known as Peking Man.

Left: The remains of H. erectus pekinensis were found, from 1927 onwards, at intervals until a few years ago, in the Dragon's Cave near Choukoutien, some 40km (25 miles) south-west of Peking. This form of H. erectus has been dated, with some uncertainty, to about 450,000 years ago. Sites were occupied for long periods and judging by the thickness of the fragment of hearth, it would seem that fires were kept going for years. The utensils are rough and ready.

Homo erectus pekinensis

scious, that is thinking. Can it honestly be said that man really knows himself? He knows about his past, he knows something of his present, but he knows little about his future.

Let us dwell a little longer on his past. The form *H. sapiens* was slow to emerge while *H. erectus* was still widely distributed. Of course there are plenty of uncertainties regarding the interpretation of various finds. A highly interesting discovery of part of a skullcap in 1965 at Vértészöllös, near Budapest, can be dated back about half a million years. It was first attributed to a *H. erectus* but according to some distinguished authors, various characteristics, especially the curvature of the internal cavity and the bulge of the nape of the neck, were already those of *H. sapiens*. A hypothetical calculation of the brain capacity of this skullcap arrived at a figure of $1400cm^3$ ($85in^3$), which seems somewhat excessive. Also found at the site were crude stone tools and the traces of hearths.

Four fragments of skulls revealed

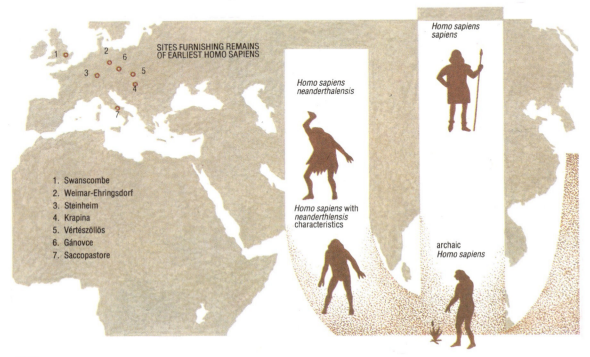

SITES FURNISHING REMAINS OF EARLIEST HOMO SAPIENS

1. Swanscombe
2. Weimar-Ehringsdorf
3. Steinheim
4. Krapina
5. Vértészöllös
6. Gánovce
7. Saccopastore

Homo sapiens sapiens

Homo sapiens neanderthalensis

Homo sapiens with neanderthlensis characteristics

archaic Homo sapiens

by Louis Leakey at Kanjera, East Africa have been dated to about 400,000 years ago. Here too there are several features that point to a higher level of evolution than *H. erectus*.

The skulls discovered at Steinheim on the Murr, near Stuttgart, West Germany, and at Swanscombe, on the Thames in England go back some 200,000–250,000 years. These skulls have a large cap, a fairly pronounced ridge over the orbits, a rounded nape, a face less inclined than that of *H. erectus* and less pronounced cheekbones. These are characteristics which point the way towards those of modern man.

Another group of slightly later finds (Riss–Würm interglacial, about 150,000–100,000 years ago) show typical *H. sapiens* features, but chiefly elements that are later to be found in Neanderthal Man. Examples include the remains from Weimar–Ehringsdorf, East Germany; Krapina, north of Zagreb, Yugoslavia; Gánovce near Poprad, Czechoslovakia; and Saccopastore, on the north-eastern outskirts of Rome Italy. The bones are very large, the skull is elongated and the brain capacity is 1070–1280cm$^3$ (65–78in$^3$). There is a more varied selection of stone objects.

What conclusions can be drawn from these data? The form *Homo sapiens* is ancient; many features of modern man are outlined at least 250,000 years ago, if not before. Other characteristics are more obviously-associated with Neanderthal Man. It almost seems as if *H. sapiens* was waiting for a long time in the wings and that during a certain phase he yielded the stage to Neanderthal Man. It is hard to say whether things were quite like that but we can nevertheless try to answer some of the problems.

# The cavemen that never were

Neanderthal Man is undoubtedly the most famous of all prehistoric men, as well known as the tyrannosaur in the world of dinosaurs, and surrounded by just as much mystery.

The scientific name *Homo neanderthalensis*, applied in the late 19th century, was based on finds of various bones in a gorge of the Neander valley in Germany and subsequently at other sites in Europe. Reconstructions, based on the later discovery of a skeleton at La-Chapelle-aux-Saints in the Dordogne, France, showed a shambling, ape-like hunchback with

*Opposite: A map of sites furnishing human remains belonging to forms preceding the species Homo sapiens. At the top is the skull from Steinheim on the Murr in West Germany and in the centre the skullcap from Vértésszöllös, near Budapest in Hungary.*
*Below: The skulls from Weimar-Ehringsdorf, East Germany and Saccopastore, a site now on the outskirts of Rome, finds which make it possible to describe a form of H. sapiens already closely resembling Neanderthal Man.*

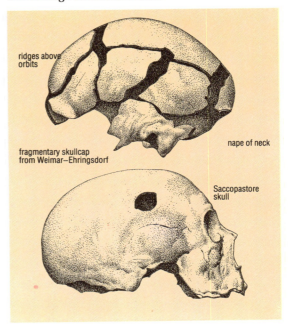

ridges above orbits

fragmentary skullcap from Weimar–Ehringsdorf

nape of neck

Saccopastore skull

bent knees and club in hand, rather like a fairy-tale giant. This was a misconception, for the individual in question was an old man whose bones were deformed as a result of arthritis. The Neanderthals were certainly not hunchbacked, nor did they walk with bent legs. A similar error is usually made with regard to their way of life. They are commonly called cavemen, yet the truth is that these people never lived in caves. Their settlements were occasionally established near to a cave entrance but were, in most cases, encampments set up beneath jutting rocks that provided natural protection or even groups of large huts containing a number of hearths.

*Below: A cast of the famous skullcap found in 1857 in a limestone cave of the Neander river valley, near Düsseldorf, West Germany. On the basis of this discovery, in 1864, the first description was given of the human form nowadays called* Homo sapiens neanderthalensis. *The characteristic ridges over the eye orbits are clearly visible.*

MANUFACTURED ARTICLES OF MOUSTERIAN CULTURE

hand-axe     scraper     bone clasp (?)     scrapers     point     knife     scraper

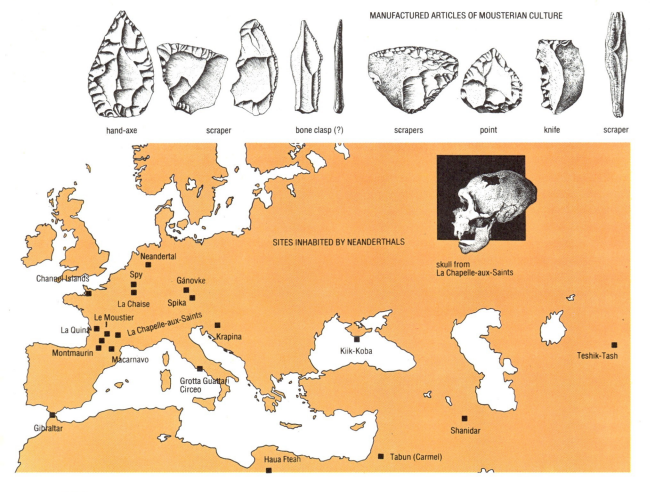

SITES INHABITED BY NEANDERTHALS

skull from La Chapelle-aux-Saints

Neandertal
Channel Islands
Spy
Gánovke
La Chaise
Spika
Le Moustier
La Quina
La Chapelle-aux-Saints
Krapina
Montmaurin
Macarnavo
Kiik-Koba
Teshik-Tash
Grotta Guattari Circeo
Gibraltar
Shanidar
Haua Fteah
Tabun (Carmel)

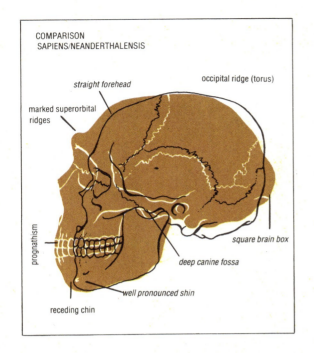

COMPARISON
SAPIENS/NEANDERTHALENSIS

straight forehead

occipital ridge (torus)

marked superorbital
ridges

square brain box

prognathism

deep canine fossa

well pronounced shin

receding chin

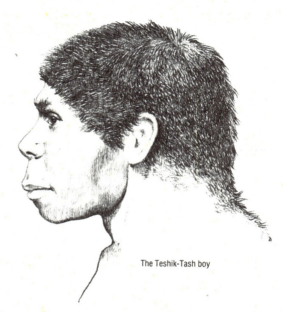

The Teshik-Tash boy

*Opposite: The sites that have furnished the principal remains of* H. s. Neanderthalensis.
*Opposite centre: Some examples of the Mousterian culture, associated with the Neanderthals.*
*Above: The outline of a modern human skull superimposed on that of a Neanderthal.*
*Above right: A profile of the nine-year-old boy buried at Teshik-Tash, Uzbekistan, USSR.*

The scientific name in general use nowadays is *Homo sapiens neanderthalensis*, implying a close relationship, as a subspecies, to modern man. The fact that other names continue to be applied to this as well as earlier and later forms (Paleanthropinae for the Neanderthals, Archanthropinae for *H. erectus* and preceding species, and Neanthropinae for the 'new men', our immediate ancestors) shows how much uncertainty and disagreement still prevails in this field of study.

What were the Neanderthals really like? For an answer we can compare the skull of a modern man with that of a Neanderthal. In this way one can attempt a reconstruction as accurate as that made of a nine-year-old boy whose skull was found at Teshik-Tash in Uzbekistan, USSR.

The lower jaw is large and sturdy, and the rami, or branches, have a not very pronounced canine fossa. This is the hollow in the top part of the rami, which in the mandible of modern man is very deep, so that each side appears to end in a fork. There is a space between the last molar and the ascending part of the lower jaw. In modern man there is no such gap, as many of us who have had the last molars or wisdom teeth extracted are aware, simply because they do not have enough room to grow.

There is absolutely no projecting part corresponding to the chin. The cheekbones are very strong, in keeping with the muscular, rounded cheeks and help the huge lower jaw to chew food efficiently.

Both the upper and lower jaw are markedly prognathous, projecting forwards together with all the teeth. The bones at the base of the nose recede slightly. Above the orbits the characteristic ridges, clearly visible in

255

the skullcap found in the Neander valley, form a double-arched visor.

The forehead is receding, whereas in modern man it is almost vertical. The cap of the skull is very long and has a typical ridge, almost a shelf (the occipital torus) in the nape region. This feature is not very pronounced in modern man.

The average brain capacity is higher than that of present-day man: 1438cm$^3$ (88in$^3$), with maximum limits of up to 1700cm$^3$ (104in$^3$). The average capacity of our own skulls is 1400cm$^3$ (85in$^3$), exceptionally up to 2000cm$^3$ (122in$^3$).

Among other characteristics of the skeleton, all the bones are stronger than the equivalent bones in modern man. The limb bones are a little shorter. The height of the Neanderthals evidently varied, among adults, from 150 to 165cm (59–65in). The arm movements were broader than our own. Both arm and forearm could be rotated at a wider angle because of the form of the shoulder-blade.

The big toe of the foot was perhaps set more widely apart than the other four. This peculiarity, probably of use for running, is evident from the footprints preserved in the soil of some settlements.

The Neanderthals lived in various places, mainly in Europe and Asia, almost at the limits of the zone which, during the Würm, was covered by the icecaps. They were people of the North, accustomed to cold. Björn Kurtén, paleontologist and anthropologist, has suggested that they were light-skinned, perhaps with fair or reddish hair, and with blue eyes. It is a possibility.

Where did the Neanderthals come from? They were derived from types represented by the skulls from Ehringsdorf and Saccopastore. Later they went through a proto-Neander-

*Below: Examination of the teeth of the Neanderthals reveals series of oblique scratches. It is thought that these marks may have been made because of their habit of eating meat by stuffing it into the mouth and then slicing off the parts that were hanging out with flint blades that scraped against the teeth. This was undoubtedly an effective way of tackling fairly tough food.*

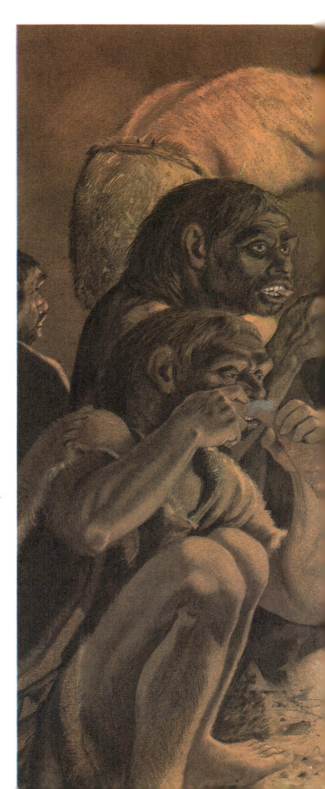

*Right: Neanderthal Man learned how to make fire and retain the embers. The remains of hearths, common in all the Mousterian settlements, show us that the Neanderthals cooked or at least scalded their meat on red-hot stones around the hearth. Probably the heat of the fire also served to make fish edible.*

hearth surrounded by stones

Once the firebrands were removed, the meat was roasted on the red-hot stones.

*Homo sapiens neanderthalensis*

thal phase and then a 'classic' phase. Taken as a whole, the subspecies *H. s. neanderthalensis* lived just under 150,000 years ago (Riss–Würm interglacial) up to 40,000–35,000 years ago (at the peak of the Würm glacial), and thus a little more than 100,000 years.

They lived as hunter–gatherers and would not have been short of food. It is wrong to imagine life in a Neanderthal community as a desperate struggle for survival. The bones 'speak'. They are the skeletons of strong, healthy individuals, nourished on a balanced diet, with plenty of protein. Microscopic examination of thin section of bone shows a very solid internal structure.

The Neanderthals hunted mammals of various sizes, including rhinoceroses, giant deer, mammoths and horses, as well as birds and fishes. They ate the meat in a special way, cramming it into the mouth and then cutting off the protruding parts with stone knives. This is proved without question, according to F.E. Koby by very thin parallel scratches on the front teeth revealed under the microscope. Other authors claim that the Neanderthals used their front teeth as pincers and all-purpose tools, to grip objects, tie knots and so forth; thus the scratches might be the result of such activities. Koby's theory nevertheless finds support in the fact that some Eskimo populations still eat meat in this manner today, often not cooking the food at all. The Neanderthals also ate vegetables and cereals.

We have many striking examples of Neanderthal culture. Above all, they made stone artefacts of great precision and refinement, objects which have been attributed to the Mousterian culture (from Le Moustier in the Dordogne, site of many important finds). They manufactured almond-shaped hand-axes, scrapers, blades and points. These weapons and tools were made from flakes previously chipped roughly from larger blocks of stone. This form of working in several stages justifies our imagining a group of individuals engaged in a kind of assembly-line production.

The Neanderthals buried their dead; this is why so many of their skeletons have been found in such a perfect state of preservation. They are definitely not the fragments of corpses that happened to be preserved by accident, as was the case with *H. erectus* or *H. habilis*.

Why did the Neanderthals entrust their dead to the earth? Did they believe it might bring them to life again? Was the earth envisaged as the great mother within whose body the dead person had to be placed curled up like a foetus in the female womb? Alternatively, were the dead bent double because their limbs had been bound, so that although they might live again they would not be capable of returning to disturb those who were still alive, to beg their share of food? We can only guess at the answers.

*Opposite: A Neanderthal community funeral. This reconstruction is partially based upon finds in the cave of La Ferrassie in the Dordogne, France. On the floor of the cave were a number of small artificial mounds; they were clearly heaps of earth to cover dead bodies, hence genuine graves. Stone utensils and sometimes flowers were buried with the dead. The idea was certainly to consign the corpse to the ground, perhaps with the view of bringing it back to life – a belief based on attentive observation of seasonal cycles whereby each seed that fell on the ground came to life again, becoming a new plant.*

*Insets: Photographs of the prints of feet and knees of Neanderthals discovered in the Bàsura cave at Toirano, near Albenga, Italy. The layer of soil which was muddy 50,000 or so years ago turned to stone with the passage of time, preserving this fascinating evidence.*

*Homo sapiens
neanderthalensis*

# New men

Before the Neanderthal man vanished about 35,000 years ago, the Neanthropinae or 'new men' made their appearance in Europe. The oldest examples, documented from 45,000–40,000 years ago, are attributed to the subspecies *Homo sapiens fossilis*. There are no marked differences in the skeletal formation between this and modern man, known scientifically as *Homo sapiens sapiens*. In fact, we ourselves are these 'new men'. We have to question ourselves, just as Linnaeus suggested, in order to know our direct ancestors, and to imagine, from signs of their activities, how they influenced the environment and made an impact on their world.

Among the most interesting remains of Neanthropinae are those of Combe–Capelle, in the Dordogne, and Předmosti, near Přerov in Czechoslovakia. The most noteworthy of the non-European sites that have turned up neanthropic skeletons, are Niah in Sarawak in Malaysia and Florisbad in South Africa. More recent remains, dating back 20,000–25,000 years, are those from Cro-Magnon, another site in the Dor-

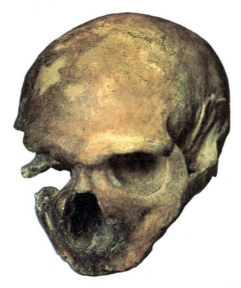

*Below: Neanderthal Man practised cannibalism, certainly as a magic-religious ritual. Perhaps important dead persons, either a clan elder or an enemy, were beheaded, the occipital foramen enlarged and the brain removed and then eaten. This kind of operation was carried out on skulls found at various sites, especially on the one discovered in the Guattari cave of Monte Circeo, south of Rome (below left). Very often the teeth of the skulls were filed in order to prevent the dead returning to beg for food.*

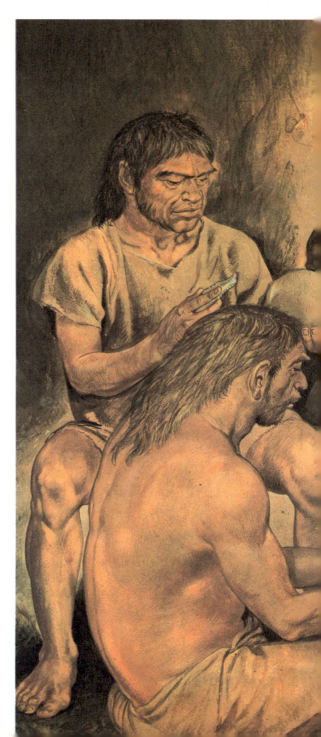

dogne. The human form known as Cro-Magnon Man is certainly an extreme type with very special characteristics. These are individuals 180cm (70in) and more in height, with very strong bones and with typical, almost rectangular orbits or eye-sockets. The term Cro-Magnon Man should not rightly be used to describe all the Neanthropinae collectively, for it applies only to one variety of new man.

Let us therefore consider the chief characteristics of the Neanthropinae in general. The forehead is like ours, that is, high and not receding. The skull is, as a whole, rather short. There is hardly a sign of ridges above the orbits which are thus well divided

Homo sapiens neanderthalensis

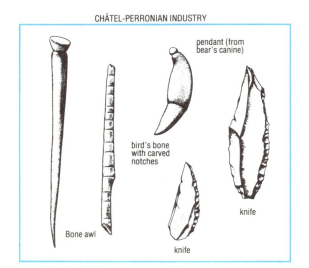

**CHÂTEL-PERRONIAN INDUSTRY**

pendant (from bear's canine)

bird's bone with carved notches

knife

knife

Bone awl

**AURIGNACIAN INDUSTRY**

awl

pendant (bone)

scraper

blade

awl

scraper (two views)

grooved awl (two views)

at the root of the nose. The chin is pronounced, the cheekbones are strong, the canine cavity is deep and forked, there is no ridge at the back of the skull and the jaws are not markedly prognathous.

What is the history of the Neanthropinae? It is hard to give a reply, particularly one that takes into account all the available facts; and there seem to be too many facts. So we should perhaps do better to examine

*Left: Manufactured objects of two typical cultures associated with the Neanthropinae (Homo sapiens sapiens).*
*Below: Neanthropic hunters receive from a shaman-sage amulets and other objects which, through magic, can help them during the hunt.*
*Opposite: A close-up of the cast of a skull of an aged Cro-Magnon Man. The teeth have fallen out because of the individual's advanced age.*

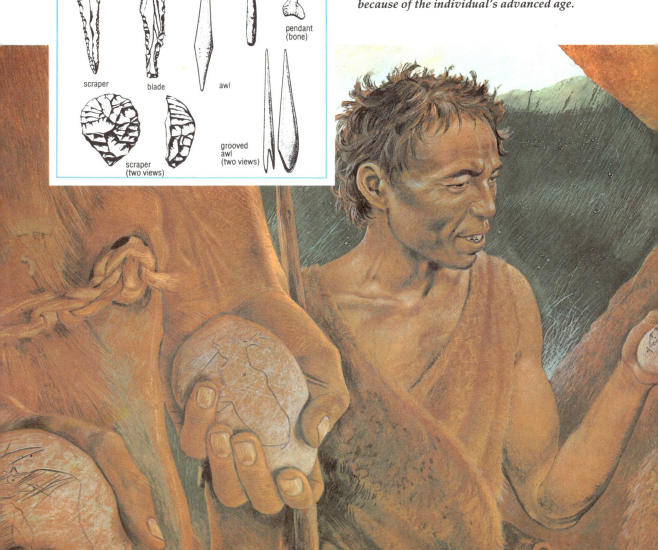

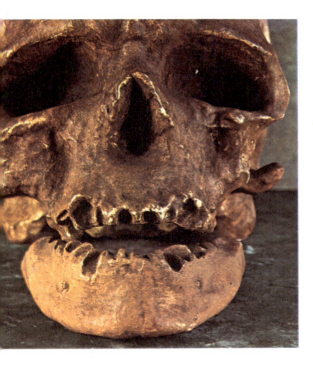

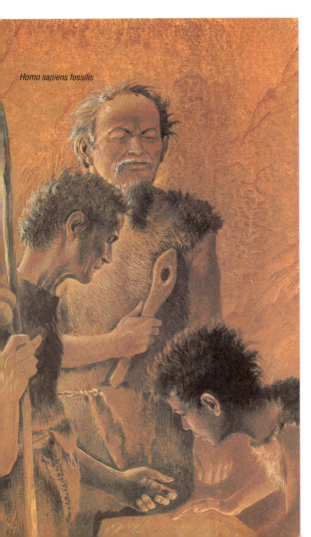

Homo sapiens fossilis

the problem from another angle, and ask what could have happened to the Neanderthals.

At European sites we see what amounts to a substitution of paleanthropic Neanderthals by neanthropic newcomers. But elsewhere, especially in the Middle East, there is evidence of the existence of populations with mixed characteristics. The skulls found in caves on Mount Carmel, near Jerusalem, represent a type halfway between that of a classic Neanderthal skull and a neanthropic skull. Furthermore, there is a striking difference, as we have seen, between paleanthropic and neanthropic skulls. It does not seem possible that one type could have evolved into the other. The intervening time is too short and no environmental change of any significance has been recorded for that period about 40,000 years ago. The Würm glaciation was still in progress, even though there were brief phases when the climate was hardly much harsher than it is today. It may be that the individuals from Mount Carmel were the result of crossbreeding, descended from classic Neanderthals and from an emergent form, derived perhaps from the earliest specimens of *H. sapiens*, Steinheim, Swanscombe, Kanjera and the like, which had evolved quite inconspicuously. Admittedly, there are few signs of such an evolutionary line. There are very interesting remains from Border Cave, between Lesotho and South Africa, which have neanthropic features and are probably older than the earliest neanthropic specimens either from Europe or the Middle East. The possibility that part of the evolutionary process of the Neanthropinae took place in warm, sunny regions, has led some authors to suppose our direct ancestors were dark-skinned.

The Neanderthals of Europe did, in some areas, have to contend with adverse climatic conditions. It is possible that the advance and retreat of the ice literally isolated some communities. It may be that such conditions were so common and widespread that these Neanderthals became extinct. Other Neanderthals, however, prospered in the Middle East and crossbred with the new men. These mixed populations might then have enjoyed wide distribution; perhaps Europe was repopulated by these 'halfbreeds'. In any event, the new men came to be represented by a vast range of local populations, which can be explained both by the process of parallel evolution and by successive waves of migration. It is quite possible that every one of us, members of *H. sapiens sapiens*, has a drop of Neanderthal blood in our veins.

Within a fairly short time the Neanthropinae spread all over the Old World. Even today, however, we do not know whether America was first reached by representatives of these new men by way of the Bering land-bridge from Asia or, prior to that, by people who lived at the same time as the Neanderthals. The oldest human remains, Paleo-Indians, discovered in California, USA have been dated to about 48,000 years ago. It is possible that one evolutionary line of Neanthropinae developed on American soil. As for Australia, the earliest evidence of human presence dates from some 60,000 years ago.

# The real and the imagined

The discovery of tools and weapons has enabled paleontologists to distinguish a number of cultures or indus-

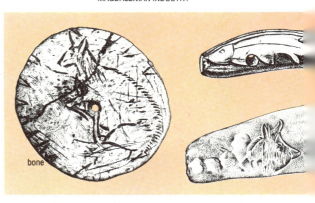

*Above: Objects made from various materials (bone, teeth and stone) with animal figures. Upper Paleolithic art had undoubted magic-religious significance. Pictures, engravings and inscriptions with the images of animals were designed to bring success in hunting.*
*Opposite: A reconstruction of the ritual killing of a sham bear clad in a real skin. Details of this picture are based on finds at various sites. The man on the right brandishes a spear-thrower.*

tries associated with different communities at different times. The Mousterian culture of the Neanderthals was followed by neanthropic cultures, named after the sites or regions in France where the artefacts were originally found. The principal cultures are Aurignacian, Gravettian, Solutrean and Magdalenian. These had their distinctive forms and techniques. The objects which were produced, both in western and eastern Europe, over a period of about 25,000 years, included flint hand-axes, spear points, blades, knives and awls, bone needles and quartz daggers, charms and other ornaments made from bone or carved from animal teeth, and statuettes in stone or ivory. The craftsmen who fashioned them were able to think in abstract terms. These objects were made with a definite idea in mind. For example, they are symmetrical, partly for practical reasons but also because they satisfied a taste originating from close observation of nature. Animals,

limestone flake

Homo sapiens sapiens

flowers and leaves all possess symmetry. These people also looked at themselves and decided to adorn their bodies, and so they made rings and fashioned necklaces from teeth, animal vertebrae and shells.

As time passed, people tended more and more to combine what they could see and touch with what they could merely imagine; and so art was born. The cave-painting of the Magdalenians had magic-religious meaning. By drawing or painting animal images on a cave wall, a dark, hidden, secret place, the artist thought he could, by magic, reduce the dangers of the hunt, bring it luck and success. By touching carved images of the prey or wearing an animal amulet round the neck, a man thought he would be able to hunt better and everyone would eat more. By observing nature, people learned how to reproduce its forms but, more importantly, to understand its workings. The many images of pregnant women show that the craftsmen who made them were well aware of the reproductive cycles of animals. The celebrated female figures known as Venuses all have large breasts, huge buttocks and a swollen belly. It was thought that these images could, by magic, cause women, and also female animals, to have more babies. Yet images of humans, on cave walls, for instance, are few and far between. The fear was that the use of magic on the human form might harm the real person. Many of the animal images on cave walls show signs of having been struck or bear marks that are meant to convey wounds. These, too, are magic actions designed to bring good fortune in future hunts. Rough statues were sometimes covered with the skin and hung with the skull of a bear. By touching this image, hunters

from Brassempouy
(Landes)

from Lespugne
(Hauts Pyrénées)

from Laussel
(Dordogne)

from Willendorff
(lower Austria)

*Left: Four of the female figures in full or bas-relief known as Paleolithic 'Venuses'. These statuettes were designed, through magic, to induce fertility in women or, more generally, in female animals. The Brassempouy head is more like a portrait than any of the others and is probably a fragment.*

*Below: The walls of the famous Lascaux cave in the Dordogne region painted with animals. This cave was accidentally discovered by four boys in 1940 and is now closed to visitors.*

were 'guaranteed' to capture a bear the next day.

The artistic output of the Neanthropinae cannot, however, always be interpreted in terms of magic. Undoubtedly, beautiful and realistic images were believed to have more effective magical powers, but it is also likely that ornamental objects were beautiful simply to please and perhaps to show the importance of the persons wearing them. Some of these articles were clearly made for particular individuals. Burials involved rituals that were perhaps similar to those of the Neanderthals, that of bound corpses and the use of red ochre. But the trappings were often elaborate as well, including many objects of more than ordinary value. The well made, precious object would be useful to the dead person elsewhere, but it also indicated rank to those still living, and was thus a symbol of social prestige.

Until about 12,000–10,000 years ago, the Neanthropinae lived quite well. There was plenty of prey such as horses, aurochs, mammoths, woolly rhinos and the cold but dry climate enabled them to store their meat. Vegetables such as fruit, roots and cereals could be gathered in seasonal cycles. There were various kinds of hearths inside their shelters beneath rocks and their huts that were often supported by the tusks and bones of mammoths.

During the period that followed the end of the Paleolithic, when the effects of the ending of the Würm glaciation were already being felt, humans were confronted by a serious crisis due to the extinction of many large animals. Populations often moved to areas near lakes or along the sea coasts, seeking their food in the water. They ate vast quantities of molluscs and hunted both aquatic animals and birds. This period is known as the Mesolithic.

# Time of crisis

The long period of cultural evolution which we have just described is generally known as the Paleolithic

Homo sapiens sapiens

(old stone) Age. Actually, the people who lived at this time used materials other than stone for making their artefacts: bone, teeth, ivory, amber and shells. At one site, diggers even found a trilobite, this fossil having been picked up for its curiosity value and perhaps used as an ornament. One of the Venuses from Dolní Veštonice, in Czechoslovakia was made from a mixture of clay paste and dust of animal bones, baked in the fire. Technically, therefore, it is a terracotta statue.

The term Paleolithic, which comes from only one of the materials used for practical and artistic purposes, is nevertheless generally used to mark the dividing line between two cul-

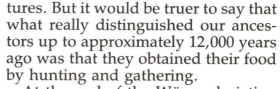

tures. But it would be truer to say that what really distinguished our ancestors up to approximately 12,000 years ago was that they obtained their food by hunting and gathering.

At the end of the Würm glaciation there were marked changes in various environments. A new interglacial, in which we still live, began. The climate turned milder, floods were frequent as the enormous masses of ice melted and, above all, some of the animals that had been adapted to cold became extinct. Hunters now had to go after smaller animals and, in certain regions, people began to eat molluscs, crustaceans and fish. Elsewhere they were compelled to feed on birds and rodents. Some settlements, in areas near the sea or close to lakes, were furnished with thick walls consisting of the remains of meals, shells, for example. This form of 'kitchen waste' is a feature of many sites on the coasts of Denmark, Japan and Brazil.

The name given to this period of crisis is the Mesolithic (middle stone) Age. During the Paleolithic, hunters had improved on the hand-thrown spear by propelling it with a spear-thrower, so giving added range. Now they learned how to make and use bows and arrows. Certain animals, too, began to be protected. The wolf, especially, had by this time been domesticated, developing into forms of dog similar to modern alsatians. Such dogs were provided with shelter and scraps of human meals. They helped protect the community against harmful animals such as rodents, possibly served as food as they could, if necessary, be killed and eaten, and were taken along on hunting expeditions. Dogs would not have been of much use in hunting mammoths, but must have been a help in chasing smaller animals such as rodents, hares and small carnivores.

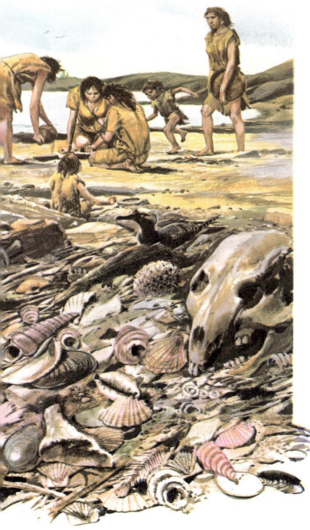

# Farms and cities

In some areas of the Near East (Palestine, present-day Turkey and northern Egypt) streams had, and still have, seasonal phases. After the rains they become torrents, and a little later they turn muddy or even dry up. These watercourses are called wadis. Local people, observing the irregular cycles, discovered that the water gave seeds the chance to germinate; and they realized that if they kept a few seeds aside, protecting them from the rains and floods, they could use them for growing new plants the following season. It is probable that observations and conclusions of this nature had already been made during the later part of the Old Stone Age and perhaps by the Neanderthals themselves, although they would not have had to face real food problems, given their very gradual rise in numbers.

The Mesolithic crisis compelled man to make a decision. He changed his diet, so that it now consisted mainly of cereals, which he himself produced. In other words, he became a farmer. At about the same time he began raising livestock, protecting certain animals which could provide him with food and other useful products such as milk, from sheep, or assistance, as was the case with the dog. Since this diet was rich in carbohydrates, the result was an increase in numbers. Groups became larger.

Storing cereals, even in areas that did not have a dry climate, became a possibility thanks to the discovery of pottery. For the first time, people began to manufacture containers, like bowls, jugs and jars – utensils that were strong and waterproof. The discovery may have been accidental. The floors of huts were usually covered with clay and perhaps the heat generated by the hearths 'baked' the

*Opposite: Above 10,000 years ago man turned to agriculture as a systematic practice, saving seeds from season to season in order to obtain new plants. This 'revolution', which marked the start of the Neolithic, occurred for the first time in certain parts of the Near East. The new diet, rich in carbohydrates, soon led to a great increase in the size of the population. Cereal crops were harvested with sickles made from small blades of flint mounted on horn or wooden handles.*
*Below: The different stages of preparing the first loaves of bread.*

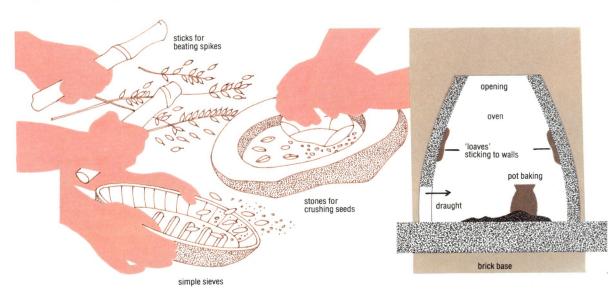

sticks for beating spikes

stones for crushing seeds

simple sieves

opening

oven

'loaves' sticking to walls

pot baking

draught

brick base

Homo sapiens sapiens

ground. Deep storage bins or silos were built to contain the grains of barley or wheat. Indeed, the community as a whole learned to protect, to hide and to defend this form of wealth.

The earliest barns and granaries were a sign that groups were beginning to be distinguished by what they had. A community could be counted rich because it had a certain capital in cereals, and another, not so fortunate, might resort to aggression or theft in order to appropriate such food and wealth. Communities began to build defensive barricades. Villages grew into cities, with walls and towers. Jericho, in modern Israel, was the first of the world's cities, dating back to over 8000 years ago. Individual or group quarrels developed into wars.

Very soon members of a community began to do different jobs; some individuals were engaged in the production of cereals, meat and other livestock products, some in defence and offence, and a selected few as the learned sorcerer-priests in giving advice on sowing and livestock rearing. Naturally, the soldiers and the sorcerer-priests did not produce food. They had to be supported by the rest of the community. The soldiers took action against actual dangers, the sorcerer-priests against more vague dangers for which they advanced far-fetched explanations. Yet the prestige of these non-productive groups steadily increased. This contributed towards social and class distinctions.

This cultural period is known as the Neolithic (New Stone) Age: but it is more notable for being the age of pottery, agriculture and livestock rearing. It was the period when civilization was born.

The processes set in motion then have never stopped. Man has sys-tematically ransacked every part of the planet to produce his food. He has destroyed forests in order to create cultivated fields; he has killed large numbers of 'harmful' animals to protect a few others. What Ernst Mayr called 'despecialization', which came about as a result of using human intelligence, has not enabled man to adapt to new environmental situations. Instead, the impact of our species has been so strong that in practice the entire planet has been transformed into our own ecological niche, our exclusive province.

# Survival

The transition to the stage of systematic food-production has been called the Neolithic revolution – a peaceful revolution accomplished with the very simplest of weapons. The first was a billhook consisting of a wooden or bone handle and a series of small stone blades set in a groove and held together with pitch. The other was a small enclosure to accommodate and protect the first animals which were eventually to become domesticated.

Over the centuries man improved the means for altering his environment. Fertilizers consisting of the excrement of people and animals of the village were superseded by artificial fertilizers produced by giant chemical industries. The patient task of separating useful from useless plants was simplified by the large-scale and drastic application of herbicides. So as man's ecological niche became ever more extensive, it also became increasingly degraded, polluted and poisoned.

We know that some living forms managed to survive for thousands, even millions, of years because the

*Right: A table showing statistics of the steady increase in the world's human population from the emergence of the genus* Homo *to the present day. This increase has been quite staggering during the past couple of centuries and particularly in the 20th century. Every region on Earth is now populated. The greatest concentrations are in urban centres, not only in the great cities of Europe, America and Japan but also in the fast-developing cities of India, South-East Asia and the Philippines.*

*Below right: Children of a Third World country. The major problem of our time is not so much that there are too many people but that there are too many, like these children, who are hungry or starving. Many of these youngsters will not live to be adults, others will spend their entire lives afflicted by deficiency diseases, due to the lack of essential elements in their diet, for example, in proteins and vitamins. Elsewhere economic necessity involves the using up and frequent squandering of vital resources. The grim lesson we have to learn is that there can be no further excuse for waste; either we shall all be saved together or we shall all perish together.*

| INCREASE IN NUMBERS OF HUMAN POPULATION | | |
|---|---|---|
| Period | Estimated numbers | Significant events |
| 1,500,000 years ago | some thousands of individuals | |
| 12/10,000 years ago | tens to hundreds of thousands | Neolithic 'revolution' |
| 7000/6000 years ago | several millions | first riverside empires |
| AD1 | 250 million | |
| AD1000 | 350 million | In 14th century Black Death kills perhaps 100 million people. |
| AD1500 | 450 million | Conquest of New World; massacre of natives kills perhaps 15–19 million people. |
| AD1800 | 1000 million | |
| AD1900 | 1650 million | World War One: 8 million dead. |
| Today | 4000 million | World War Two: 15 million fighting men, 35 million civilians, killed. |
| AD2000 | 6500–7000 million | |

ecological niches to which they had adapted were not excessively despoiled and harmed. Today many species, which in the natural course of things would not be threatened, are on the verge of extinction because man has hunted them or has drastically altered their natural habitats. Could *H. sapiens sapiens* also be one of these endangered species?

# Man and evolution

Darwin grasped the principles of evolution by observing and analyzing the results of selection in natural surroundings. In the Galapagos Islands he saw the various types of tortoise which had become different as a result of isolation and finches which had adapted to different habitats and available foods. He also pointed out the striking diversities between extinct species, such as *Megatherium*,

and other living species which perhaps had the same habits. He took a keen interest in the results achieved by raisers of livestock. Cattle and sheep exhibited the very characteristics that man had chosen to give them. Darwin understood how the natural process of evolution worked, partly by seeing what man had done and was still doing by experimenting with living species he had raised. Today we can calculate the effects of human actions on a global scale, how people have altered the world, and we can also see how our own species has changed as a result of such actions.

These are not changes which have anything to do with our body. We know that we are the same as the Neanthropinae who lived during the Würm. The differences are really of little significance. But we are well aware of the enormous gap in cultural

The photographs on these pages show some animals which have survived while the majority of closely related species have become extinct. Some of them are described as 'living fossils'. A brief list is given in the table on the opposite page.

*Opposite, below:* The horseshoe crab, a fairly near relative of the gigantostracans, enormous sea-scorpions widespread during the Silurian and Devonian.

*Above:* The kiwi, not a living fossil but certainly a type of bird unlike any other living form. The kiwi has totally reduced wings and cannot therefore fly; its feathers are threadbare and it lives in burrows. The bird survives in one part of its original habitat, the wooded areas of the two main islands of New Zealand, not yet destroyed by human interference.

*Right:* The tuatara, last representative of a group of reptiles which flourished, with similar forms, in the Triassic. This animal survives today only on some of the lesser islands off New Zealand. The tuatara often takes refuge in winter in the nests of certain marine birds such as shearwaters and petrels.

development. This, then, is the type of evolution we need to examine in order to find out where and how man went wrong and also to determine whether or not he can make amends.

On the one hand there is the natural process: man the product of natural evolution, *Ramapithecus*, *Australopithecus* and *Homo* representing the main stages of development. On the other hand there is the cultural, unnatural process: modern man the slave of habit, custom and ritual, man the inventor of a social structure that

*The living fossils are animals which have had to contend with many changes in their environment and managed to adapt successfully. Many more creatures were incapable of doing so and thus became extinct. Added to these are some species whose extinction has been brought about by man, and many others seriously threatened today.*
*Left: A brief list of species that have become extinct in recent times and those in danger of extinction.*
*Below: A giant turtle from the Galapagos.*
*Opposite: A pair of mountain gorillas.*

crushes him, man the ransacker of a vast ecological niche which he is making steadily poorer. What we can deduce by observing the results of the first process is fairly comforting. It is sometimes said that we are prisoners of our motor cars and buses: yet most of us are quite capable of walking or running for quite some time before getting out of breath. It is also said that we are slaves of mass-communication, of the media; but we do not have to telephone a friend who lives next door to give them news, and we do not have to sit in front of a television screen to appreciate the setting sun. Our body, with all its capacities, including intelligence, has not changed.

We can still communicate knowledge and can still care for others as well as ourselves. Yet our cultural evolution has brought in its wake enormous dangers. Evil is a product of the society man has created. It is a cultural evil not to spread culture, to withhold education and knowledge; and it is a cultural evil to keep one-third of the world's population in a state of poverty and underdevelopment. The very term, underdevelopment, sounds like a dirty word for it

*Is man a species threatened with extinction? Looking at the present world situation, it has to be admitted that our own extinction may indeed be quite close at hand. Are we then to end up in some museum of the future with a label stating 'the only species that managed to destroy itself'? We must all do what we can to make sure this never happens. By looking at our ancestors (like these children who are in a museum examining the skull of one of the oldest men found on American soil), we can understand that human beings have come a long way in hundreds of thousands of generations, that many errors have been committed and that such mistakes need to be put right. There is no time to be lost. Prehistory has barely come to an end and what we call history is merely its brief continuation; yet it has been stained by bloodshed. War and famine are social evils and if we created them we have the power to abolish them. Our survival is in our hands.*

runs contrary to the development which our species, like all others, should always strive to attain. It goes against evolution.

What can be done? Get rid of the scourges of our so-called civilization – wars, spending on arms, consumer madness, indoctrination by advertising. Realize the full potential of food resources and, above all, ensure that they are fairly distributed. Make our culture, our knowledge, our expertise, available to all. The rich countries must invest more heavily in educational facilities for those countries in need of them. Everything possible must be done to make sure that this money is not wasted. The mass media should be aware of their true responsibility, namely to inform and educate the people of the so-called 'backward' countries. The wealthier nations should invest less in the industrial sector and more in livestock raising and agriculture. It is important, too, to educate people to have fewer children. And it is essential that we clean up our planet, Earth, in the fullest sense, so that it remains habitable. Can such a programme be successful? It is an immense task. Yet there is no time to lose. Every minute people are dying of hunger and the Earth becomes a bleaker, less hospitable, less friendly place.

We should bear in mind that no natural process can be reversed. All that can happen is for things to come to a stop, as the living fossils have done. The path of evolution is cluttered with fallen species which have been unable either to stop or to go forwards. In *our* evolutionary process, which during the past few thousand years has been predominantly cultural, a change of direction is possible. Indeed, it is essential.

# INDEX

# Illustration Credits